Praise for *Barely Visible*

"Somers remains unflinching in her love for her son, leaving readers with the hopeful advice that 'life has a way of working itself out.'"
—BookLife Review

"*Barely Visible* is a powerful first-person account of one mother's journey in raising an autistic child, and many readers will undoubtedly relate to her story. I applaud the author's candor and vulnerability."
—Eric Endlich, Ph.D., Psychologist & Founder,
Top College Consultants

"A heartfelt and skillfully written memoir that stands out for its unvarnished honesty and authentic voice…making it a perfect read for those who are on the hunt for a memoir with real substance and heart."
—Readers' Favorite Review

"A reflective and humorous journey that should resonate with any parent."

—*Kirkus Reviews*

BARELY VISIBLE

MOTHERING A SON THROUGH HIS
MISUNDERSTOOD AUTISM

KATHLEEN SOMERS

SHE WRITES PRESS

Published 2025
Printed in the United States of America
Print ISBN: 978-1-64742-882-2
E-ISBN: 978-1-64742-883-9
Library of Congress Control Number: 2024923077

For information, address:
She Writes Press
1569 Solano Ave #546
Berkeley, CA 94707

Interior Design by Kiran Spees

She Writes Press is a division of SparkPoint Studio, LLC.

Names and identifying characteristics have been changed to protect the privacy of certain individuals.

For my mother
for never failing to remind me that life has a way—
a way of working itself out.

And of course, for Jack
You are my why.

Contents

Author's Note

In 2007, my son Jack was formally diagnosed with "Asperger syndrome." The term was still in its infancy. In 2013, with the publication of the American Psychiatric Association's *Diagnostic and Statistical Manual of Mental Disorders*, the syndrome was removed, and the symptoms are now included within autism spectrum disorder.

The phrase "Asperger syndrome" originated with Hans Asperger, an Austrian physician noted for his early studies on atypical neurology, specifically in children. Today, some are highly offended by use of this term because of allegations that Hans Asperger supported the Nazi regime's goal of eliminating children who did not fit with the Nazi ideal of a homogeneous society.

I use the term frequently throughout this book because those were the words in use at the time of my son's diagnosis, and for better or for worse they became our norm. Use of those words represents *my experience only*. It does not represent any racial, political, or neurodivergent beliefs or prejudice in any way. To those people who perceive it as offensive or incorrect, I offer my sincerest apologies.

Prologue

Today's game was unlike the rest, so it killed me to be late. I had spent all morning catching up on yesterday's remaining errands, and I was missing the start. Rushing down the gravel path, I was surprised to find the parking lot full. I had expected a much smaller turnout. I found that the only spot remaining was in the far corner next to the dumpster. Begrudgingly, I parked my car beside a weekend's worth of half-eaten hot dogs and empty Gatorade bottles. It wasn't the best, but it would do. I grabbed my chair from the trunk and headed for the field. A blanket of blue hovered overhead, and the temperature had topped out at a glorious seventy-eight degrees. It was a perfect Sunday afternoon for baseball.

As I approached the field, I could see that my options for a viewing spot were limited. I had my chair, so it didn't matter that the stands were filled. Though given the number of parents crowding the fence, it seemed unlikely I would find a spot to set up. There was barely enough room to slip myself in, let alone a chair.

Scanning the field, I found one small opening near third base and made my way through the cluster of parents, none of whom I recognized. I propped the now useless chair against a nearby trash can and wedged in close to the fence. Jack was already there, having come with his father. He wasn't taking his usual position today, so it took me several moments, but I finally found my son standing across the field at first base next to a dark-haired boy who looked to be about eight or nine years old.

Chaos surrounded them.

The field was cluttered with boys and girls of all ages. Mixed among them were the familiar faces of boys that Jack played with regularly, most of whom were chatting and laughing with one another.

A father was playing the role of pitcher, though he stood just six feet away from home plate. Softly he tossed a plastic ball to the batter, a small girl in a bright pink dress. "That's an odd choice of attire for a baseball game," I mumbled, reminding myself though that this wasn't your average game.

She took a determined swing at the ball, missed, and nearly toppled over, but it didn't stop her from jumping back over the plate. She readied herself for the second ball, and this time sent it rolling across the grass. As shouts of encouragement rang out, pure enthusiasm twirled off her. In her excitement, she was oblivious to the parents urging her to run to first base. The volunteer at her side gently took her hand and led her down the baseline, and as she bounced along, I saw Jack bend down to say something to the boy next to him. The boy gently rocked back and forth and shook his head as if to say yes but didn't move. Jack wrapped his arm awkwardly around the boy's shoulder and guided him to second base.

There were already two other children there. One was lying in the grass, kicking his sneakered feet in the air; the other was fiddling with the buttons on his shirt. A boy who looked to be nearly an adult wandered back and forth between second and third base, patting his head and muttering, while a redheaded girl in a wheelchair waited patiently at third for someone to push her home. I watched it all unfold with astonishment.

The day's game had been organized by our local little league in an effort to make baseball accessible to children with disabilities. Regardless of age, sex, or disability, each child was paired with a teenage volunteer to help guide them. When I first heard the idea, it made perfect sense, though given Jack's own disability, I wasn't quite sure how he would fare in this volunteer role. Even though he was fourteen, having Asperger syndrome meant he was easily frustrated and bored. I didn't know if he would make it through the game without losing interest or if he would understand how to guide his young buddy. I questioned if he would even talk to him.

The game went on for the better part of an hour, and there didn't appear to be any rules. Everyone was given the opportunity to circle the field and score a run, whether they hit the ball or not. As each one crossed home plate to the waiting praise of supportive parents and grandparents, I was overwhelmed. So many children—so much worse off than Jack—and all of them right in our backyard. In this context, Jack's disability seemed like barely more than a scraped knee.

There were several moments when I found myself wanting to motion to him, to get his attention and urge him to interact with the little boy next to him. If nothing else, I wanted him to laugh and joke with his teammates volunteering alongside of him. I wanted desperately for him to connect and engage more fully, or to at least look like he wasn't bored out of his mind, but I had been making more of an effort recently to take my hands off the wheel. I let go of my expectations and breathed a sigh of relief once the game was over.

As Jack, his father, and I headed out into the parking lot, I heard a woman's voice calling us. "Excuse me," she repeated as she grew closer, and I turned to see that it was the mother of the young boy with whom Jack had been paired.

"I just wanted to thank you," she said, catching her breath, "for giving up your Sunday afternoon for this." Turning toward Jack, she went on. "I really appreciate you being so nice to my son."

I thought that Jack really hadn't done all that much. But the simple fact that he was here and had interacted with this complete stranger, and that he had made it through the entire game without losing his patience or having a meltdown was a significant accomplishment. He had done quite a bit without anyone even being aware of it.

"You're welcome," Jack replied, glancing at her just briefly before looking away. He barely acknowledged her further as she went on to tell us how difficult it was for their family, dealing with her son's autism—and how lucky we were. He shuffled from one foot to the other and rubbed his eye in agitation before cutting her off midsentence.

"Can we go, Mom?" he asked and turned abruptly toward the car. The woman was taken aback.

I had to hand it to my ex-husband. He didn't miss a beat and handled the situation perfectly. He was very gracious in telling the boy's mother that we appreciated her gratitude, going on to delicately point out that she was the lucky one. Her son's disability was obvious, and because of that, people were likely to be very understanding and tolerant. He explained that Jack, too, has a disability, but it's one that few people can see. On the surface, he appears normal, and when he acts otherwise, which is most of the time, people see him as being rude and assume he's poorly disciplined.

Her expression changed to one of apology, and suddenly my heart was as blue as the sky. Blue for this mother and her son—and blue for Jack. He could be counted among this group of kids. And yet he couldn't. He attended a regular school, took regular classes, played on regular sports teams; he did many of the things you would expect a regular teenager to do.

On which side of the fence did he fall? On some difficult, unpredictable-version-of-normal side—or the truly disabled side?

It's a question I've asked myself countless times.

CHAPTER 1
The Unthinkable

It was a clear, cold Saturday morning in mid-January. I was boxing up holiday decorations before hauling them to the spare room on our third floor, where they would sit for the next eleven months. I wondered why, year after year, I went to such lengths to decorate the house for just one holiday. It was something to do, I suppose.

I climbed the last few steps to the top as a heavy cold sank over me. The windows no longer fit the frames quite right, and at this time of year, the third floor of our century-old Dutch Colonial was an icebox.

I surveyed the tiny space. The tattered antique rug beneath my feet offered little protection from the cold. The discolored shreds of wallpaper that still clung to the bare walls were a gentle reminder that, at one point, we had had plans for this room. Our starter home was certainly loaded with architectural charm, but it was short on modern space, so this small room had been transformed into a glorified dumping ground.

I gazed at seven years' worth of discarded possessions—our motorcycle helmets that never saw the road trips we talked about, the dumbbells that didn't interest me enough to lift them, the unopened box containing the sewing machine and an accompanying career idea that never made it off the ground. They were all relics of past excitements and big dreams that had faded as much as the rug I was standing on.

I set the boxes down with a sigh and something closer to apathy than resentment, when I felt a pinch. I had felt the same sensation in my midsection earlier that day, not exactly a tickle, but not quite pain, either. I was bleeding lightly, so I doubted I was pregnant, yet something was off. Maybe I would grab a pregnancy test when I went out later in the day, just to be sure.

We hadn't been trying all that hard. I think the decision to have children was made purely out of boredom. It wasn't that life was lacking in opportunities; it was simply a matter of Andrew having little sense of adventure, and me following his lead. The idea of parenthood was not a natural one for us. I never saw myself as the motherly type nor did I think I could possibly be a good one. It just seemed to be the obvious next step in our life. Not allowing any of it too much thought, I finished up with the decorations, handled some odds and ends around the house, and set off on my usual Saturday errands.

Later that afternoon, I stood at the bathroom sink, fumbling to unfold the directions for the pregnancy test. I wasn't expecting my sudden nervousness. I didn't know what I wanted this stick to tell me. Were we ready for a baby? Would I be disappointed if the result was negative?

Moments later, I found myself looking down at a plus sign. It had to be wrong. I scanned my reflection in the mirror, searching for some indication that the test strip was being honest with me. I didn't look any different. And if the result was accurate, why was I bleeding?

Andrew had been gone all day and was only in the door a minute or two when I blurted the news.

"I have something to show you." With a grin, I waved the stick in front of him, and immediately he understood.

"Are you serious?" He was in disbelief. Some couples try for years to conceive. We had been at the plate just two or three times and somehow managed to hit a home run. The newest father-to-be was obviously pleased with himself. He dropped his keys on the table and wrapped his arms around me with a kiss. "I thought you said you got your period."

"I thought I did, but the bleeding is so light, I figured I better check. And sure enough. . . ." I held the stick steady so he could clearly see that the test was positive.

"I can't believe we're going to have a baby," he added.

Andrew's positive reception of the news contributed to my sudden enthusiasm. Despite not feeling any natural inclination toward motherhood, the thought of creating a life, welcoming a person into this world, and filling a clean slate with all the details a life is comprised of had taken hold of me.

Monday morning arrived, and being the early bird, I found myself impatiently checking the clock every ten minutes, waiting for my doctor's office to open. I finally reached the receptionist at 9:10 a.m.

"I need an appointment as soon as possible. I did a pregnancy test this weekend, and it was positive. I want to confirm that it's accurate," I stated proudly.

"Dr. Ewing can see you Thursday afternoon," she informed me flatly.

"Thursday afternoon? You don't have any openings today?"

"I'm sorry, that's the first opening we have." Clearly, she didn't understand my urgent need to confirm this, and she put me down for a 2:15 p.m. appointment on Thursday.

Sure enough, the test was correct. I was six weeks along. "Should I be concerned about the fact that I'm bleeding?" I asked.

"A little bit of spotting isn't abnormal at this early stage of pregnancy. Just try to take it easy for a while." The doctor went on to recite the expected litany of instructions before sending me on my way. "Get plenty of rest, eat a well-balanced diet—and no smoking or drinking. I'll see you again in a month, and we'll do an ultrasound."

I shared the details of my appointment that evening with Andrew. "She says there's nothing to worry about."

"I hope she's right," he replied, sounding uneasy.

Over the years, we had often discussed what it might be like to start a family. Each time we talked about it, he had openly voiced a fear that we would be the ones from our circle of friends to run into issues. Becoming a parent should be the highlight of your life. But what if the unthinkable happens?

Over those next four weeks, Andrew was extremely supportive. He had always treated me like a princess, but pregnancy had elevated me to queen status. Despite all his attention, I was on a roller coaster of emotions. I wanted to embrace the excitement. I wanted to plan ahead for a nursery and think about the adjustments I would make to my work schedule. But I was feeling a tug I couldn't ignore. The bleeding had persisted, signaling to me that the little pinch I felt early on, the not-really-a-tickle-or-a-pain, wasn't normal.

Andrew was aware of my issues, but I knew he didn't understand the depth of my concern, and I didn't want to pile on stress if it was unwarranted. I didn't want him jumping to conclusions when there was no concrete proof of a problem. Instead, I turned to my mother. She had had four other children before me, so I figured she knew a thing or two about pregnancy.

"Stop worrying," she insisted. "You're being overly sensitive, and that's normal the first time around."

I knew she was right. Worrying needlessly would do more harm than good. I didn't want to look like an overly dramatic newcomer to this age-old process of reproduction, so I decided to hold off until the following week.

Much to my relief, the ultrasound showed nothing out of the ordinary. I had my doctor's assurance that this was a viable pregnancy and there was no reason to anguish over my body's apparent lack of cooperation. I left her office with a sense of hope. I could put my fears aside and focus on doing all the right things and enjoy the changes that were unfolding.

As the next couple of months passed, the bleeding subsided, and my nerves settled. There was no longer anything to signal a potential problem. My body shape had visibly changed, and for the first time, I felt the gentle kick of a tiny life growing inside of me. With that, a palpable seriousness set in. In a few months' time, we would be parents.

At five and a half months along and feeling proud of myself for making it this far, Andrew accompanied me to the hospital for my routine, midpregnancy ultrasound. The bleeding I was experiencing had stopped completely. The baby was tossing about more and more each day, and in general, I was feeling good.

The technician greeted us with restrained warmth, jaded I'm sure by countless enthusiastic pregnant couples before us. I'm certain our excitement was nothing new, or maybe the ability to remain emotionless was just part of the job description.

"We've had a bit of a rocky start," I said, "so we're anxious to see something. Anything. But we don't want to know the sex!" I added quickly.

"Don't worry, I won't give it away," she promised as she coated my rounded belly with a cold gel and began scanning the contents inside. She said little as she moved the device back and forth.

"Tell me about the rocky start you had," she said finally.

"Well, I wasn't even sure I was pregnant at first. I was bleeding for the first couple of months. But my doctor said it was nothing to worry about." I offered that last piece of information as if saying it aloud would guarantee its reality. I searched her face, looking for some explanation of why she had asked, but she simply continued with the scan. After ten minutes, she put down her wand and excused herself. It may have been my imagination, but I could swear she was trying to suppress a look of terror. Andrew and I searched the screen, then looked at one another dumbfounded. To us, it looked like nothing more than an abstract, colorless mess of curves. To trained eyes, the monitor was a billboard for disaster. We were about to be blindsided.

A few moments later, the technician returned. "You can get dressed now," she instructed. "I'm going to have you talk with the doctor on duty. His office is at the end of the hall when you're ready." With barely a smile, she backed out of the room, pulling the door closed. I remember that moment as clear as if it happened yesterday. We were about to become *that* couple—the one that gets the terrible news we'd feared from the start. The couple that has everyone else shaking their heads and saying, "Oh, how sad" or, "What a shame." My hands trembled. Barely able to button my blouse, I steadied myself before stepping into the hallway.

At the end of the hall, we found an antiseptic office with a perfectly sterile marriage of metal furniture and fluorescent lighting. As the doctor introduced himself, my eyes wandered the walls bearing his credentials. Who was he, and could we trust him to interpret our ultrasound accurately? He didn't waste time with pleasantries as he pulled up the images on his desktop monitor and began to speak in a routine voice. To him, the images were nothing more than a road map. To us, they were everything—our baby, our future family.

"Your ultrasound images are revealing some inconsistencies in the baby's development. We're seeing three separate issues, and were it just any one of these issues, we would not question it, but the fact that there are three is cause for concern." He pointed to the amorphous shapes on the screen as he described each of the three problems. It was at that point that I tuned out. All I could hear was, *Three strikes, you're out.* The doctor matter-of-factly recommended that we have an amniocentesis, gave us the phone number for scheduling, and tried his best to offer some assurance.

We rode home in silence.

We hadn't been home long when the phone rang. It was my mother calling to check in. I hadn't even managed a hello when I burst into tears and told her what had happened.

"There's something wrong with the baby," I sobbed. I know she asked me question after question, but I didn't process a single one. It didn't matter; I didn't have any answers. All I could muster was one "I don't know" after another. In my mother's typical fashion, she took immediate control, stating that first we needed to find out exactly what was wrong with the baby and what we would need to do to care for him or her. And then we would face it head-on.

"We will love this baby like any other baby," she kept saying.

Why did she always have to be so damn practical? I wanted to believe her, but could I actually do that? It was another answer I didn't have, and supplying yet another "I don't know" allowed me a little time to lean on her.

The results of the ultrasound, combined with those of an amniocentesis and a barrage of obscure tests over the next six weeks, pointed to a freak chromosomal disorder that had a one in one hundred thousand chance of occurring. What had taken place was so unusual that there wasn't even a name for it, other than "a duplication of chromosome 9p." From what the doctors knew, only nine people in the country were living with the disorder. They couldn't be certain, but they believed it would not impact physical appearance as Down syndrome would. In other words, our baby would *look* normal—as if that were some consolation. It would, however, greatly impact mental ability.

Two things determined how badly the baby would be affected— when the duplication took place, and how much of the chromosome had duplicated itself. Of course, we were not among the fortunate. Duplication had taken place at conception, not at some point down the road in the fetus's development. This meant that every cell of this baby was affected. Equally as awful was that the entire chromosome had duplicated itself, not just a portion. Every parent's worst fear was staring us in the face.

And we had no idea what to do.

Andrew was in shock. I, on the other hand, was not. I had felt every ounce of this ugliness coming. That didn't mean I was any less grief-stricken. I can recall several moments during that period of testing—of realization, of devastation, of the pain sinking in— where I did nothing more than sit, rock, and cry until I was senseless, knowing I had no choice but to kill my baby. How do you come to grips with that?

In an effort to stay sane, I threw myself into researching "duplication of chromosome 9p." We hadn't yet entered the twenty-first century, so finding answers was not as easy as asking Google. We needed to rely heavily on what information the doctors were able to provide. The doctors' knowledge of the disorder was limited, but the bulk of what we were told was correct.

Generally speaking, an infant with this disorder could be expected to face developmental delays, intellectual disability, and behavioral problems. Okay, that's not the end of the world, I thought. A lot of children have trouble meeting milestones and issues with behavior. I had to keep reminding myself, though, that our case was worst-case.

Our baby would have difficulty learning to crawl and walk, and he or she would experience a long list of other issues such as low muscle tone, difficulty feeding, and failure to gain weight and grow at the expected rate. "Failure to thrive" were the exact words, and the growth deficiency could begin before the baby was even born, which is known as "intrauterine growth retardation." Those words terrified me.

The list went on—and on.

We had been told that our child would likely look normal, despite the massive impact of this disability, but that didn't appear to be the case. I continued on to find that there were multiple characteristics regarding appearance we could expect to see in our baby—small head circumference; a wide mouth with downturned corners; a prominent, bulbous nose; large, low-set ears; a short, webbed neck. *What does that even mean?*

And then there were the parts that stopped me in my tracks: severely delayed language development and learning disabilities that would only get worse with age; curvature of the spine; hip dislocation; genital and kidney malformations; protrusion of a portion of the intestine; heart defects that could lead to life-threatening complications; and hydrocephalus, which results in fluid accumulating in and around the brain, leading to abnormally high pressure within the skull, swelling of the head, neurological impairment, seizures, irritability, vomiting, headache, loss of coordination. . . .

There was no end.

I read everything I could find, which at the time was not a lot, and every path led me to the same four words: "more research is necessary."

After an afternoon of digging furiously for information, I was exhausted. I was still pregnant, and the demands of a long, hard day at six and a half months took their toll. I was brushing my teeth when I heard Andrew come into our bedroom. He didn't say a word; he didn't need to. His silence betrayed him as he collapsed onto our bed. I peered around the corner of the bathroom door, and I knew—the bottom had fallen out from beneath him. To see him struggling to find answers in this desperate moment drew every raw emotion inside of me to the surface.

I rinsed the toothpaste from my mouth, wiped my face, and went to sit on the bed beside him. The gravity of our situation had finally come down on him, and he was falling apart.

"I knew this was going to happen. Why us? Why did this have to happen to *us*?" He was at an absolute loss.

"It's going to be okay," I said. "There has to be a reason."

"What kind of reason could there possibly be?"

"I just don't know. . . ." I let the words trail off and float in the air. Not knowing somehow made it easier. I would rather not know than be forced to accept this cruelty.

Andrew broke down. "I don't think I can do this."

"Do what?" I countered. I knew exactly what he meant, but I needed him to say the words—to make it okay for me to concede as well.

"We can't have this baby. I just can't do it."

As much as I wanted to, I couldn't run and hide. I took a deep breath. "I know." I finally said as I wrapped my arm around him. "I can't do it, either."

CHAPTER 2
Why Us?

Now that we had as much information as possible, we were certain we couldn't see this pregnancy through. Despite wanting to believe differently, we knew that our baby wouldn't have a normal life. I couldn't see bringing a child into this world knowing that he or she has not even a fraction of a chance, and the thought of placing our child in an institution was unimaginable. Together, we agreed there was only one choice.

By the time testing was complete, I was twenty-six weeks along and beyond the legal limit in Pennsylvania for terminating a pregnancy. We were referred to two doctors that would terminate at such a late stage—one was in Colorado, the other in Kansas. We decided to go to Kansas, reasoning that it was a few hundred miles closer. As if it mattered.

I don't recall who provided us with contact information for the Kansas clinic, but it was up to us to schedule the procedure, and it was the hardest phone call I've ever made. After explaining our situation, the woman at the other end of the line carefully spelled out what we needed to do and patiently answered every question, including the ones I asked twice. She told me that they had an immediate opening, but that would mean scrambling to make flight arrangements and flying to Kansas within a couple of days of having been handed this gut-wrenching news. The alternative would be to wait another two weeks.

I was overwhelmed. I didn't know where to begin in terms of processing this. How could I possibly kill a baby that I now so desperately wanted? Before I could simply "end it," I needed to grieve. I needed to come face-to-face with what we were experiencing and about to do in order to have the strength to see it through. We decided to wait the two weeks.

Those fourteen days overflowed with turbulent emotion, continuous second guessing and sheer terror. We shed an unrestrained flood of tears. I found myself getting in the car more than once just to drive. I didn't know where I was going—anywhere that I wouldn't feel pain. I would inevitably end up at my parents' house each time, as if they could magically fix things like they had when I was a child. On one of those nights, my father set a bottle of whiskey on the table in front of me. I pushed it away. Reaching for a small glass from the cabinet, he poured some.

"It might make you feel better," he offered. Reluctantly I took the glass, sipped the whiskey, and felt a warmth come over me, so I sipped a little more. And immediately I felt guilty.

"I can't do this. It's not good for the baby. I've spent the last seven months doing everything I'm supposed to do." I instantly realized the ridiculousness of that statement and how it made no difference. We were about to kill the baby. I drank the whole glass, set it on the table—and poured myself another.

Our support system of family and friends went into action immediately, making the necessary arrangements and minimizing the burden of organizing our trip. My brother worked in the hospitality industry, and after a few calls, we had lodging for the week. My girl-friend's father worked for one of the major airlines, and he took care of arranging our flights. Both were small blessings that went a long way.

The biggest hurdle was our insurance company. The cost of the procedure was not cheap, and they refused to pay for it, indicating that it was an elective procedure. I suppose, yes, this was our choice, but we were making this choice out of necessity for the good of every-one involved—including our insurance company. Over the course of two days, I made twelve calls, talked to seven different people, and finally found someone in charge that had some compassion for what we were going through. They finally agreed to cover the expense.

All the pieces were now in place. We just needed to follow through.

As we boarded our flight that Sunday afternoon, the flight atten-dant noted that I was glowing. "How far along are you?" she asked, obviously concerned about our decision to fly so late in the preg-nancy. She had no clue where we were going or what dreadful deed we were about to carry out. I forced a smile and choked back tears.

"Thank you," I murmured. "I'm seven months along." I didn't share with her that in another week I wouldn't be pregnant.

The clinic warned us in advance about our arrival, urging us to steel ourselves against the antiabortion protesters that gathered daily to picket, point fingers, and hurl expletives at arriving patients. As we turned into the parking lot, my anger rose.

"How dare they judge us!" I snapped. "This isn't some casual deci-sion. Don't these people understand that we want this baby?" Andrew reminded me not to engage, and I did my best to stare straight ahead, focusing instead on the one-story painted brick building beyond them. Its blunt simplicity felt right at home in this nightmare.

The inside of the clinic was a perfect complement to its exterior. Its lackluster appearance bore a striking resemblance to the office of Dr. Three Strikes You're Out. We were greeted by the typical request to fill out paperwork, and as I sank into an unadorned gray chair, I surveyed the people around me. They were couples that looked just like us. They *were* us.

I had envisioned termination of this pregnancy as being a quick procedure. Just get rid of it, let us get on with grieving, and eventually we'll pick up the pieces. But it didn't work that way. The clinic's standard procedure required that we participate in a weeklong process—in this bare environment, with these other couples. I didn't see how we could possibly share this catastrophe with strangers, and I convinced myself that we didn't belong here. We weren't murderers.

After I returned the clipboard to the front desk, a nurse escorted me into a small room where she handed me two pills and a cup of water. "Take these," she said warmly. "It's a mild sedative that will help to relax you. Give them a little time to take effect, and then I'll take you in to meet with the doctor." I returned to the plainness of my chair and sat with Andrew in silence for twenty minutes.

A short time later, the nurse escorted us into the doctor's office. Unlike the waiting area, it was a warmly lit, calming space. Two brown leather armchairs hugged one another closely in front of a richly carved wooden desk, as if to say that this appalling conversation we were about to have was okay. With the exception of the doctor's certificates covering one wall, the entire room had the look of a lodge.

I knew right away that Dr. Miller was a very compassionate man. He would have to be to put his life on the line every day in order to help people like us. He had endured being shot and the clinic being firebombed—I knew this from the small amount of information I had been able to find on him. Yet day after day he continued his practice of helping couples to terminate late-stage pregnancies, regardless of their reason. Our initial meeting was brief, with him not asking too many questions—he knew all he needed to know—nor telling us more than we could handle. I absorbed almost none of what he said, only that he would see us shortly in the examination room.

Feeling myself collapse emotionally, I barely noticed the nurse that had entered the office. As I tried to regain my bearings, she led us to an exam room where she prepared me for an ultrasound. Although I knew the moment would eventually come, there was no advance warning that this moment was *the* moment. We had just arrived. Shouldn't there be some sort of extensive preparation? Couldn't we talk about this a little while longer?

Dr. Miller entered the room and sat down in front of the machine's monitor. He studied the images briefly before turning toward me to rub a small amount of anesthetic on my belly. Using the images on the screen to guide him, he inserted a needle into my abdomen and injected a fluid into the baby's heart to stop it from beating.

Just like that.

Just like that, my insides shifted from the constant fielding of gentle kicks to complete absence of movement. It was all at once devastating and eerie. The baby's daily dance had been setting the pace of my days for the last few months, and now it was gone in a matter of seconds.

I was paralyzed.

Maybe this whole process was by design. Maybe we would have resisted or changed our minds at the last minute if we were given more time to think. Day after day, the clinic saw couples just like us—couples forced into terminating pregnancies that were very much wanted. I had to trust that they knew what they were doing.

Once the doctor was certain that the baby was no longer alive—had he just asked me, I could have assured him—he guided my feet into the stirrups at the end of the table.

"I'm going to insert seaweed sticks into your cervix. Over the next few days, they will work naturally to dilate your cervix. Once it's fully dilated, we'll induce labor so you can deliver the baby."

"*Deliver* the baby?" I guess I hadn't given any thought as to how this was supposed to go, but they couldn't possibly expect me to go through delivery. I shot a look at Andrew as his head dropped in defeat. He wanted nothing more than to carry this heavy weight for me, but there was nothing he could do.

We were told to go back to our hotel, get some rest, and return the following morning. We left the clinic completely disconnected from the world around us. The overwhelming emotion of everything that had just taken place, combined with the sedatives I had been given, left me nauseous and spinning. What little breakfast was in my stomach was soon all over the parking lot.

Over the next few days, while we waited for my cervix to dilate, we underwent extensive group counseling with the other five couples that had chosen this same week to endure their own version of hell. Initially I wanted nothing to do with sharing our story, but after listening to the others, I came to understand that this was as difficult for them as it was for us. I began to open up. It was during those sessions that these strangers became real people to us. They were couples from all over the country that were living the same nightmare, because of illnesses, disabilities, or disorders whose names didn't matter.

Somewhere around ten o'clock on our fourth night, my water broke. Scared and unsure of what to do, Andrew called Dr. Miller. Thirty minutes later, both he and his nurse arrived at our hotel to check on me. While I was floored by their thoughtfulness and a level of attention that went above and beyond, I wondered to myself what they needed to check on. It wasn't as if they needed to make sure the baby was okay. The baby was dead.

How quickly I had detached myself.

Because my water had broken, there was no choice but to induce labor the next morning. I was assigned to a bed behind a curtain in a large community-style examining room, where the nurse injected me with a drug to induce labor. In less than an hour, I began feeling contractions. In little over an hour, I was writhing in pain, and the knowledge that there would be no happy ending to my efforts only magnified the torture. I rolled from one side to the other, moaning, crying—resisting. I lost sense of time. My resistance to the game plan duped me into thinking I had been left alone for hours to struggle. I barely even noticed that Andrew was by my side the entire time, feeling absolutely helpless. It was a small victory when the doctor finally examined me and signaled to the nurse that I was ready for delivery. I was given a twilight medication, wheeled into the delivery room, and that's the last thing I remember.

I wasn't surprised to find that Andrew was next to me when I awoke. In his constantly attentive way, he immediately asked how I felt. Without answering, I asked the one thing I had wanted to know all along.

"Was it a boy or a girl?"

"It was a girl," he said quietly.

Suddenly, it was all real.

She was real. Knowing that I had been given a daughter versus a son changed everything. My mind jumped to all the things *she* could never do, all the things *she* would never be. In that moment, there were a million thoughts behind my grief—and only blank space ahead of it.

A few moments later, Dr. Miller pulled the curtain aside and entered my makeshift hospital room. In a comforting but matter-of-fact manner, he told me that everything had gone well and as soon as I felt up to it, we could leave for the day. Before turning to go, he paused and asked the unthinkable: "Do you want to see the baby?"

The thought had never crossed my mind. But then, the thought that any of this could ever happen to us hadn't, either. I didn't hesitate. It wasn't something I needed to think about.

"Yes, I want to see her," I insisted as I turned to Andrew, assuming he would want the same.

"I can't do it," he admitted. The look in his eyes told me that he didn't want to be forever left with that visual, whereas for me, having it was imperative. I needed something concrete to let me know that this had been more than just a horrible dream, some proof to carry with me that I was more than just the victim of freak circumstances—I was a mother. Maybe I hadn't achieved motherhood in the full sense yet, but I had given of myself so completely for this baby, in ways that demanded a level of selflessness that felt virtually impossible. And if that isn't what makes a mother, then I don't know what does.

The following morning, Dr. Miller and his nurse welcomed me privately into his office. I felt so alone. The leather chairs that had initially appeared sympathetic and supportive were now assaulting me with the nauseating smell of cowhide. I wanted to run away. And yet I wanted to hold on for dear life.

"Before I bring her in," Dr. Miller began, "I want you to know that in all my many years of doing this, I've never seen such obvious proof that a couple has made the right decision. She is significantly disfigured." I guess that original assumption regarding "duplication of chromosome 9p" had been wrong after all. Our daughter would not have looked normal—he could see it—and sadly, I was comforted by that news.

Dr. Miller stepped out the door and moments later returned with a tiny bundle wrapped in a pink blanket. As he lowered her into my arms, I began to cry. I cried so hard I couldn't see through my tears. All I could manage was an apology. Over and over, I told her how sorry I was, how much we loved her and wished we could keep her. I told her it was all so unfair and assured her that she was in a much better place.

I don't know how long I sat there with her in my arms. Dr. Miller and his nurse didn't say a word, and they didn't rush me. They simply sat and allowed me the time I needed. Eventually the tears slowed, and for the first time, I saw my baby girl. I studied her face—her pink cheeks, her tiny nose and soft lashes. I memorized the lines of her pouting lips and her fingers, barely longer than a paper clip. I didn't see one ounce of the disfigurement they said was there. I only saw my love for her.

After some time, I told Dr. Miller that I was ready. I kissed her wrinkled forehead and whispered goodbye before he gently took her from my arms and left the room. When he returned, he handed me a folder that contained both a birth and death certificate, and a set of photos of the baby wrapped in the same pink blanket. It was a bit twisted, in my opinion—posed "newborn" portraits—as if we would be leaving as proud new parents. It took me a long time to understand why they were given to us. At some point later it became clear—one look is all it takes to understand the severity of her condition.

Somehow, we survived that week in Kansas and walked away clutching the slightest glimmer of hope. It was tragic, yet it was fortifying. We had started the week with no desire to know the baby's sex, and we certainly had no intention of naming her or bringing home her ashes, but all of that had changed by week's end. We took solace in believing we had done the right thing. We spared our innocent daughter from a cruel existence, and we allowed ourselves a second chance.

We named her Angela Marie.

I couldn't possibly see it then, but we were never meant to have her. As devastating as the experience had been, it was short-lived, and it was over. The only way I could possibly move forward would be to package it up and place it on a shelf. Eventually, it would be a distant memory—I hoped.

CHAPTER 3
A Second Chance

We returned from Kansas at the beginning of July. I'm certain it was my bleak mental state, but I swear it didn't rain once the entire month. From there, the months trudged along in black-and-white while the rest of the world sped by in technicolor. As I grieved for a daughter that I never had a chance to know but fell instantly in love with, I longed for someone to push the play button. I wanted nothing more than to get pregnant, the sooner the better, and when months passed with no success, my grief turned to despair.

It was just a few days before my thirty-third birthday, and again I found myself, in tears, on the phone with my mother. We had said goodbye to Angela at the end of June, and here it was the end of October, and I wasn't pregnant yet.

"Why is it taking so long?" I pleaded.

"Be patient, honey. It will happen." I could tell by the tone of her voice that she was heartbroken. She couldn't bear to see me so unhappy. I wanted to believe her, but in the midst of grief, it's impossible to see beyond the moment.

A colleague at the time suggested that I make an appointment to see his wife, who just happened to be the head of obstetrics and gynecology at a nearby well-regarded hospital. Perhaps she could offer reassurance that there was no physical problem preventing me from conceiving. I had nothing to lose, so I made an appointment.

I had met Dr. Roberts only once before but immediately felt comfortable with her. She was incredibly understanding, and she was also all business. I didn't want anyone's pity, and I certainly didn't need to be given false hope. We talked through everything that had happened. After examining me, she assured me that my body had healed perfectly. There appeared to be no physical reason why I shouldn't conceive. She also sensed that I needed more and referred me to a fertility specialist whom she knew well. We both knew she did it more for my mental health than anything else. I took the doctor's number, thanked her profusely for her time, and went home to schedule yet another appointment. I felt as though I could tell my story to anyone simply by linking together the countless appointments that I had been to over the last thirteen months.

The first opening the specialist had was three weeks away. I asked the receptionist if they could call me should there be a cancellation, and she assured me they would. It had been almost six months since we had been to Kansas. Perhaps my stress was easing a bit, because my disappointment over the delay didn't feel quite as overwhelming as it would have two months earlier. It's true what they say about time: it heals. And I was slowly accepting the age-old adage that all things happen for a reason, and what's meant to be will be. If we were meant to be parents, we would. But the thought had crossed my mind—after our decision to play God, maybe we no longer deserved a baby. Despite my mixed emotions, Andrew and I didn't ease up on our efforts.

On Friday of the following week, as I was hanging Christmas decorations and feeling unexpectedly cheery, the phone rang. It was the specialist's office. A patient had cancelled, and they had an opening to see me on Monday. I took the appointment, despite having a strange sense that I might not need it. I had been feeling all afternoon as if my good mood over the last few days was because of more than just an adjustment in my perspective. Something about me seemed to have changed physically.

After meeting with the specialist, I received exactly the news I expected: there was no reason I shouldn't be able to conceive naturally and have another baby. With that assurance, I promised myself I would put the thought of getting pregnant aside for a while. Instead, I focused on the upcoming Christmas holiday, and my good mood somehow remained.

We were hosting Christmas Eve dinner. Early that afternoon, while I was busy with preparations, I thought about the fact that I was a few days late. I fought the impulse to do a pregnancy test. I didn't want to ruin the holiday with another month's worth of disappointment, but eventually my impulsivity got the best of me. I put down my measuring spoon, snuck up to the bathroom, and grabbed the extra test that had been sitting in the medicine cabinet. Five minutes later, I found myself a bit confused and a lot frustrated. Half of a plus sign had appeared. Not a whole one. Half. I threw the stick in the trash and shrugged it off as being defective. The day after Christmas, I would get another test. As I descended the steps to the kitchen, a smile spread slowly across my face.

It wasn't a minus sign.

I spent the rest of the day running between the kitchen and the bathroom. I checked that little stick fifteen times, and each time I saw the same thing—a plus sign. Even though it wasn't fully formed, I began to have a little faith in what it was telling me. What better Christmas gift could there possibly be?

———

Just as I had known from the start with Angela that everything was wrong, I knew from the start with this baby that everything was right. I had no twinges of pain, no spotting of blood, and no negative gut feelings, and surely lightning couldn't strike twice. Still, after that horrendous experience, I insisted upon an amniocentesis, despite the possible risk of miscarriage. I felt a connection with Dr. Roberts that I didn't feel with my own doctor, so I asked if she would be able to perform it. She didn't hesitate, and we scheduled it for a Wednesday in March. I would be sixteen weeks along by then.

When that Wednesday finally came, I was petrified. I knew I had nothing to fear, but that didn't stop my imagination from getting the best of me. Before beginning, Dr. Roberts urged me to stay calm. All signs had been positive so far, and getting myself worked up would only make her job harder. She told me to relax and think positively. The first step would be an ultrasound, which was the part I feared most. It was like opening the door to a dark attic room, fearing what might be lurking. Nonetheless, I took a deep breath and told her I was ready. After viewing several images on her screen, she paused to empty her instruments onto the tray beside me.

"Hmmm, that's strange," she said.

I filled with panic. Those were not the words I wanted to hear. "What's wrong?" I asked with trepidation.

"Normally my test tubes have pink lids, and today they have blue ones." Andrew and I looked at her, not understanding at first, then looked at one another and smiled. I breathed a sigh of relief and settled back as she led us through the procedure, pointing out various positive signs as she went.

"I'm confident that the results will come back as good news," she assured us. "I would also expect the baby to arrive sometime around

August twenty-fifth." She left us with a smile as we beamed at one another.

A week went by before we received the results. "I have good news for you," she said. "Everything is normal."

"Oh, thank God." I exhaled, not realizing I had been holding my breath. To say that I was relieved was an understatement. By this time, we had had enough surprises, so I asked to know the sex. Sure enough, those blue lids had been no coincidence. It was a boy.

As soon as I ended my call with Dr. Roberts, I dialed Andrew. The moment he picked up, I screamed into the phone, "It's a boy! And he's healthy!"

"Oh, thank God!"

"I know, that's what *I* said!" We spent a few minutes on the phone, wallowing in the good news, before he promised to be home early so we could celebrate.

Those positive results were more than just good news. They were permission: permission to plan, to decorate the nursery, to have a baby shower and start thinking about names. Most importantly, they gave us permission to be happy, even though that happiness was tinged with guilt. There was a sadness to being so happy about having a healthy baby when we had just let go of a very unhealthy one. Something about it seemed so careless and selfish.

Still, from that point forward, my pregnancy was a joy. We moved my office from the second floor of our house to the third, to an extra bedroom opposite the dumping ground. It would allow us to have the nursery right next to our bedroom. We borrowed a crib and changing table from Andrew's sister, who no longer needed them, and chose colors for the baby's room. We also compiled a list of everything we would need as new parents, so the grandmothers-to-be could organize a baby shower. The biggest problem we faced was settling on the name. We went through every possibility and narrowed it down to several but failed to land on the perfect choice, so throughout those remaining months, I simply called the baby "bud."

In the early morning hours of a hot and humid August Friday, I was awakened by mild contractions. The pain was disorganized enough that I questioned if it was really time, so I lay awake for several hours, trying to decide what to do. When six o'clock finally rolled around, I knew I needed to get moving. If this baby was coming today, there were a lot of loose ends to tie up. I took a deep breath and thought for a moment about the day. It was the twenty-fifth—the baby's due date. Little did I know how foretelling it was that this boy of mine was about to show up precisely on time.

I nudged Andrew gently. "You better get up. I've been awake since two thirty, and I'm pretty sure I'm in labor."

"Wait, what?" He startled in confusion. "Are you sure? Did your water break?" He jumped out of bed, now fully awake, and frantically reached for his pants. "Do we need to get to the hospital?"

"Relax. My water didn't break, and I have work to do, and I'm not going to the hospital only to sit there for twelve hours because it's a false alarm. Go to work, do what you need to do. I'll call the doctor, and we'll go from there."

We were polar opposites in that moment. His head was spinning, not knowing what to do first, and I was as cool as a cucumber. It was only with the promise that I would touch base with him within a couple of hours that I was successful in getting him out the door. Before calling the doctor, I climbed the three floors to my office, sat down at my desk, and dashed off an email to clients letting them know that today was the day, and assuring them that my support network for the next six weeks was in place. I packaged up project files and sent them off to my team with the appropriate instructions for completion, telling them I would check in when I returned home from the hospital.

Once my work situation was under control, I made my way down the three floors and down one more to the basement so I could transfer clothes from the washer to the dryer. I checked the stack of bills on the kitchen table to make sure none needed to go out right away, and I took a quick peek in the fridge to make sure there were enough leftovers to last Andrew for a day or two. I don't recall what other miscellaneous items I tended to before packing my toothbrush and a few other last-minute things—there had to be at least half a dozen—and once I was confident I had checked everything off the list, I called my doctor.

"If your contractions are only five minutes apart, what are you waiting for? You really should get to the hospital," she insisted.

"Yes, but they're not consistent. They *were* five minutes apart, and now they've spread out again."

"Well, okay, but don't wait too long. As soon as they become organized again, get to the hospital."

I hung up and called Andrew. As I waited for him to pick up, I looked at the clock. It was already nine forty-five. He was almost an hour away, and I wanted him to have a substantial meal before we left for the hospital. "You better come home. It might be a long time before you have a chance to eat again."

"Okay, I'm on my way," he replied hurriedly. He arrived a short time later, and within thirty minutes of his arrival, the contractions were coming fast and hard.

"You better eat a little faster," I chuckled, "because we need to go!"

We arrived at the hospital shortly after noon. Of course, my contractions not only slowed, they almost stopped. But after walking the halls for less than an hour, I was ready for that epidural I missed out on the first time. I speak from experience when I say that an epidural is a huge plus when it comes to childbirth. There was another difference too—I was far more mentally, emotionally, and physically prepared for this delivery, and I was 100 percent focused on what was about to take place. We were about to have a son. And in stark contrast to my first time, which had a predetermined tragic outcome, labor and delivery was a cinch.

With one last push at 7:03 p.m., our little boy finally arrived. By all indications, he was a healthy, normal baby. I'm assuming every new mother that cradles a baby with ten perfect fingers and toes feels as though her child is a gift. But for us, this beautiful baby was so much more. His birth was a defining moment. It marked the end of a journey that had been fraught with overwhelming heartache. I looked down at his perfect being in my arms and whispered, "Hey, bud." Two tiny eyes popped open and looked straight into mine. I'm certain that his big sister was looking down on him at that moment—and cheering him on.

CHAPTER 4
World of Change

The road from point A to point B is rarely straight. In our case, we had taken a wrong left turn and traveled through a pitch-black tunnel, but after a thirteen-month detour, we finally appeared to be on the right path. We had a beautiful baby boy, and we were excited to experience parenting.

We had until Sunday, when the hospital would send us home, to decide on the baby's name. His middle name would be Andrew, but we still hadn't settled on a first name. Jonathan was at the top of our list, and Jonathan Andrew felt solid. It was a mouthful, but we would call him Jack for short, and with his light hair, fair skin, and blue eyes, Jack seemed to suit him. We informed the hospital of our decision, and with a few lines of elegant black script and a raised seal on a small sheet of parchment, our son was official.

Sunday morning brought ninety-four degrees of heat and high humidity. It promised to be a typical August steam bath, but I didn't mind. I couldn't be happier. Andrew, on the other hand, couldn't be more frightened.

"Are they really going to let us take him home? Don't we need a license or something? We have no idea what we're doing."

I laughed at his incredulousness. "Yes, they are going to let us take him home. We don't need a license, and there is no owner's manual. We'll figure it out," I assured him as he carefully snapped the car seat into place before helping me into the warm car. I didn't dare say it, but I was scared to death too. We had learned firsthand that anything can go wrong. But I wouldn't allow those thoughts to take hold. Jack was here, he was healthy, and he was now the center of our world.

I had made all the necessary arrangements to be off from work for at least six weeks, but Andrew could only be home for the first ten days. It's amazing how well acquainted we became in that first week with this third member of our household. Jack had three cries, and I could distinguish each: "Feed me now, I'm starving"; "Good God, it's been a long day, I'm exhausted"; and "Oh shit, I've made a mess of things."

Once Andrew returned to work, my mother jumped in to help, coming each day to fold laundry and clean dishes or take Jack for a walk while I napped. She relished the opportunity to dote over her new grandson, and I was grateful for the support, though I knew I couldn't depend on her forever. Eventually life would need to return to normal, and I would need to get back to my career as a graphic designer. Having a type A personality meant that my days had always been routine. For nine months, Jack had been the perfect copilot, not forcing much change to that routine other than the occasional reminder to stop and refuel with an afternoon nap. But now that my sidekick was present in the flesh, adding him to the daily mix proved more mentally challenging than I anticipated. The creative process needs to flow without interruption, and newborn babies are the definition of interruption. I found myself needing to learn the difficult art of "stop and start." Being creative on demand was hard enough. Being creative on demand in short spurts felt virtually impossible. I found myself wishing I could play the role of mother—and only that role—indefinitely.

It was an especially hard day in the first few weeks of my return to work. Jack had been irritable most of the day, and I had hit a brick wall with a project. A quick glance at the clock told me I would need to get dinner underway. Even with the care of a baby added to my daily plate, I was determined to maintain my image of the perfect wife and have a hot dinner on the table every night.

I had planned on making chicken cutlets, a dish I could normally manage with my eyes closed. I was successful in prepping the chicken, but I had no sooner gotten it in the pan when Jack began to cry—again. It wasn't like him to fuss all day, and I worried that he was sick. Hoping that he simply wanted attention, I lifted him from his swing, cradled him in my left arm, and returned to the stove. Without realizing it, I had turned the heat too high, and the cutlets were already starting to burn. I tried flipping one or two, but they were sticking to the pan, so I shifted Jack to my shoulder to grab a spatula, and the jostling started him crying again. While soothing him with one arm, I wrestled the chicken with the other, inadvertently pushing the pan right off the stove. The chicken was still sliding across the floor when the door opened and Andrew entered. Tears began a slow descent down my cheeks.

"I can't do this," I cried.

"Do what?" he asked.

"I can't manage all of this. I can't work, take care of Jack, and make dinner every night. It's too much."

"You have to do it," he responded with a shrug. The expression on his face told me it wasn't up for debate. I glared at him. I wasn't sure what stunned me more: his total lack of sensitivity, or my immediate concession to his way of thinking.

Yes. I had to do this.

Jack was a permanent part of the equation now. We couldn't afford for me not to work, and we needed to eat every night. These were my responsibilities as a mother and wife, and I wouldn't admit defeat. Nor would I ask for help. I won't say it came naturally or even all that successfully, but somehow, I pushed past the hurdles and adjusted my daily routine to accommodate Jack's presence and my added role of mother. He was four months old to the day when he started sleeping through the night, and it was a blessing. I would put him down at eight o'clock in the evening and not hear a sound from him until eight o'clock in the morning.

I had gone from getting out of bed each day pre-Jack at seven thirty to now getting up at five thirty. If I could raise myself at five thirty, surely I could manage five o'clock. And what harm could one less half hour of sleep do? My new norm became four thirty. It enabled me to work for a few hours, and then devote all my attention to Jack when he woke.

When the Jack clock struck eight, I put work aside to dress and feed him before taking him for a long walk in his stroller. By ten thirty he was ready for his first nap, and like clockwork, I could count on having a solid hour and a half for more work. In the afternoons, I fed him lunch, then trotted off to the grocery store to gather supplies for dinner. By two o'clock he was ready for his second ninety-minute nap, and back to work I would go. Once Jack woke, I started dinner so it would be ready by the time Andrew returned home. If I didn't need to go to the grocery store, I took Jack to the park. If it was raining, I subjected us to daytime television. Marking his milestones and celebrating his growth became my central focus. And all the while, I snapped one photo after another. *Click, click, click.* "Oh, wait, you look so cute in that outfit from Aunt Pat. . . ."

Click.

Four thousand photos later, Jack was a year old.

———

There hadn't been any indication during that year that something might not be right. I remember thinking that Jack was a little bit slower to develop in some areas than some of our friends' kids, but I wasn't sure it was cause for concern. At four weeks old, a bright toothless smile spread across his face for the first time, and from that point on, he rarely cried. By six months, Jack was sitting on his own, but at ten months he had yet to start crawling. That worried me, so I consulted the expert.

"Do you think I should be concerned?" I asked my mother. "How old was I when I started crawling?"

"Hmm, let me think. You were about nine months old. But I wouldn't worry—all kids are different. Your brother didn't start *talking* until he was almost *four*. I thought for sure there was something wrong with him, and look at him now." True enough, my brother was the epitome of perfection.

She had put my mind at rest. Jack would start crawling when Jack was ready, and sure enough, at ten and a half months he finally began. One Sunday afternoon, at thirteen months, he hoisted himself with the help of a doorknob and took his first steps—and never looked back.

Eventually I got so good at juggling everything, my days began to spin by. Life was a merry-go-round.

Working woman. Nurturing woman. Dutiful woman.

Working. Nurturing. Dutiful.

Work. Nurture. Do.

Although I was successful in finding a rhythm for navigating Jack's ever-changing first year, I had lost sight of the woman. I had too much on my plate, and I was exhausted. Despite the fact that I loved having Jack at home, by the time he reached sixteen months, I had run out of steam. I needed a break, and he needed socialization.

"We need to move," I announced one evening as I pushed a spoonful of mashed peas past Jack's lips.

"What are you talking about?" Andrew asked in surprise.

"We can't stay in this house forever. We need more space, and with Jack walking now, being on this busy road makes me nervous. I want a quiet yard where he can play without me having to worry." My exasperation was obvious. "Plus he needs to start spending time with other children, and I don't have much confidence in any of the day care around here."

Andrew backed off, unable to argue. For a starter home, the neighborhood was fine, but as a suitable place to raise a family, it was far from ideal. I hated the thought of giving it up, but I knew it was time. One afternoon, after several months of searching, I stumbled upon a listing for a home that appeared to have it all.

This is it, I thought and called Andrew at work. "I found a house," I told him excitedly. "This might be the one—it's perfect—an English Tudor on two and a half acres."

"How much?" he asked.

"Well, it's a little beyond our price range. But it can't hurt to look. Maybe we can talk them down." Andrew agreed and promised to call the realtor. Later that week, after visiting the property and viewing the house, we talked seriously about making an offer.

"You have to admit, it's perfect," I said. "This is the only house we've seen that's unique. I don't want your average two-story Colonial. I want something that has as much character as this house. Besides, you'll be closer to work, and the property is beautiful."

"But it's a lot of money," he countered.

"Let's lowball them. Maybe they'll accept our offer, and if they do, we can take the down payment out of savings and replace it once we sell this house." I felt a sense of urgency. On the surface, I didn't want someone else to get it. Deep down, I had this notion that improving our lifestyle would somehow calm the restlessness that had taken hold of me.

Andrew finally gave in. "Okay, I'll call the realtor in the morning, and we'll make an offer."

The phone rang three times before I heard my mother's voice on the other end.

"We got the house!" I screamed, almost not believing it.

"That's great!" she exclaimed. "I hear there's a wonderful pre-school just down the road. Apparently it has an excellent reputation, not just as a school but for day care as well. You should look into it."

"I will," I said, jotting down the name. I couldn't believe this was happening.

After just five weeks we had an offer on our house—for our asking price—and we would have until April to move out. Andrew set to work on renovating the new house; I focused on getting us packed and ready to move. That included getting Jack enrolled in day care for three half days a week. I had done my due diligence, and sure enough, the school my mother had told me about had an excellent reputation. Although we wouldn't be settled in the house until April, Jack was scheduled to start at the beginning of March. There would be a bit of back-and-forth for a while, but I was willing to deal with it. This would be good for Jack and for me as well. I longed to return to a reasonable routine.

Although the first few days were a challenge, Jack adjusted to day care quickly, and I breathed a huge sigh of relief. He went off each day happily and without hesitation. Monday through Wednesday, he was gone all morning and returned so exhausted that he slept all afternoon. My mother filled in on Thursday and Friday, arriving at the house by midmorning, freeing me up to work the rest of the day. Maybe I would survive this motherhood thing after all.

CHAPTER 5
Autopilot

One Thursday afternoon, while on the phone with a client, I heard my mother return with Jack from the supermarket. She appeared in the doorway to my office just as I hung up the phone.

"Something strange happened while we were at the store," she said uncomfortably.

"What's that?" I responded, only half paying attention as I made notes from my call.

"Well, I was pushing the cart down the aisle when another woman passed us with a little boy in her cart. He looked to be about the same age. Jack reached out and hit the boy. For no reason."

"How come?" I wondered aloud.

"I don't know," she responded. "It was very strange. I've never seen him act like that."

Even though she was my barometer for motherhood, and I was still highly inexperienced, I was too preoccupied with work and shrugged off her comment as overreaction. Jack was eighteen months old; I assumed it to be typical behavior for a toddler. Although I let her comment slide and she didn't mention the incident again, something about it tugged at me. Generally, Jack was all smiles, but on occasion he could turn nasty, and it seemed as though it was always in public.

On the flip side, his quirky behaviors at home made us laugh. While most little boys were playing with cars and trucks, Jack was playing with pots and pans. Not just one or two—*all* the pots and pans. Every morning, the kitchen cabinets were emptied. Every pot, pan, and plastic container was pulled out and arranged in the order of the day across the kitchen floor. I gave up trying to put them away—they would just end up back on the floor, stacked and ready for Jack to stir, blend, and whisk his heart out. When he wasn't at day care or napping, it was all he was doing.

"I told my parents we would join them at the beach for a week," Andrew informed me one evening a few weeks later. "Can you manage that?"

I glanced at the calendar but doubted it would be a problem. It was the end of July, and business generally slowed during summer. "Yes, that's fine," I replied. Our time at the beach with Andrew's family was always the highlight of my summer—we never went anywhere else—and I did enjoy them, so I was grateful to go. "I hope Jack likes the beach more than he did last year."

I thought back to the previous year's trip. Jack wasn't quite a year old yet, and he didn't seem to like anything about the beach. Both the sun and the heat agitated him, and he cried every time he got sand on himself. "I've never seen a kid that doesn't like the beach," Andrew's mother had commented.

"Yeah, hopefully this year will be different," Andrew said. "Do you think we should pack the pots and pans?" he added with a chuckle. Although I laughed along with him, we left the contents of our kitchen behind.

Our first evening there, Andrew's father decided that we should have dinner out.

"Why don't you go, and I'll stay here with Jack?" I offered.

"Why would you do that?" My father-in-law's question was laced with a tone of, "You must be crazy."

"I don't want Jack ruining everyone's dinner. He's too young to eat out."

"That's silly," Andrew's father fired back. "How will he ever learn how to behave in a restaurant if you don't take him out?"

Andrew stepped in. "The last few times we've taken Jack out with us, he's been really tough."

His father roared, "Tough? How could he possibly be tough? He's only two! You tell him, 'Sit in your seat, and don't move!'"

I'm certain my eyes rolled at his tough-guy mentality, but I didn't say a word. It was a nice idea, but as of late, it wasn't working with Jack. He would throw silverware, or leave the table and wander. It's not that we thought this was okay. We tried to control him, but it seemed his behavior was getting away from us. He was becoming uncontrollable. Jack did what Jack wanted, no matter what we said or did.

How could Jack be smarter than us? Maybe Andrew's father was right—maybe we needed to be tougher on him, do a better job of disciplining him. Wanting to prove myself, I gave in and agreed to dinner out.

There were nine of us. We hadn't been seated long when Jack started rolling around in his seat. He fidgeted for a bit, stood up, sat down, then stood up again.

"Jack, here . . . ," I said, handing him the crayons and coloring page that the restaurant had provided. "Why don't we color for a bit?" Jack took the crayon from my hand and appeared to be interested. I relaxed a little and tried to enjoy myself. I said a little prayer that we would survive this event.

Approximately thirteen seconds later, Jack was hurling the crayon across the table.

"Jack! Stop doing that! Don't throw the crayons." I tried to redirect him, but he was out of his seat and across the restaurant so fast, I had no choice but to chase him.

I snatched him and signaled to Andrew that I was taking Jack outside. I felt like a failure in front of his family, and I knew we would never hear the end of this. Andrew and I spent the rest of dinner taking turns with managing Jack, most of the time away from our table.

The incident left us frustrated. It was difficult to pinpoint the problem and verbalize it. It wasn't as though we weren't disciplining Jack, and he generally wasn't a bad child. At home, he wasn't a handful at all. It was when we were in public or around other people that he would act up. It was like he knew exactly when and how to push our buttons—and was doing it purposely. Being unable to explain Jack's behavior made us want to look past it, so we wrote it off as being part of the "terrible twos."

As Jack continued to develop, our marriage was chugging along blindly in the background. My days no longer aligned with Andrew's. His schedule had never changed, while mine had turned upside down completely. He adored Jack, but he had little understanding of what it took to care for him while maintaining a business and a household, while still being someone's partner. Whether we realized it or not, we were losing sight of one another.

I suppose that's the same new-parent story everyone reads. Children come along and marriage goes by the wayside, but there was more to what was happening between us than just the standard new-parent overload. I was knowingly distancing myself from our marriage—filling my life with distractions. I had thought that improving our lifestyle by moving into a bigger, better house with a big yard would somehow improve our relationship. I was beginning to sense that even having a child was simply a Band-Aid.

My thoughts kept drifting back to what Dr. Miller had told us and the other couples during our counseling sessions in Kansas: "Traumatic experiences such as this will often lead to difficulties down the road. Don't be surprised if your relationship begins to feel the strain." At the time, I couldn't even fathom that thought. That would never happen to us. Our relationship was the constant that enabled me to push through the pain that had crippled me for months. How could it possibly break into pieces?

As our days, weeks, and months continued to drift by, I found myself analyzing the relationships of everyone around me, wondering where I had gone wrong. Andrew loved me, of course, but it was only as long as I fit the mold of who he wanted me to be. I couldn't understand why it had taken me so long to see it. If ever I spent too long talking to one person at a party, I would get a disapproving look. I constantly monitored the length of my shorts and the sheerness of fabrics. None could be too short or too revealing. Eventually I gave up on wearing anything sleeveless for fear that my bra strap might show. Andrew would consider it inappropriate. When we were young, it all seemed okay. I believed he was keeping me in line—saving me from myself. As the years passed, I buried myself in the belief that our relationship was solid and safe. Normal. The exact point at which I had lost sight of myself to be this man's partner didn't matter. What did matter was that having Jack suddenly woke me up to how ridiculous my behavior had been.

I could hear my mother making a cup of tea for her lunch. She must have put Jack down for his afternoon nap already. Unable to focus, I wandered out of my office, down to the kitchen, and sat at the table beside her.

"I need your advice," I said nervously.

She could sense that something wasn't right. "What's wrong, honey?"

"I don't know, Mom. I'm just not happy."

"What do you mean, 'not happy'?"

"In my marriage." There, it was out. "I feel like I made a mistake in marrying Andrew, but now we have Jack, and we just moved and . . . and I don't know what to do." I could feel myself cracking.

"Did something happen? Is he having an affair?" she asked, surprised by this sudden acknowledgment.

"No, nothing happened, and I doubt Andrew would ever cheat on me. I . . . I just . . . I was so naive. I had no idea of what having a life partner even meant." I couldn't stop. I had to get my regret out in the open.

"Well, honestly, I never thought you and Andrew were right for one another. What attracted you to him?" She was throwing me a line, hoping to pull me to safety, yet I felt a stab of betrayal.

"I don't know. I thought he was cute, I guess. If you didn't think he was right for me, why didn't you say anything?" I choked back tears, knowing that I was about to tumble into an abyss.

"I thought you knew what you were doing. I didn't want to interfere." She rested her hand softly over mine. "Don't cry. Listen, the two of you need to get yourselves to a marriage counselor. And if counseling doesn't work and you feel that getting divorced is what you need to do, your father and I will stand behind you 100 percent."

There she was again—that matter-of-fact, no-bullshit woman who doubled as my mother. How could she make it sound so easy?

"I don't want to get divorced," I cried, "but I need to be me. I can't continue being someone I'm not, just to make Andrew happy. I'm not even sure he loves me. He just loves the idea of me. I don't want Jack growing up thinking that he needs to be anyone other than who he is, just to please someone else."

It would be twelve or fifteen years before I would recognize the immense value of that statement. How can you teach a child to live up to their full potential if you're not doing it yourself?

Just prior to Jack's third birthday—and after months of agonizing, assessing, justifying, and flip-flopping—I had cemented my decision to leave Andrew. It was a tremendously stressful time. The air between us was thick with anger. Andrew was devastated and couldn't understand how or why this was happening, and I hated that I was hurting him.

"Karen told me today that I'm in an abusive relationship." We had been cleaning the dinner dishes in silence one evening when Andrew hurled this at me, as if he were trying to explain away my insanity.

I paused. "That's funny. She told me the same thing." Obviously, our marriage counselor wasn't too interested in helping us save our marriage. I knew then that neither of us would be seeing her again, together or separately. I put down my sponge, turned off the water, and looked directly into his eyes. "All I'm asking for is thirty days. Please," I begged, "can't you go live with your parents for a month?"

"And not see my son?" For Andrew to think that I would keep him from seeing Jack was ridiculous. That was not my intention.

"No, of course not, but I need time to think," I insisted, though I knew in my heart that thirty days apart wouldn't change anything.

"I'm not going to walk out on my son." Andrew was firm.

I had to look away. The pain in his eyes sliced through my heart. "Then I'm going to start looking for a house."

"You can't be serious," he said, grabbing my arm and forcing me to face him.

"I'll take money from our savings for the down payment, and we can deduct it from my share later."

"Why don't you just rent an apartment for six months?" he pleaded.

That idea made the most sense, but I knew that if I bought a house, the financial commitment would stop me from going back to him. I was acting on autopilot. I was second-guessing myself at every turn, but I knew that I needed to follow through. The only reason I could offer Andrew was that I needed to be me, both for myself and for our son.

I turned to look at him. He was flattened, just as he was when he realized that having Angela wasn't something he could handle.

"You might not see it now"—I floated the words delicately—"but someday we'll get past all of this, and I guarantee you our relationship will be special."

The look of disgust on his face broke me in half. "I guarantee *you—that* will never happen." He snatched his jacket and stormed out the door, slamming it as he left.

I didn't invest much effort in my home search. This time around, it wasn't about charm or having the pool I had always wanted. My priority was Jack and finding something that was close to Andrew so the transition between two homes would be as seamless as possible. The following morning, I reached out to the realtor who had sold our first home, explained my situation, and asked for his help.

"I'm shocked," was his response. "I never would have guessed that the two of you would split. You seemed so happy together."

"Well, a lot can happen in a year and a half." Not wanting to get into the complex emotions and self-reflection that drove me to such a significant upsetting of the apple cart, I left it at that. It was all so complicated. Andrew and I had been happy together—for a long time. We never fought, and from a nuts-and-bolts perspective, we had a very functional marriage, a great working relationship. I was having a hard time understanding it myself.

The realtor agreed to pull some listings together for me, and that evening I found myself sifting through a pile. I emailed him with a list of properties I wanted to see, questioning how soon I could see them. If I didn't maintain momentum, I risked changing my mind. Over the course of the next two days, I looked at five homes that met my criteria. Only one felt right. I quickly arranged for a second viewing to get my parents' input, and they agreed if I could manage it financially, it would be perfect. The following day, I made an offer. One day later it was accepted, and a settlement date was set for just three weeks out. The whole process took less than a week.

There was no turning back.

I lay in the dark that first night in this strange house—it was far from being a home just yet—paralyzed by loneliness, staring up from a mattress on the floor at the blank walls closing in on me. I wondered which would come first: would I cry myself into a cold, dreamless sleep, or would I be swallowed whole by this foreign, empty life surrounding me? I had walked out of my "dream life" with nothing more than my clothes and my office furniture, letting Andrew keep everything else. I was doing enough damage as it was; I didn't feel entitled to anything more. My mattress and the family room furniture had been delivered, but it would be a couple of days before Jack's bedroom set and my own would arrive, so Jack was staying with Andrew. Lying there in blackness, it hit me: my time with my son had suddenly been cut in half, and it had been my own doing.

How could I have done that to Jack? How could I be that selfish?

I was scrambling to find reasons that I could give everyone in order to explain the madness I had created. I never imagined my life would end up in this empty space. There was only one thing I was certain of—I couldn't allow myself to be weak. I had to stay on course regardless of the hurdles in front of me, so I kicked my heartache and self-doubt out of the room and welcomed the tears that would carry me through a restless night.

When morning came, the sunlight streaming through my bedroom window cast a brighter hue across a still unfamiliar horizon, and I felt new resolve. I needed to make this work, and the only way to do that was to tackle the arduous process of settling in—to a new home, a new life, and a new way of being. I was living on my own for the first time in my life and it scared the hell out of me, but I would not let it beat me.

Jack became my focus. It had been little more than twenty-four hours, but I felt as though I had been away from him for days. I couldn't wait to see him and hold him. I felt the need to reassure him. I needed to reassure myself.

CHAPTER 6
Phase du Jour

Although I had purchased a home and we were living separately, Andrew and I had not made any moves toward divorcing. There had been some truth in my needing time away from him. Just being separated allowed me time to think and gain perspective. I didn't want to rush this. I was feeling so much internal confusion that I wasn't even sure I wanted to follow through, and I felt I owed it to both Andrew and Jack to at least try. Maybe after some time apart it would be possible to work things out.

In the first few months of our separation, we had no formal pattern of custody. Andrew couldn't bear to be without Jack for more than a couple of days, so Jack would stay with me for two nights and then with Andrew for two nights. Back and forth we went, two days on, two days off. We also made an effort to spend time together as a family on the weekends, whether it be to watch a movie or spend Saturday afternoon at the park pushing Jack on the swings. It felt natural and easy, but it also felt strained. Andrew still wanted to kiss me good night, and that simple act, something that had always been so comfortable, suddenly felt awkward. Time apart was forcing me to see the sad truth that life with Andrew was easy because it didn't challenge me. All I needed to do was be the way I had always been, and everything would be just fine. The only problem was that I wasn't growing. In that respect, my life had fallen flat.

Spending time together was also sending Andrew mixed messages. He wanted to believe that we could fix things, but I didn't have intentions of moving back in with him. I would steel myself every time the phone rang because I never knew which Andrew I was going to get—my husband of twelve years who still loved me and would do anything to have me back, or the man engulfed in anger because he had been hurt so deeply and needlessly.

On one of the afternoons that Andrew was scheduled to pick up Jack from school, my phone rang.

"Hello?" I answered gently.

"Hey," Andrew replied. Thankfully, his voice was calm and not tainted with anger. "I need to share something with you," he went on. "You're not going to believe what just happened."

"Is everything okay?" I worried that something was wrong with Jack.

"Yes, Jack is fine, but you're not going to believe what he did. You know how I have that stack of CDs in my truck?" Andrew always had at least fifty music discs piled on the seat of his truck. There were more in his truck than in our stereo cabinet. "I was trying to get Jack out of his car seat, and I knocked the entire stack off the seat. They were all over the ground."

"Okay . . . ," I said slowly, not knowing where this was going.

"Jack took one look at them and said that Sheryl Crow was missing. I asked him what he meant by that, and he just said that it was missing."

"I'm not following you."

"I took a look through the mess on the ground, and Jack was right. That new Sheryl Crow CD that I just bought wasn't in the pile. I looked all around the truck and found it under the front seat. He took one look at the pile and knew instantly that it was gone."

"Like that scene . . . ."

"Right, like that scene in the movie *Rain Man*." Andrew finished my thought. "It was exactly like that scene where Tom Cruise drops the matches, and Dustin Hoffman counts them in three seconds flat. It was the strangest thing. Jack took one look and just knew."

I wasn't sure what to make of Andrew's story. Maybe Jack just got lucky.

In the background, Jack's fascination with cookware was ongoing. It lasted so long that we began to think he might have some innate passion, a budding career path that he didn't knowingly choose but rather one that chose him. You hear of that happening. "He's been swinging a golf club ever since he learned to walk." Professional golfer. "She was coloring inside the lines at age two." Graphic designer. "He's always had an interest in trains." Amtrak engineer. With so many hours of practice, Jack must have become adept at crafting exquisite dishes, and I could practically taste his future title of world-class chef. But that bubble burst abruptly when Jack cast the cast iron aside—and took up driving. There would be no more retreating to the kitchen after day care. He was finally in the driver's seat.

Literally.

Every moment at home that Jack wasn't eating, sleeping, or being bathed was spent in the driveway. Whether it was my car or Andrew's truck, Jack would open the door, climb onto the front seat, and position himself on his knees behind the wheel. There he would stay, steering himself toward fantastical make-believe places. If a storm were to whip up, he would furiously flip on the windshield wipers, vanish the storm from his mind, and move on to some other magical setting. As long as the keys were out of reach, we agreed to let him have his fun.

As Jack cruised his way toward being a race car driver, he also acquired another unusual habit. He became oddly attached to my purse. At first, he simply wanted to take it along on every imaginary trip he set off on. Eventually, one or two of his toys began appearing in my bag. When Jack began putting things in my bag, I found it endearing and didn't think anything of it. It wasn't until he started emptying my bag of all its contents and filling it with his own, and then wanting to carry my bag everywhere that it became an issue. So, as any open-minded woman would do, I took my son shopping and let him pick out his own bag.

Over the next six months, Jack's obsession with bags remained. No matter where he went, he had his bag of the day in tow. Some became obvious favorites. There was a red Winnie-the-Pooh tote bag that accompanied him everywhere, always filled with the belongings Jack deemed most important.

One afternoon, I found that a package had been wedged into our mailbox along with the regular mail. It was addressed to Jack. The return address indicated that it was from my brother, and I was instantly curious. It wasn't Jack's birthday, and I couldn't imagine what it might be.

"You got a present in the mail today," I told Jack when I picked him up from day care that afternoon, "from Uncle Tom."

"What is it?" Jack asked excitedly.

"I don't know. You'll have to open it when we get home."

Jack tore the package open in three seconds, and I burst into laughter. Clearly, my gay brother had decided to have a field day with Jack's bag phase. Leave it to him to find a purple, heart-shaped sequined handbag. And I mean *purple*.

Jack was thrilled.

Andrew, on the other hand, was not amused.

"Can't you see he's lashing out?" was the question I heard repeatedly. Andrew believed that Jack was clinging to different objects and repeating the same behaviors because he was trying to make himself feel better about the separation. Well, that was true. Jack was trying to make himself feel better, but not because Andrew and I had split. Jack was trying to cope with circumstances that we weren't even aware of yet.

Despite Jack's enthusiasm over the heart bag, it was a bright yellow makeup case, which had been a free gift with a cosmetic purchase, that became his constant companion. Jack clung to that bag as if it contained his last will and testament. When my parents took him to have his picture taken with Santa, they tried taking it from him for the photo, but Jack refused. Santa himself couldn't pry it away, and we ended up with a Christmas photo of Jack on Santa's lap and the yellow makeup case on Jack's lap.

At the age of four, Jack moved onto wristwatches, belts, and plaid button-down shirts. The wristwatch interest was the most pronounced and lasted the longest. I don't even recall where the first watch came from or what type of watch it was, but Jack wouldn't go anywhere without it. Each time he saw a man wearing a watch, he would check to see which arm it was on. If that person had the watch on the left arm, and Jack had his on his right, we would need to stop and switch, and it got complicated quickly. Going to a mall was a major challenge; forget going into the city completely.

There was another phase during Jack's fourth year, and I have to admit, this one was my favorite—the suit phase. I'm not sure what prompted it. I just know that at my four-year-old son's request, I found myself buying him a three-piece suit, and he wanted to wear it everywhere. One evening we needed to run to the supermarket, but we wouldn't be going anywhere until he changed into his suit. Everywhere we went, Jack went in his suit. When we arrived at my aunt's house that year for Thanksgiving dinner, with the entire family in jeans and warm sweaters, my cousin wanted to know who brought the accountant. I knew then that my son was destined to stand out. Jack was committed to making a fashion statement every day.

Jack's cooking up of imaginary recipes, his fascination with driving, his interest in accessorizing—it was all just the beginning of his obsessive-compulsive behaviors. Jack became acutely fixated on one thing for a period of time, and as quickly as each obsession began, it was just as quickly replaced by another.

From Corvettes and suits, Jack moved on to collecting all things Pokémon, Yu-Gi-Oh!, and Bakugan. He wasn't interested in playing any of these Japanese character games; his main objective was solely to acquire as many characters and cards as possible.

From there, he transitioned to collecting sports cards of all types—baseball, basketball, football, and hockey. This was at least something we could understand. The trading of sports cards was big business, and it was a hobby that Andrew had always had interest in as a boy, so he set about teaching Jack the ins and outs. If he were to care for his cards properly, they might someday be worth a lot of money. Jack was instantly hooked and quickly became an afficionado. He learned how to use pricing guides to determine a card's worth, making note of every player's statistics. He carefully protected the valuable cards with plastic sleeves and even attempted to keep them organized. But then he decided, "Nope, I'm done with this," and the thousands of cards were dumped in big Tupperware bins and relegated to a shelf in a closet. His obsession had switched to jigsaw puzzles.

The puzzle phase was short but fascinating. Jack could dump the puzzle on the floor, take one look at the picture, and correctly assemble all the pieces just as quickly as you could put them back in the box randomly. We found ourselves buying puzzle after puzzle simply to test him.

Our heads were starting to spin.

CHAPTER 7

Mounting Concern

As Andrew and I stumbled our way through the divorce process, we found ourselves wrestling not only with our own emotions but with a child whose behavior was becoming less than exemplary. Concern was building, at home and at school.

At four, Jack was now a regular at his preschool. He had graduated from three half days to three full days a week, while my mother continued to pick up the slack on Thursdays and Fridays. Both Jack's teachers and his grandmother agreed that something was not quite right. He was meeting goals at a slower pace than the other kids—when he decided he was ready—and he had begun showing aggressive behaviors.

Every parent that has a child in day care or school knows that when the school calls, the news isn't good. Your child is either sick or in trouble. "Sick" means complete disruption to your day, and "in trouble" could mean any one of a hundred bad things. So of course I was apprehensive when I saw the school's number on my phone one Tuesday afternoon.

I was informed, much to my horror, that Jack had thrown a rock at another student during recess, the daughter of one of his teachers. Jack had hit her in the head.

From day one, Miss Jo had been one of Jack's biggest supporters.

If she didn't fully understand him, she at least had the skills and patience to manage him. She possessed some otherworldly knowledge that enabled her to keep Jack in line both academically and socially. She seemed to know what Jack needed most and appeared to be truly invested in helping him, unlike so many others that we would encounter down the line. Rightfully so, we revered her.

Jack's throwing a rock at her daughter changed that. Permanently.

Miss Jo assured us numerous times that "it was fine," kids do stupid things, and all that mattered was that Ellie wasn't seriously hurt. But it wasn't fine. Her demeanor toward Jack changed. Of course, she continued to do her job and fulfill her obligation to him. But she no longer provided him with the extra attention or understanding he so desperately needed, and her interaction with us went cold. Lasting physical harm had thankfully been avoided, but permanent emotional damage had been done. Jack's actions managed to have an eternally negative impact on everyone other than Jack.

I'm certain now that all the turmoil of our divorce acted as a smoke screen for Jack's behavior. In struggling my way through a tough separation, I had been oblivious to the fact that my feeling of "needing to get through each day" with Jack wasn't normal. It wasn't just because I was a single mom trying to maintain a business and a new home and rebuild my personal life. It was because Jack was difficult. How and when did all this happen? As we were laughing our way through each one of his phases, his issues had been piling up in front of us. I woke up one morning and the laughter was gone, replaced by confusion and frustration.

Why was he so tough?

That fall, at the age of five, Jack moved into kindergarten. We weren't surprised at the end of that year when they informed us that Jack wasn't ready to move on to first grade. He was behind the other kids in writing, math, and just about everything else. His birthday fell close to the cutoff, so we had a choice: move him on to first grade and have him be the youngest in his class, or have him repeat kindergarten and move forward the following year as one of the oldest. The last thing we wanted him to do was struggle more. We figured if he had the advantage of age, he was likely to be more mature, with potential for being a leader rather than a follower. It was decided that come the new school year, Jack would repeat kindergarten at his current school in the mornings, then go off to Mrs. McGeehan's kindergarten class at the local elementary school in the afternoon. With a game plan in place for the upcoming school year but still a few weeks of summer left, I decided to take him to Disney World. I wanted to travel with him and provide new experiences.

The trip was everything you would expect—Jack had the ridiculously lucky pleasure of shaking Mickey's hand at the afternoon parade, we rode the monorail to the Magic Kingdom and back more than once, and we exhausted every ride ticket on the Buzz Lightyear ride. We spun that route 262 times, at least. Jack was enjoying himself, and so was I.

Until. . . .

It looked like any other trash can in the park, but when we walked past, it moved and talked. Its mouth opened and closed in time with prerecorded messages such as, "I'm hungry for some trash!" or, "Yikes, I smell like garbage today!" Every child that passed by the can was enamored. They wanted to follow it, engage it in conversation, and hug it. Not Jack. He walked right up to it and gave it a swift kick—followed by another, and then another. And then he began punching the lid of the can.

I grabbed him and apologized to the stunned families around

us. I reprimanded him and thought about a suitable consequence. I also wracked my brain for an explanation. Jack's response to what should be a playful moment of interaction was anything but playful. He completely misunderstood the friendly intent and that it was supposed to be funny, and worse, these strange episodes were becoming more frequent. With each new occurrence, I grew more bewildered.

After returning from our trip, Jack began his year of double kindergarten, and it would prove to be more successful than his first year. According to Mrs. McGeehan, Jack "functioned well academically, took pride in his work, wanted to learn, and even contributed to classroom discussions." I'm not sure how intense kindergarten-age discussions might be, but he was contributing. Academically, he seemed to be making some progress.

Socially, it was a different story.

Jack was impolite. He had no clue what to do or how to act around strangers, hiding behind me any time he was introduced to someone new. He could also become very withdrawn around my parents, which made no sense. The two closest people in Jack's life next to Andrew and me were my parents. Jack had been spending two full days a week with them for the last few years. They certainly were not strangers. But Jack could be really affectionate with my mother at one moment and hitting her the next. He also seemed to prefer adult activities to the typical ways in which a five- or six-year-old boy would play. He would jump at the chance to rake leaves with my father but wasn't all that interested in playing with cars or Lego blocks. He insisted on doing everything his own way, in his own time.

With prompting from Jack's teachers, Andrew and I agreed to have Jack evaluated by a school psychologist toward the end of his second kindergarten year. It was at this point that our relationship took its first step toward healing. Granted, it was the tiniest of baby steps, and neither of us was aware that it was happening. We just knew that we needed to get on the same page regarding Jack, and we needed to get there quickly.

When the evaluation arrived, I carried it into the house, placed the rest of the day's mail on the kitchen table, and opened the large envelope holding a thick stack of pages. I skimmed its contents quickly. There were testing scales of all sorts, with numbers that meant nothing to me. My eyes jumped right to phrases like "at risk" and "below average." After repeatedly seeing the words "impulsive," "disruptive," and "aggressive," I resigned myself to reading the evaluation in its entirety and lowered myself slowly into a chair. I skipped all the generic details—the names of teachers that had provided input, a description of the setting in which the tests were given, even the information that Andrew and I had provided—and I went straight to the results. What I read unnerved me, but I took it slow, wanting to understand every detail.

Jack is demonstrating delays in the development of learning concepts, social skills, gross motor skills, and all areas of readiness development. His fine motor skills are age appropriate, as are his self-help skills and his ability to process sensory information.

I questioned what gross motor skills were, exactly. According to the pocket-size dictionary I kept in my kitchen's junk drawer: "Gross motor skills are those used to move your arms, legs, and torso in a functional manner. They involve the large muscles of the body that enable such functions as walking, jumping, sitting upright, and throwing a ball."

Something clicked. And crawling, maybe?

Jack's communication skills revealed a moderate delay in his understanding of language. Spontaneous communication was within normal limits, with the exception of needing cues or reminders from his mother to use greetings or farewells.

Okay, a moderate delay was not as bad as a severe delay. And how many times have we encountered a parent with their child, and the parent has to say, "Susie, say hello to Mrs. So-and-So"? I went on to read the input from his teachers. None of it was anything we hadn't already heard, but to see the details collected in one place, printed clearly in black-and-white, was distressing.

Jack acts impulsively in school and has a difficult time sitting still. He struggles to maintain focus and concentration. Jack is often disruptive to the activities of other children and often destroys things that the other children are working on. He rarely follows instructions from adults and rarely uses his free time in an acceptable way. He rarely takes turns with toys and other materials and rarely demonstrates self-control. He does not demonstrate empathy with other children or adults. However, he makes friends easily, laughs and smiles with other children, and asks for help when needed.

Destroys things—that other kids are working on? Good God, where had I been? Why wasn't I aware of all of this horrible destruction? I knew his behavior was problematic, but I had no idea to what degree. Small consolation though—at least he laughed and smiled with the other kids.

I had to force myself to keep going.

At home, Jack plays alone, next to others, or with a group of children.

Uh, no. At home, Jack plays alone or next to us. There are no others. There are no kids in Andrew's neighborhood, and any time he tries to play with kids in our neighborhood, it doesn't last long. Referring back to the previous observation, it's clear why.

He can be aggressive with adults and peers, has difficulty following directions and paying attention in a group. He tends to overreact to correction, is easily upset, has tantrums, and can be defiant. He can be loving, affectionate, and helpful. . . .

How can he be both aggressive and defiant, and affectionate and helpful all at the same time? I know it to be true. He's my son, and he can be all those same things in one breath. But why did it look so ridiculous in writing?

He has an excellent memory and loves the outdoors.

Loves the outdoors? Jack hates being outside. It's either too hot or too cold. The sun is too bright, or the wind is too strong. He only likes being outside when it involves one of his latest obsessions.

Jack tends to be impulsive and has a flip-switch personality. He is obsessive or excessively observant about things, including accessories that he and other people wear.

Gee, ya think? With a closet full of discarded bags, belts, plaid shirts, and a three-piece suit, I would say yes, he was obsessive about accessories. The more I read, the more upsetting it was. Jack needed to learn basic concepts for literacy and math. He needed to practice balance skills to keep up with other kids. He needed to learn how to focus, concentrate, and process information. Jack's needs were endless, it seemed. Was there any part of him that was normal and positive?

Sitting there dumbfounded, I caught a glimpse of a photo on our refrigerator of a four-year-old Jack on an amusement ride, smiling from ear to ear. It had been taken at a local amusement park the previous summer. What can't be seen in the photo is the little girl in front of him whose hair Jack had pulled and was now crying. He didn't know the girl. They'd had no interaction, and his actions were completely unprompted and downright mean. Why had he done that? Worse yet, why had he taken so much pleasure in doing it? His behavior that day made no sense.

Reading this report, it was now a bit clearer.

Because the school recommended establishing an individualized education plan, or IEP, for Jack, the lines of communication were opened. As the end of the school year approached, we received another report from Jack's afternoon teacher. Mrs. McGeehan's observations confirmed my belief that all preschool and kindergarten teachers must be saints.

Jack is in need of strategies for self-discipline and socialization among his peers. Jack tends to shy away and avoid eye contact if reprimanded. Socially, he tries to play but teases or grabs toys from peers instead of asking for them. Additional behaviors with which Jack has had difficulties include: leaving his seat at inappropriate times, running through the classroom, bothering other children when they are trying to listen, taking toys away from other children when they are playing with them. He also bit a child but did not break the skin.

Oh God, please tell me you're not serious. Please tell me that my child did not *bite* another child. Please tell me that someone assured that child's parents that we are *not* raising an animal. And *please*, please let this all disappear. We are good parents, I promise—even if we are divorced. I picked up the phone to call Andrew, desperate for some sort of answer or explanation. "Have you seen the most recent report from school?"

"Yes," he replied in defeat. "I just don't get it."

"Neither do I. What do we do?"

"Didn't your mother say that there's a psychologist working in her office?" On the days when my mother was not watching Jack, she worked as a medical assistant in a doctor's office and she had mentioned Dr. Casey, suggesting we should talk to him.

"Right, Dr. Casey. He's not a psychologist. He's a pediatric neurologist."

"Why don't you call her and see if she thinks we should make an appointment?"

I hung up with Andrew and dialed my mother at work. After relaying the information from the school and our uncertainty over what to do, my mother agreed that making an appointment wasn't a bad idea. Dr. Casey's first opening wasn't until the end of June, and it was only April, but after talking it through, Andrew and I agreed it was necessary. We wanted—and needed—the second opinion.

CHAPTER 8
Not So Fast

Throughout this period of testing with Jack, my personal life was settling down. I no longer had an ounce of doubt about the decision I had made. Andrew and I did not belong together. We were two and a half years out from our separation. It was time to finalize our divorce and move on with life. I wanted a relationship, and I was ready to invest time in the right person. I was also hopeful about bringing another significant male figure into Jack's life, provided I could find the right one. In light of everything that was unfolding, the description for Mr. Right was becoming more complicated. He would need to be a highly skilled individual.

Of one thing I was certain—I wasn't willing to settle. I had achieved a comfortable level of independence, and I was self-sufficient. I had my own business, calling the shots. I was living in a beautiful house surrounded by wonderful neighbors that did their best to look out for me. For the first time, no one was telling me how I should go about my days. I didn't need a man to take care of me. I had never needed some*body*. I wanted some*one*. Someone who was willing to let me be me—good or bad.

As I embarked on this new stage, I never shared with any of the men I dated the fact that Jack was tough. My instinct was to shield them from him as much as possible. I knew he was difficult, and I wasn't yet committed to the reasons why he was difficult. I thought if I could keep Jack out of the picture long enough, maybe I could secure the relationship, and introducing him into the equation would then be easier. Or maybe I was just hoping that if I avoided it long enough, Jack's behavior would somehow improve.

I made it my fault. Blaming it on our divorce was far easier than acknowledging that something had gone wrong with the recipe. I did this to Jack when I left Andrew. I scribbled all over his young life with the indelible marks of my own unhappiness and dissatisfaction. I don't know what made me think I could hide the cracks. Jack's faults were far more obvious to the world than they were to me. I had no other children. I had no real experience with children. I had no idea how they were supposed to be, so I went about my days with blinders on. He would improve. He would have to.

Even if I had been fully aware and educated about what made Jack so difficult—even if I had honestly shared all of his issues and acted as his greatest advocate—his behaviors still would have been misunderstood and met with rejection. No one wanted to try and understand him or find the patience to deal with him. On the surface, he was a pain in the ass. Few were interested in digging deeper, and to those few men that I did introduce into Jack's world, he made it painfully clear that they were not welcome.

That same spring, while joining my brother in Colorado for a reunion of colleagues, I met Paul. I had worked with many of these same people over the years and had grown to know some of them quite well, so I was certain it would be fun. Having never been to Colorado was added incentive.

Paul, a native New Yorker transplanted to Boulder, was one of those joining the weekend's festivities that I had never met. That Saturday, he invited everyone to his home in the canyon just outside of town. I was instantly enamored with his setting high above Boulder. As the weekend progressed, I found myself enamored with Paul as well. The feeling appeared mutual, and we agreed to keep in touch.

Because we were living in different states, our relationship began as nothing more than innocent flirtation over email, phone, and thousands of miles. It wasn't until the following January that we acknowledged a desire to see one another again in person. I made plans to visit him in Boulder, and without question there was chemistry between us over that first long weekend alone. As far as we both knew, the weekend we had just shared was a one-off. We had enjoyed each other for a few days, we would continue to talk for sure, but now it was back to reality with neither of us knowing what was to come.

Paul dropped me at the airport well in advance of my flight. Despite having checked its status before leaving Paul's house and being assured it was on time, I reached my gate to find that it was now delayed by thirty minutes. Over the next hour, that delay grew from thirty to sixty minutes, then increased to ninety minutes, stretched further to two and a half hours, and didn't stop until it had finally ballooned into a seven-hour delay.

Shit.

It was Sunday. Andrew was scheduled to bring Jack back to me at seven o'clock that evening, but now I wouldn't be getting home until ten thirty. I dialed Andrew's number. He answered with his usual hello, cordial enough but still laced with annoyance.

"Hey, how's it going?" I tried to sound casual but wasn't terribly successful, so I jumped right to the heart of it. "I have a slight problem."

"What's wrong?"

"My flight's delayed. I won't be home until ten thirty. Any chance you could keep—"

Andrew cut me off. *"What? Are you kidding me? What about Jack?"*

"Can you keep him overnight?"

"No, I can't keep him overnight! I have plans!"

I get it. Andrew has a date, and I'm wrecking everything. I'm always wrecking everything.

"You have no business—as a mother—flying halfway across the country for the weekend!"

"Andrew, you're being ridiculous. Things happen. Flights get delayed. It's not my fault."

"You are a rotten mother, you know that? Why can't you get a different flight?"

I had already checked and there were no other flights, but it wasn't worth the energy to try and explain that to him. "Forget it. I'll call my parents. They have a key to the house. They can meet you there at seven o'clock." I hung up before Andrew could respond, took a deep breath—and dialed my mother.

I sat in the airport for hours, second-guessing everything I had done in leaving Andrew, questioning all my intentions, contemplating whether or not I truly was a rotten mother. I should have expected that Andrew's reaction would be explosive, but I was honestly surprised by it. He was always arguing that I had stolen his time with his son. Here I was giving him the opportunity for an extra night, and his not wanting it made no sense to me. I sat there cursing Andrew for being a jerk and chastising myself for being a rotten mother—and believing that the latter was more accurate.

A week later, Paul's mother, who lived in Manhattan, suffered a heart attack. When he called to say he would be coming to the East Coast the following weekend, I was excited but also caught off guard. I hadn't expected to see him again so soon and wasn't sure how it would impact my schedule with Jack, and subsequently what kind of conflict I could expect with Andrew. I agreed to drive up to the city to meet him, nonetheless.

Paul had grown up in a boutique hotel owned by his family on East Fifty-Fourth Street. With his mother ill and still living in the penthouse alone, he began making frequent trips to New York. With a free place to stay right in the heart of the city, I found myself joining him at every opportunity. Before I knew it, we were engaged in a whirlwind relationship. When Paul wasn't coming to New York, he was flying me out to Boulder, and in just a few months' time, he was talking about marriage—and life with me *and* Jack—in Boulder.

Whoa, could we slow this thing down a bit?

Realistically, the logistics of our relationship made no sense. Paul was fifty-five with no children and living halfway across the country. I was forty with a six-year-old that I had no intention of uprooting. Andrew and I were divorcing, yes, but Andrew and Jack were not. Taking Jack away from his father, for any reason, was not an option.

We also couldn't ignore that I had a full-time job. Because of his family's hotel business, Paul was fortunate enough to retire in his early forties, but I needed to be at my desk every day in order to pay my bills—and that left little quality time to spare. When Paul came east to stay with us rather than in New York at the hotel, he needed to find ways to occupy himself. Being completely out of his element, that was far easier said than done.

But he had jumped right in, headfirst, and he was making it easy for me to enjoy him. I was learning a tremendous amount from him both mentally and emotionally, and the long weekends with him, whether in Boulder or New York City, provided an escape from my day-to-day. When we were together without Jack, it worked. It was when he began coming east regularly that it became stressful. Each time, he stayed a bit longer, and he was making it clear that he wanted to live as a family. He wanted to sleep in my bed and have a say in disciplining Jack, yet neither Jack nor I were ready for that level of commitment. Paul persevered nonetheless, respecting the boundaries I had set and continuously searching for common ground with Jack, going to great lengths to find ways to connect with him.

One Monday evening the phone rang.

"Hey, sweetie," came Paul's usual greeting. I found it comforting. It was one part cheerful, one part secure, and all parts caring. "Listen, I had an idea. When I come out this weekend, why don't we take Jack up to the city and spend the night? We can take him to the top of the Empire State Building, Times Square—and even P. J. Clarke's for one of their burgers. We'll stay at the hotel. I'm sure he'll love it. What do you think?"

Paul rattled off his plan so quickly, I didn't have a chance to interject. I could sense that he was enthusiastic about this idea and I had to admit, it wasn't a bad one. Besides, Jack had never been to New York City.

"That sounds like fun, but what if Jack doesn't like it? I'd hate for you to be stuck on the road with him if he's not having a good time."

"How could he not like it?" I could see that Paul had made up his mind. I also realized that I couldn't shield him forever from Jack's ability to turn any situation into a train wreck, so I agreed. It was only one night, I told myself. How bad could it be?

Saturday morning's to-do list took a bit longer than usual, which meant we didn't get on the road until close to one o'clock. It was almost three-thirty by the time we arrived. Jack had been fine on the ride up, but I could tell he was getting hungry. After leaving our bags at the hotel, we headed out into the crowded streets toward P. J. Clarke's, promising Jack that this would be "the best burger he ever ate," building it up to be larger than life. Unfortunately, the only thing larger than life that afternoon was the line snaking out of the restaurant and all the way around the corner.

"It'll move fast—let's wait," Paul suggested.

I glanced down at Jack as he was rubbing his right eye—never a good sign—and I knew we didn't have much time.

"No, let's just go somewhere else. Whatever's closest." I could sense Paul's disappointment, and I was kicking myself for not having planned this very well. Jack's window of accommodation was generally half closed, and at any moment he could slam it shut. I should have put errands aside in order to capitalize on his best times of the day. We settled on another restaurant nearby, and I asked for a booth by the window, hoping that a bit of people watching would help to keep Jack entertained.

He squirmed and fidgeted the entire time. He complained when his burger arrived covered in mayonnaise and refused to eat it. Needing to wait while they prepared another only worked against us, and I could see that Paul was frustrated.

"Maybe after we eat, we should go back to the hotel and let Jack nap for a while." I made an effort to salvage what was becoming a tense situation. Jack was being tough, but he was also only six and sometimes he did still need a nap. I could see that Paul didn't get it, but he agreed with my suggestion.

Fortunately, an hour nap did the trick. It restored Jack to a pleasant mood and provided Paul and me with a respite. Now that everyone was happy, we set off into the madness of Times Square. We wound our way in and out of stores, stopped every now and again to watch a street performance, and marveled at the spectacle of lights in every color imaginable. Jack was captivated.

We headed into the Nike store with its multiple levels and wall after wall of shoes. Jack had never seen such excessive sneaker-ness. The lights of Times Square? They were nothing compared to the flagship Nike store. He went from being captivated to being hypnotized. Several pairs caught his attention, and I knew that if I didn't divert it quickly, he would become fixated for the duration of our trip.

"Come on, Jack," I said, taking his hand and urging him toward the down escalator.

"Can I get a pair?" he begged. "Can't I just try them on?"

"How about if we come back tomorrow? We still have a lot to see." It took a bit of coercing, but eventually the promise of a return trip seemed to pacify him. I had bought myself some time. Come tomorrow, I was sure I could find some reason why we couldn't come back. Better yet, maybe he would forget.

As we continued on with our sightseeing, Jack made it perfectly clear that he wasn't about to forget anything. "Why can't we go back and get sneakers?" he asked repeatedly.

"Because, Jack, we have other things to do." I suddenly found myself engaged in a game of redirection. Fortunately, we were approaching FAO Schwarz. "Look, there's the toy store I was telling you about!"

I expected some enthusiasm, but Jack's attention had shifted to a man juggling two hot dogs and a mustard bottle at a nearby food cart. "Can I get a hot dog?"

"You already had dinner. How about if we go in the toy store and then go get some ice cream?" Paul proposed with a definite edge of irritation.

"I want a hot dog," Jack insisted.

I looked at Paul, attempting to gauge his thoughts on the situation.

"If he wants a hot dog, get him a hot dog." Paul was clearly making an effort to be patient. I squeezed his hand and smiled, letting him know that his concession was appreciated.

After Jack inhaled two hot dogs, we made our way into the two-story wonderland on the lower level, with its colorful sea of stuffed animals and NYC-themed characters. After being amazed by the endless shelves of fluff, we took the escalator to the second level. And there, Jack saw the giant piano keys embedded in the floor, inviting anyone to tap out a melody using their two feet.

There was a clearly visible, organized line of people waiting for their turn at the big keys, but that didn't matter to Jack. He breezed right past it, jumped on the piano, and completely disrupted another boy's fun. After Jack bumped into him and gave him a brazen shove, the stunned boy shied away in defeat, leaving Jack free to jump his way from one side of the piano to the other. Once again, I found myself taking him by the arm and apologizing to anyone willing to listen.

After pounding the piano keys, Jack bounced from one section of the store to the next, wanting just about everything that caught his eye. He just wanted anything. I finally gave in and bought him a stuffed bear wearing an NYPD uniform, wanting to placate him so we could remove ourselves from this disaster as quickly as possible. I justified my weakness by thinking he should at least have a souvenir from his first trip to New York City.

He was sufficiently worn out by the time we began our walk back to the hotel. Clutching his new friend, Jack trudged along a few feet in front of us, stopping every so often to make sure we were following. Paul took my hand and we strolled along behind him, avoiding discussion of what had just taken place in the toy store, talking instead about our plans for the following day. I could sense that Paul wanted to provide his thoughts on how things should have been handled, but I also knew he understood I wasn't willing to have that conversation. Jack was my responsibility, and it was up to me to figure out how to handle him. The next time Jack turned to check on us, he stopped to let us pass. Without warning, he came running up from behind and forced his way between the two of us, breaking our hands apart.

I laughed. "A little jealous, Jack?"

Paul didn't see the humor. "You're not going to let him get away with that, are you?" he shot at me.

"What are you talking about?"

"Don't you think it's time you made it clear to him that I'm here to stay? I am equally as important a part of your life as he is." Paul's tone was angry.

I stared at him for several seconds. Without uttering a word, I grabbed Jack's hand, pulling him toward me, and headed down the street. "Let's go, Jack."

"Kat, don't do this," Paul ordered from behind.

Stunned, I didn't say a word. I tightened my hold on Jack's hand and quickened our pace.

"Where are you going?" he shouted, as I kept moving. I was not going to let him dictate my relationship with my son and his place within that picture.

Paul caught up to us, grabbing me hard by the arm. "Kat, what are you doing?"

"We're going home."

"Kat, no," he begged, but his remorse was brief. "If you leave, we're through. I mean it—our relationship will be over."

I stopped in my tracks, pulled Jack close to me, and got in Paul's face, roaring, "Let me tell you something—*he's my son*! Do you get that? He is *tough*, I know that, but *he* comes first! No one else comes before him, not even me. I don't know who you think you are to suddenly make the determination that you are as important as he is. I'm . . . I'm . . . I just can't believe this." I was at a loss for words.

Passersby were staring, walking wide circles around us, and I realized I was screaming. I took Jack's hand, and we left Paul standing alone on the sidewalk. He trailed behind the entire walk back, catching up to us as we reached the hotel.

"Kat, please, don't do this," he pleaded. "What are you going to do, drive all the way home?"

What was I going to do? I hadn't exactly thought this through. It was already after nine o'clock. It had been a long and trying day. The last thing I felt like doing was getting in the car and making the two-hour-plus drive home.

"We are not spending the night with you," I said. "I will find us a room somewhere, or we'll go home."

"We're in Manhattan—do you have any idea how much a hotel room costs in Manhattan, if you can even get one? And you don't want to make that drive at night. Just stay here. I'll get another room."

Of course—Paul owned the hotel. He could get as many rooms as he wanted.

"Fine," I said, as I pushed Jack through the lobby toward the elevator. I pressed the button for the top floor, and the two of us went up alone without saying another word to Paul.

What on earth just happened?

I shocked not only Paul with my street performance but myself as well. Such an explosive manner was completely out of character for me. I have never coexisted peacefully with conflict, but in that moment, I was overcome by some unseen certainty, some absolute confidence and level of conviction that I had never felt before—about anything. Was there real truth in those feelings, or was it all just some inner need to prove Andrew wrong, shed my cloak of guilt, and lay claim to my innocence? Standing up and making my presence known was proof that I was not a rotten mother. This handful of a child, no, let me correct that—this *truckload* of a child—was my responsibility. Regardless of what I might want for my own life, his needs would never take a back seat to mine. By so forcefully vocalizing it, I was accepting that challenge. I wanted to believe it, and I shuddered at the massive amount of work I had to do in order to get it right.

After getting Jack settled with a movie, I eyed the minibar. I needed something to calm the storm raging in my head. Paul had told me how these things work. Even if I did nothing more than remove an item and put it back, I would be charged for it. I swung the door wide and removed a miniature bottle of vodka. I twisted the cap until it snapped off and gulped the liquid down in one shot.

I stopped myself for a moment.

Should I?

One by one, I pulled every last item from the minibar. Jack and I split bags of chips and cookies while I twisted the cap from another bottle of vodka, then opened a beer. I rested my eyes on Jack as I welcomed the beginnings of decompression.

God help me.

A ringing phone woke me from a deep sleep the following morning. I shook off the cobwebs quickly enough to realize it had to be Paul.

"Hello?" I answered quietly.

"Kat, look, I am so sorry about last night. I was wrong to—"

I cut him off. "It's fine. Just forget it, okay?" I didn't have the strength to make a mountain out of this. More importantly, I didn't want Jack being exposed to the negative energy. "As soon as Jack is awake, I'll pack up and we'll go."

"Please don't go. Please stay. Let's get some breakfast and do the things we had planned on doing today. I spent all night thinking about it, and I understand where you're coming from. Please, I don't want it to end this way."

Deep down I knew that Paul could never understand, but I didn't want it to end this way, either. I hesitated, but then said, "Okay, we'll stay for a while."

I let Jack sleep a bit longer while I showered and did my best to reassemble the minibar. A wave of guilt washed over me as I assessed the monetary damage caused by my rage the night before. I couldn't determine the root of the anger that had caused my outburst. Was it really Paul's reaction to Jack, or was it this constant feeling of pressure to defend my son's behavior—and my own inability to control it in the first place?

We headed to breakfast at one of Paul's favorite places, and Jack was a complete angel from start to finish. His behavior was unlike any I'd ever seen from him. He was nice to Paul, he was well-mannered toward our waitress, and he didn't complain once, not even as Paul and I lingered over our tea.

"How about we go back and get those sneakers you wanted?" Paul suggested to Jack.

"Can we?" he asked excitedly, stealing a glance at me to make sure it was okay.

I gave Paul a look that said, *Are you sure you want to do this?* His eyes said yes, so I turned to Jack with a measured smile. "Sure. Let's go get some sneakers, and then we'll go to the top of a really big building and see all of New York City from the sky."

Turning to Paul, I added apologetically, "By the way, I owe you for the minibar."

CHAPTER 9
Someone? Anyone?

That particular weekend ended on a good note, but without question, Jack was brilliant. He didn't want Paul around, and he was masterful in making it such that Paul didn't want to be around. Trying to balance life with the two of them wasn't easy. We had weathered the Times Square incident. But we were always one step away from another upheaval. My only hope of holding it together was to keep the two apart as much as possible. I restricted my time with Paul to weekends without Jack, whether that be in New York or in Boulder. Time without Paul was spent keeping Jack busy.

Andrew had suggested that we enroll Jack in karate lessons, thinking he might be receptive to the discipline it teaches because he would think it was fun. His sister's two boys had taken classes, and it had a positive effect.

Jack's first lesson was on a Thursday night. The studio was halfway between Andrew and me, so he planned on meeting us there. He wanted to attend the first class. Of course, Andrew wanted to attend anything and everything pertaining to Jack.

Trying to get Jack out the door on time was a struggle. With every cinch of his beginner's white belt, he insisted that I retie it.

"Jack, we're going to be late. We need to go." My annoyance was bordering on anger.

"But my belt isn't right. You have to fix it," he insisted.

"Jack, your belt is fine. Let's just go." I took a deep breath as I buckled him into the back seat. It wasn't more than a four-minute drive to the karate studio, yet in that time, Jack had managed to completely dismantle his uniform. When I saw that he had untied the belt that I had already tied seven times, I lost it. "Jack! I told you to leave it! It was fine, and now it's a mess!"

"It wasn't right," he said.

I quickly wrestled with the belt, tied it again, and hurried Jack through the doors of the studio. Andrew was already there, and he knew from the scowl on my face that something was wrong.

"The belt wasn't tied right," I informed him through clenched teeth. Andrew understood immediately and thankfully took it from there.

"Hey, buddy," he exclaimed, "you look really cool in that uniform. Are you excited?"

"Yeah," Jack replied as he glanced around the room, sizing up the other kids. "When's it going to start?"

"Soon. Let's go meet your instructor." As he led Jack away, he looked over his shoulder at me. His eyes said, *Relax, he'll be fine.*

I took my forty-seventh deep breath of the evening, took a seat in one of the plastic chairs lining the wall, and waited for class to begin. After introducing Jack to the instructor and giving a few last words of encouragement to his son, Andrew sat next to me. Glancing at him, admiring his ability to be calmly positive, I put my aggravation aside. We were on time, and no one there had any sense of my stress.

Jack was one of the taller boys in the class, so he was assigned a spot in the last row, and I knew from the start it would be problematic.

That was one of the things we were learning through development of his IEP—Jack needed to be front and center for his attention to hold.

The instructor started the kids jogging in place as a warm-up. The minute they started moving, you could tell some were naturally athletic. Those particular children moved with a rhythmic uniformity, while others flopped about randomly. There was nothing rhythmic about Jack's movement.

Disorganized.

Erratic.

Haphazard.

Those were all better adjectives to describe the senseless, borderline bizarre motion he displayed. His arms were flailing from left to right as if he were throwing punches at a ghost that only he could see. His knees were almost touching his chin at one point as he exaggerated every up and down motion of his legs.

Jack then took off running wildly around the studio, weaving his way in and out of the other kids. Andrew jumped out of his seat.

Thankfully the instructor got to Jack before Andrew could. "Hey there, cowboy," he said calmly, "this isn't a rodeo. Let's get back to your assigned spot." Effortlessly, he was able to redirect Jack and restore order to the warm-up exercise.

Once he felt their blood was flowing sufficiently, the instructor settled the kids down and gathered them in a circle on the floor. He talked with them about the importance of balance and stance before demonstrating a basic punch.

"Okay, let's get up and form one line," he announced. "One at a time, I want each of you to run up to the mirror, stop, pretend you're a big, strong tree—and then throw a punch. Do you think you can do that?"

"Yeah!" the kids shouted in unison, excited about their first opportunity to perform a real karate move. One by one they ran to the mirror, stopped, and threw their punch. All of them were far from being experts, but each performed the motion with some degree of competency.

Except Jack.

Jack ran to the mirror, stopped—and stuck his tongue out at himself.

No punch. Just a tongue.

A few parents laughed, but that didn't stop Jack from getting right back in line. And it certainly wasn't going to stop him from upstaging himself. When Jack approached the mirror his second time, he stopped and struck a pose. We're talking full-on runway model pose. Jack wasn't in karate class; he was strutting down the catwalk.

As soon as the class was over, I gathered Jack's things, took him by the arm, and pointed him in the direction of the door.

"You have quite a comedian there," one of the fathers snickered.

"Yes, thanks," I replied. I didn't need to engage; I just wanted to leave as quickly as possible.

Fortunately, Jack's second karate lesson was not a repeat performance of his first.

It was worse.

It was also obvious that some of the parents were annoyed. We had made a mistake. Jack was not cut out for karate, and it wasn't fair for him to ruin the class for everyone else. We knew that we wouldn't be bringing him back, and once the lesson was over, Andrew approached the instructor to let him know.

"Look, don't worry about it," he said. "Not all kids are cut out for karate." That's what he said, but what I'm sure he was thinking was, *Thank God that kid's not coming back.*

Clearly, karate wasn't the solution to keeping Jack busy. While we searched for an activity that would capture his energy, we coordinated playdates with his friends from school. After two or three times of Timmy or Lucas coming to play at our house, it seemed as though they all had an excuse for not coming back. Jack went through friends at breakneck speed. There were Adams and Carters, Matthews, Zachs, and Kyles. Only on one occasion would Jack be invited to someone else's house.

I had dropped Jack at Noah's around noon, and as the two boys ran off to play, I thanked his mother and told her I would be back at five o'clock to get him. I arrived at their door that afternoon feeling relaxed. I had just had five full hours to take care of things around the house, run errands, and decompress. Noah's mother, on the other hand, looked as though she had been through World War III. I assessed the look on her face, trying to gauge the extent of the damage when, out of the corner of my eye, I saw Jack crawling across their floor on his hands and knees like a wounded dog.

"Jack! Get off that floor!" I ordered. I was afraid of the answer, but I asked, "How was he?"

"He was . . . uh . . . well. . . ." She had obviously surrendered, and I guessed that the takeover had occurred somewhere around twelve thirty, if not twelve fifteen. "We had an interesting afternoon," she added.

What I heard her saying was, *Your son won't be coming back to this house.*

Jack was never invited back—and I never pressed for the details. I already knew them, maybe not specifically, but I got the general idea. My child was a handful and, more and more, he was not welcome in peoples' homes, nor did any of his "friends" want to come to our home.

Because no one seemed to want to play with Jack, the job fell to Andrew or me. One afternoon while Jack and I were playing catch in our front yard, I stopped to chat with a neighbor walking his dog. I didn't know him terribly well, but I knew he had a few boys a bit older than Jack. He mentioned how nice it was to see a mother spend so much time with her son. I gave him a slight smile, accepting the praise but wanting to acknowledge that I probably wasn't worthy of it.

"Jack's a bit shy," I explained. "He has a hard time making friends."

"Why don't you sign him up for the local youth club?" he suggested.

He went on to explain that it was a sports organization and *the* place to go for all things intramural. I had never considered that Jack might have an interest in playing sports, and I certainly had no idea that there was an entire organization right under my nose that was dedicated to numerous types of sports for kids of all ages. After discussing it with Andrew and gauging Jack's interest, we decided it was worth a try. We signed on the dotted line, and Jack was soon playing intramural basketball, soccer, and baseball.

Unbeknownst to us at the time, Jack was destined for an intense love affair with baseball, but it was by no means an instant attraction. I don't think there was even any chemistry initially. It wasn't love at first kick with soccer, either, but there was certainly enough of a spark to indicate that Jack and soccer were headed for a hot and heavy romance. Jack appeared to possess a good amount of natural athletic ability, despite his performance in the karate studio.

While Jack enjoyed basketball, he didn't take to it quite as easily as soccer. It seemed he didn't have the same level of coordination and most games were spent flopping about the court. Nonetheless, he enjoyed playing so we resigned ourselves to cringing through each clumsy game.

Both Andrew and I were relieved. Finally, we had found an outlet for some of Jack's uncontrollable energy. It was beyond me how Jack could have no understanding of casual play, yet within the context of organized sports, he was capable of being a successful, contributing member of a team. Both had rules; why could he follow one set and not the other? I wasted little time analyzing it—the youth club was an unexpected godsend, and I was grateful. Maybe some of the dust could settle.

CHAPTER 10
The Truth of the Matter

Even though Jack was far more than Paul had bargained for, he longed for a family to call his own. He wanted desperately to be a role model for Jack, eagerly attending his basketball games and happily taking him to the zoo, but Jack was resistant at every turn. Paul still failed to grasp that he couldn't just walk in and replace Andrew as Jack's father.

Jack's nighttime routine was exactly that—routine. Eight o'clock was bath time and by 8:20, Jack was climbing into bed where I would settle in next to him, scratch his back, and tell him a story. Even the stories were routine. For weeks on end, he wanted to hear the same imaginary story, and he required that every detail be the same as the last time I told it, which I can assure you is easier said than done. I never considered any of it a problem, though. If anything, it was time I cherished. Once Jack was satisfied with the story's conclusion, I would kiss him goodnight and turn on his music.

The same music. Night after night.

"Love you, Mom."

"Love you too, bud," I said one evening before closing his door halfway and wandering back downstairs to the sunroom, where Paul had gotten comfortable with the *New York Times*.

"Jack must know the first eight songs of that CD by heart, and he probably has no clue what the other forty-two songs sound like," I commented.

He laughed. "That's silly. Why don't you skip ahead one night, or play a different CD?"

"Ha, Jack would never—"

"Love you, Mom," came Jack's distant voice, interrupting my thought.

"Love you too, bud," I shouted up to him before turning back to Paul and continuing. "Jack would never allow me to start his CD in the middle or play a different one. That's how he operates. He is the pure definition of a creature of habit."

"Maybe you need to break him of his habits," Paul offered with a slight edge.

"Love you, Mom," Jack called out again.

"Love you too, bud."

"Kat, you have to get him to stop."

I paused.

"Stop him from saying 'I love you'? Paul, he's six years old." I said, getting up and going to the bottom of the steps. "Jack, you need to go to sleep now, sweetie."

"Love you, Mom."

"Love you too, but it's time to be quiet and go to sleep." It killed me to give in to Paul's objections, but if I was going to continue this relationship, I owed him some sort of balance. Deep down I knew he was right, and that killed me more. There was no doubt that I was becoming increasingly defensive as the weeks passed. Without any children of his own, Paul was naturally less tolerant—I understood that. But there were far worse things that Jack could be doing, and I don't know how many mothers can say they've ever grown tired of hearing the words "I love you" from their child.

Of course, I said that then.

When June and our first appointment with Dr. Casey finally arrived, Jack was nothing short of an asshole. Andrew and I struggled through the entire appointment, dreading that there were two more to follow. A few weeks later, Dr. Casey spelled out the findings of his evaluation in a letter to Jack's pediatrician, a copy of which was sent to us:

I saw Jack for longstanding concerns regarding his behavior and school difficulties. He is six years, ten months old and has completed kindergarten. His parents describe him as being unable to understand rules of social behavior. He periodically exhibits anxiety and hyperactivity.

Jack entered day care at eighteen months of age; he did well until age three. He made progress in a number of academic areas. He taught himself cursive. He is good at decoding. He has always been good at puzzles and likes to draw.

He then developed aggressive and defiant behaviors. He improved socially two years ago when he entered full-day kindergarten. In the past school year, he has attended kindergarten at two separate schools. He exhibits similar problems in both places. While he describes other children as friends, he will knock their constructions over. He will do inappropriate things such as throwing snowballs at other children.

Or hitting Ellie in the head with a rock.

On review by questionnaire of his behaviors at home, his parents described him as being excessive in his perfection of schoolwork. He complains a lot about food. He can be augmentative and restless at the dinner table. However, he is not significantly hyperactive at school. His evening routines are stable and predictable; behavior with adults and peers is much less so.

"Augmentative." Most of the language Dr. Casey had used in his report was straightforward, so I tripped over that one word, thinking it an odd choice and not knowing exactly what he meant. After consulting *Merriam-Webster*, I understood. The definition of *augmentative* is "able to make greater, more numerous, larger, or more intense; indicating large size and sometimes awkwardness or unattractiveness." Yep, that's Jack all right. He makes every situation more intense, awkward, and unattractive.

Jack will say rude and inappropriate things to adults, including his grandparents. He ignores his paternal grandmother. He calls other children names. When he met a new family moving into the neighborhood, he was rude to the other father. He seems not to understand the concept of others' feelings being hurt. Jack is oppositional to both parents in their homes. Even if he is having a very pleasant day with his father, he will call his mother and complain, even lying and saying that his father is hitting him.

I felt like calling Dr. Casey and saying, "Let's cut the bullshit." Jack is oppositional to everyone and everything.

Concerning his past medical history, he was born after an

uncomplicated full-term gestation and spontaneous vaginal delivery. He had no problems in the newborn nursery, and his general health has always been good. There was no family history of developmental disabilities.

Except for that topic of my first pregnancy. Let's not forget the freak chromosomal duplication that occurred to the greatest degree of severity possible and the enormous disabilities that Angela would have had. That event is permanently etched in our family history.

Patient's general appearance was normal with no dysmorphic features.

There it is again—that reference to looking normal.

Jack was minimally verbal to me; when I spoke to him, he put his hands over his ears. I decided to start a physical examination by turning down the lights to look in his eyes. He smiled when I did this, then complied with the physical examination. He was moderately fidgety. When I was not engaged with him, he tended to move around; as I wrote these notes, he stood looking over my shoulder. He made faces at his parents and mimed to them.

And let's not forget how we sat there feeling like failures at parenting.

I next administered the Peabody Picture Vocabulary Test. His mental age scored at six years, four months. His cooperation and attention seemed to fade as this test proceeded. After physical examination, he answered my questions, but often used silly voices and made inappropriate remarks, engaging me by saying, 'Do you have monster teeth?'

I have to admit, the doctor did have very large, prominent front teeth, so Jack wasn't completely off base in asking.

In summary, Jack's history and examination are consistent with Asperger syndrome and an element of anxiety. He has been identified as having a reading disability for which he will receive an Individualized Education Plan at school. I recommend that his parents seek psychotherapy. There should be two components of this—one should consist of a form of play therapy so that Jack can learn to express himself more verbally and appropriately. Social skills group is also recommended if one is not provided at school. The second should help his mother and father to develop a behavior modification program in order to deal with his unpredictable behaviors.

That was absolutely the best word to describe Jack at that age. He was thoroughly and predictably unpredictable. It was hard to imagine anyone could develop a behavior modification program to deal with his behavior.

Asperger syndrome.

The words failed to register. We knew only that they couldn't mean anything good, and our complete absence of understanding had us wanting to rewind the moment and have them taken back. For the remainder of that summer, we did nothing. We just let those words hang out there in the air, not tethered to anything—other than our son. Today, I sit here and wonder, how could we have done *nothing*?

That fall, shortly after turning seven, Jack moved on to first grade. His behaviors persisted—right alongside our denial. With the information we'd received that previous spring and summer, we could have thrown ourselves into researching this unknown disorder. But it was easier to process and understand the more common diagnoses. High anxiety. Obsessive-compulsive. Attention deficit hyperactivity.

Disorder.

That was the word that jumped off every page of every report. Our son had a disorder. Life had suddenly stopped proceeding in an orderly fashion, and we had entered a new and permanent state of disarray. I vacillated between jumping in to arm myself with as much knowledge as possible—and blissful ignorance. The more I could learn, the better equipped I would be to help my son. But if I simply ignored it, maybe it would all go away.

As the school year started, Jack was referred to an instructional support team for his social and behavioral concerns. While Jack attended his social skills group, I subjected myself to rereading every word of every evaluation. Repeatedly I thought, *Something doesn't add up.* According to Jack's teachers, his behavior was *not* indicative of Asperger syndrome. They said so, putting it down in black-and-white and adding it to Jack's official records. Dr. Casey had just three meetings with him, whereas Jack's teachers were the trained professionals who saw him every day.

Who do we listen to?

CHAPTER 11
One Step Forward, Two Steps Back

Christmas was fast approaching, and Paul thought it would be great to take Jack to Colorado. If he could see where Paul lived, Jack may be more inclined to come around to Paul's side and see him as a father figure. I thought it unlikely, but the idea of taking Jack on such an adventure and showing him the beauty of the mountains did excite me.

The flight to Denver would be long; I knew that. My best strategy would be to pack as many activities as possible to keep Jack busy. My biggest problem might be not having a plan for the moment when the handle has been cranked one too many times and the terrifying jester pops out of his box.

Thankfully our plane had screens on the back of each seat that showed our progress across the country. Being able to see how far we had gone and how far we still had to go provided a necessary visual for Jack. Having a concrete end point on which to focus would—*fingers crossed*—keep my little Jack-in-the-plane contained.

Jack's phase du jour centered around the popular Japanese video game Pokémon, with its colorful characters and their magical powers. While out grabbing a few last-minute stocking stuffers, I had found a sticker book with thirty-two glorious pages of Pokémon adventures, each missing a character. The last few pages of the book contained the corresponding character stickers.

Thirty-two pages!

I pulled the book out of my backpack shortly after takeoff, and Jack was elated. We dove headfirst into matching each character to its appropriate place within the world of Pokémon. He was all-consumed—hyperfocused—on this imaginative world of events that he seemed to understand as if it were real. It took exactly three hours and fifty minutes to fill the book—five minutes shy of the length of our flight.

Paul glanced at me in amazement. "You are an angel," he whispered in my ear.

No, I'm just a mother.

There was still a forty-minute drive to Boulder, but we had made it through the flight unscathed, and the worst was over. It was seven o'clock Colorado time, and with the sky dark already, we weren't able to show Jack much of anything. We were still on East Coast time, so I assumed he would fall asleep in the car, but he didn't seem the least bit tired.

Funny. I was exhausted.

"Hey, Paul," Jack called from the back seat, "do you want to play twenty-one?"

Yes!

I don't know where it came from; it had easily been six or eight months since the last time Jack had even mentioned twenty-one, but he had pulled it out of thin air. Not only would it fill the gap perfectly, I knew Paul would appreciate the mental challenge. Jack's prowess amazed me—he won every time, and I couldn't figure out how.

The premise is simple: two players go back and forth counting to twenty-one by choosing to add one or two numbers at a time, no more. The first player to say twenty-one is the winner. For example, the first player can say one or two. If he says two, the second player can say three or four, and so on. I explained all of this to Paul before settling in to watch (and secretly enjoy) the oncoming slaughter. I had never seen Jack lose—I couldn't beat him myself—and I was certain that Paul was facing defeat. I'm sure there was something wrong with the fact that I was looking forward to witnessing his demise at the hands of a seven-year-old.

Jack insisted that Paul go first.

Agreeing, Paul gave it a moment's consideration before saying, "One."

Jack immediately countered with three, and the two volleyed back and forth until Paul realized he was cornered. Jack had just said eighteen, which left nineteen and twenty as Paul's only options, either of which would give Jack the win.

"You got me," Paul surrendered with a laugh—one that screamed, *Game on!* "Let's try this again."

"Okay," Jack replied smugly. "You start."

Again, the two of them went head-to-head. This time Paul chose to start with two, but the result was the same. Jack somehow managed to choose the right number each time, cornering Paul. I could see Paul calculating, I could smell his determination mounting, and I could feel it—Paul was impressed. Jack had found a way to get his attention in a positive light.

Paul slipped me a sideways glance. "How does he do it?"

I shrugged my shoulders. "No clue. I've been trying to figure it out myself, but he beats me every time."

"Okay, one more time," Paul challenged Jack. "But *you* go first this time."

I shook my head, giggling, knowing that it had nothing to do with who went first. I had tried the same thing, and the only answer I could formulate was that Jack's offer to have his opponent go first was a way of disarming them.

Wait—could Jack really be that smart?

The forty-five-minute drive felt like a small win. When we finally reached Paul's house in the canyon, I insisted that Jack wind it down and get ready for bed. We only had a few days, and I didn't want to get off on the wrong foot by completely upsetting his sleep schedule.

The three-floor house had an unusual layout, with two bedrooms and a den on the lowest level, and two bedrooms, one of which was Paul's office, on the upper level, separated by the main living space in between.

"I'll sleep down here with Jack," I told Paul as I placed our bags in one of the downstairs bedrooms.

"What are you talking about? You're not going to sleep upstairs with me?"

Uh-oh—are we about to have this discussion again?

"You know I don't think that's a good idea. Besides, it's dark down there and unfamiliar to him."

"We can leave a light on. He'll be fine."

"I don't want to sleep alone," Jack said.

I felt stuck. Paul paid for our flights and we were now on his turf, but I still felt the need to stand firm regarding our sleeping arrangements when Jack was around. Not only that, being two floors below us in a strange house, in a room with no windows, would frighten him. It frightened me. What if he woke in the middle of the night needing the bathroom and had no idea where he was going? What if he started crying and I couldn't hear him? My protective instincts told me it was okay to react that way. Paul finally conceded, not wanting to argue any more than I did.

We woke the following morning with refreshed attitudes and discovered that six inches of fresh snow had fallen, curating a perfect holiday scene. Everything was untouched, pristine, and quiet. Suddenly I was thrilled that we had come and that Jack could experience such peaceful beauty.

"What do you think, Jack? Should we go for a walk? Build a snowman, maybe?"

"Yeah! Can we?"

Paul jumped in immediately. "You should go look for the bear that lives behind the house." He gave me a wink without Jack seeing.

Jack's excitement level kicked up three notches as he went running for his boots.

"The two of you go ahead," Paul said. "I'll stay here and make some breakfast. What do you think, Jack? Oatmeal or scrambled eggs?"

"Pancakes!" Jack exclaimed.

Paul winced.

"It's either eggs or oatmeal," I called after Jack, needing to support Paul on this one. I couldn't expect him to cater to Jack at every turn, especially when we were in his home.

Jack loved every minute of our search for the supposed bear. His appreciation for the mountains and the fresh snowfall appeared sincere, and we returned to the house ready for a hearty breakfast. After eating and showering, the three of us headed back down the canyon into town. On the way, Jack and Paul picked up right where they had left off, trying to dominate one another in the game of twenty-one. Once again, Jack was victorious, claiming twelve of thirteen games.

"That's it," Paul declared. "We're going to the bookstore today, and we're getting him a book of sudoku puzzles. I guarantee you he's a whiz." The potential of Jack having some hidden higher intelligence was driving him.

Once again, I felt immediately defensive. I wanted to say, "My son is not a science experiment." Thankfully I managed to contain myself. I could see that Paul believed he had found some sort of common ground with Jack, and I didn't want to minimize that. After a full day of shopping and exploring Boulder, we headed to the bookstore to buy a book of sudoku puzzles, then stopped at the ice cream shop across the street. While we sat and spooned away at our cups—never a cone for Jack—Paul taught Jack the method behind sudoku. It only took two or three tries before Jack seemed to get it and began working on them. He continued in the car all the way back up the canyon to Paul's house. As soon as we returned, Paul checked Jack's answers. I was surprised to find that most of them were right.

"I told you he was a whiz!" Paul had an air of superiority, as if he had discovered a great secret of the universe.

I brushed it off by downplaying Jack's feat. "I'm sure they're fairly easy. We'll see what happens when he gets to the harder ones."

Later that night when Jack and I crawled into bed, he brought the puzzle book with him. "Are you going to work on those while I read?" I asked him.

"Yeah, I guess they're fun," Jack replied, flipping randomly to the middle of the book.

I settled back into the pillows and opened my own book. It wasn't one of my better choices, and my mind began to wander. I thought about Paul's insistence that Jack had some hidden talent, and it made me uneasy. I wondered if he would somehow like Jack more if he were gifted. Why couldn't he just like Jack for Jack? As I pondered this, I glanced over at Jack still working on the puzzles. I watched as he flipped back and forth from the front of the book to the back.

"What are you doing?" I asked, not sure I wanted to hear the answer.

The look he gave me told me he was questioning the number of brain cells in my head. "I'm looking at the answers. They're all in the back."

I sat straight up in bed. "Jack, you are not!"

"Yeah, I am," he insisted matter-of-factly.

I started laughing. Of course he was looking at the answers—he wasn't stupid. He was smarter than us. Why struggle though the puzzles when all the answers are right in the back of the book? The more I thought about it, the harder I laughed.

"Okay, well, don't tell Paul. This is our little secret, okay?"

I made Jack promise that he wouldn't let the cat out of the bag, and as he went back to cheating his way through the puzzles, I started thinking about his success at the game of twenty-one. If he was cheating his way through sudoku, could he somehow be cheating at twenty-one too?

"Jack, how is it that you win at twenty-one every time we play?" The expression on his face signaled that he knew something no one else knew, yet he wasn't sure it was safe to share.

"Uncle Joe taught me how to win," he eventually admitted. Jack went on to explain that as long as he's the one to say three, he can win every time. I did the backward math in my head, and he was right. If your opponent goes first, they have to say either one or two. Either way, it guarantees that three is open for the taking. If Jack is forced to go first, and his opponent says three, he still can guarantee a win by saying six, nine, twelve, fifteen, or eighteen. So it was true—my little Einstein wasn't worth all the hype. He was nothing more than a seven-year-old con man. I felt cheated. I had begun to warm to the idea of Jack having some extraordinary mental talent, but that wasn't the case; he was merely working the system. However, he seemed to have the system down pat, and that itself could be perceived as a valuable real-world talent. I settled back into my pillow, feeling the slightest sense of satisfaction.

Christmas was a success, but as time wore on, the strain of trying to fit our two square pegs into a round relationship hole was wearing on me. Daily life with Jack demanded every ounce of my attention and strength, and I had little left to devote toward helping Paul conquer the divide. Still, I wasn't quite ready to break things off. I convinced myself to focus on the positive and put more energy toward better understanding Jack's perplexities. Although I wanted to believe that Dr. Casey was wrong and Jack's teachers were right, deep down I couldn't convince myself. No part of Jack made sense to me, and without knowing anything about Asperger syndrome, I couldn't discount that it might be true. I owed it to both Jack and everyone around us to educate myself.

I came home one evening with a book by Tony Attwood. Apparently he was the leading authority on Asperger syndrome, and I swore to myself that I would read every page from cover to cover. I should have looked at it more closely before promising such a Herculean task. While the information was presented clearly and was easy to understand, the book itself was page after page of tiny, endless print. I was an artist—my world revolved around visuals. With no break in the academic action, my eyes quickly glazed over, and I gave up. Much of what I read described Jack perfectly, but none of it told me how to *fix* the situation. Jack was exhausting enough; I didn't have the energy to wade through details and piece together conclusions. So I committed myself to going about it the hard way—live through it first, pull every hair out along the way, and research later. I was going to learn about Jack's disability in reverse.

Meanwhile, in an effort to help, Paul suggested that Jack might be a good candidate for therapy. He frequently surfaced with books such as *1-2-3 Magic: Effective Discipline for Children 2–12* or *Kids Are Worth It! Giving Your Child the Gift of Inner Discipline* as a means of convincing me.

Oh, please.

I don't know why I never shared with Paul the evaluations that Jack had been undergoing. I never volunteered any of the results. I was confused regarding who's opinion was right, and I was constantly in a state of deflect and protect—deflecting whatever negative comments Paul made about Jack's behavior to both protect my son and preserve the growing fragility of my relationship with Paul. More than likely, therapy would help our cause, but there was a part of me that didn't want to give Paul the satisfaction of being right. I couldn't ignore that Dr. Casey had also suggested therapy as a course of treatment. I needed to at least entertain the idea, so I called Andrew.

"I think maybe we should look into a therapist for Jack."

He agreed. "Do you still have the list of therapists from the school psychologist?"

"I do, but how do we know which ones are good?"

"I think we need to find out which ones will accept our insurance, and go from there." Andrew offered to take on the task, given that Jack was covered under his policy. A couple of days and several phone calls later, we had an appointment with our first therapist. Her name was Lucy.

Lucy had no understanding of Jack's behaviors or appreciation for the difficulties we were facing. She had little interest in helping us untangle everything. It seemed she was more focused on the underlying tension between Andrew and me that poked through every now and again. She was not the least bit in touch with Jack or with figuring out how to help him, but marital issues appeared easy for her. She was ready to roll up her sleeves, dive right in, and have a field day.

Sorry, Lucy, we're not interested.

Three appointments later, and we were back to square one.

CHAPTER 12
A Better Fit

It was late March when Paul and I finally called it quits. He seemed not to believe that Jack would improve with therapy, and with the continued stress of our go-nowhere circumstances, Paul had reached his limit. As hard as we had tried, we simply couldn't make things work. I was fatigued by the balancing act, Paul was out of steam from giving his all, and Jack was no closer to accepting Paul. I had truly wanted it to work, for all three of us—it just didn't, and no one was saying that any louder and clearer than Jack. I had to listen.

The details of how our relationship came to an end were not important. Paul simply wasn't the right piece to fit within the puzzle of my world with Jack. He wanted to relate to Jack in a very personal way, which Jack couldn't do. I wanted to pin all our failures on Paul not understanding children and parenting, when it was really Jack not understanding people in any way. There was constant tension between Paul and Jack, a tug-of-war between two sides that had dug in and were unwilling to relinquish ground. This was confirmation that I required a partner who fully understood my obligation to Jack, my commitment to being the role model that he needed, and my duty toward meeting his needs. I also needed someone who was willing to face Jack head-on and embrace him when they clashed, rather than turn away.

As spring turned to summer, I settled into a new attitude of acceptance and patience. I felt the way I had felt those last few weeks before getting pregnant with Jack. I had accepted that Angela was gone, I knew that eventually I would get pregnant again, and I understood that I just needed to be patient. It was the same now with wanting to find a life partner—when the time was right, he would come along. More importantly, when he did, not only would I be receptive but Jack would as well.

Because I worked from home, my opportunities for meeting new people were limited, so I placed a profile on an online dating site. For the most part, the men I met were all nice enough, but none captivated me enough to hold my attention.

When I first saw Liam's profile, I was intrigued. He didn't use a single pronoun in his description of himself. No "*I* play golf" or "*I'm* interested in fishing." How does one completely avoid the use of pronouns? What kind of person feels the need to ignore such an important part of the English language?

The photos he had posted were of such poor quality that they were tough to make out. He appeared to be my type. He had dark hair, and his profile indicated that he was tall enough. Beyond that though, I had no idea what he looked like, so I filled in the gaps on my own. Despite not having yet met in person, I grew more intrigued by the day. He appeared to be smart, quick-witted, and interesting, and the sound of his voice, both solid and soothing, turned me on. We spent the first few weeks getting to know one another by way of phone, email, and instant message.

"I love to play golf."

Oh good; he's athletic. "Cycling is my passion."

"I run a futures trading program."

I have no idea what that is. I'll research it. "I'm a graphic designer."

"I'm having a tough time with this divorce process."

You have three or four more years before things start to settle down. If you're lucky. "Welcome to the club."

"I have two kids, seven and nine."

Perfect. "I have a son. He's eight."

"My daughter is a bit tough."

Yes! My son is impossible.

I asked my parents to stay with Jack the evening of my first date with Liam. It was a Wednesday, so I planned on an early night. I was both excited and nervous to meet him. It was obvious that we had a lot in common, but would the real-life version stack up to the one I had created in my mind? With so few visual cues to go on, I wasn't sure how I would find him once I arrived at the restaurant. I scanned the bar area quickly and didn't see anyone that might be Liam. There were no single men at all, which meant I must have arrived first. I breathed a sigh of relief for small miracles—let him find me.

When Liam did arrive, I was caught off guard. He certainly wasn't unattractive; he just wasn't at all what I was expecting. His hair was dark, yes. But his skin was fair, and probably at one time freckled, and his eyes were blue. Not my usual type, but what could I do? I would let the evening unfold, and much to my surprise, it unfolded naturally. We covered all the basics—learning more about each other's interests, careers, family—and we began to explore one another both mentally and emotionally. There was no shortage of interest or laughter. Yet all evening I sat across the table from Liam scanning his face for something, any element of physical similarity between the picture I had created in my mind and the real person.

—

"So how was your date?" my mother was asking before I had even closed the door behind me.

"It was good," I said, without much enthusiasm.

My mother probed. It was her nature. "Did you not have fun?"

I let out a heavy sigh. "Yes, I had fun. It's just that something was missing, and I can't put my finger on it." I was exhausted. I had been on countless dates, each time hoping it would be the one that was different, each time feeling let down. I felt especially let down by Liam, but I couldn't figure out why.

I reflected on our date from start to finish. The conversation had flowed, the laughter was genuine, and it had ended up being not all that early of an evening. A first date that is several hours long is typically a good sign. At one point, Liam used the word "simpatico" to describe the energy between us—a unique choice, I thought, and a definite point in his column. I couldn't exactly argue, either; there was an obvious chemistry. What was it then? What was tugging at me?

I sat down at my desk the following morning, and I heard what had become a familiar sound over the last few weeks—the ping of an instant message. I didn't engage in instant messaging with anyone else, so I knew it was Liam. I saw a simple "gm" on my screen. I had learned the night before that he was all about economy of typing—hence the lack of pronouns in his profile.

"Good morning," I typed, feeling he was at least worth the extra letters.

"Was fun being with you."

"Yes."

"Was thinking . . . dinner tomorrow night?"

Despite my unexplained disappointment, I agreed. Later that afternoon I called my mother to see if she would be available to watch Jack again.

"I'm not 100 percent sure I want to go," I confessed.

"Oh, honey, give it a chance. What do you have to lose? It seems to me that you like this guy. You've been enjoying just talking to him— that must count for something." It both annoyed and comforted me that she was always right, and I conceded that it couldn't hurt to give Liam a second chance. I agreed to meet him for dinner.

We had another evening of shared continuous laughter and conversation that kept me on my toes. In studying Liam's features over the course of the night, I allowed myself to let go and open the door to an unforeseen attraction. His blue eyes that softened when he flirted and pale skin that glowed to a rosy hue when he laughed were both warm and welcoming. His thick, dark curls invited me to run my fingers through them, though I wouldn't have dared. I was still struggling with some undefined miscalculation on my part, but I convinced myself not to overthink it and just enjoyed Liam's company.

In the days that followed, I tried to determine the source of my initial hesitation. What's visible on the surface is never a complete picture; I knew that. Maybe with a little time and digging, I would find that Liam truly was here to be the knight in shining armor he promised to be. For a few brief moments I allowed myself to fanta-size. Then I began to fret. What if it were true? What if we were to have a third date, followed by a fourth and a fifth, and things began to click, and—jumping ahead—Liam and I were to fall in love, become inseparable, and. . . .

I was getting way ahead of myself, but I had to in order to escape the question stalking me.

How will he react to Jack?

What's visible on the surface will turn him off for sure. If he's willing to dig a little deeper though, maybe he'll find that Jack being a handful is not the result of poor parenting and nonexistent discipline, or Jack intentionally being a jerk. It's simply because he's programmed differently than us. Though there was nothing *simple* about that—I was still struggling myself to unpack everything that meant. Every unwieldy piece of Jack's being is because he's not built like everyone else. His pieces have been assembled in a completely different order.

My wishful thinking convinced me that if Liam took the time to dig deep, he would develop an appreciation for Jack. He might even find a Jack in there he likes. My wishful thinking also knew that amount of digging would require heavy machinery.

A couple of days later, Liam and I had a third date, which rolled right into a fourth and then a fifth. Within a few weeks it seemed we were spending every spare moment together. However, the children were a priority that couldn't be ignored. While it was extremely early on, we discussed adding them to the equation and agreed that it would require a very delicate approach. Liam's concern was much greater than my own. Andrew and I were five years out from our initial separation, our divorce had been finalized, and Jack had already experienced the presence of a new significant other. Liam was still at the beginning stages of the divorce process, and his children were far too vulnerable. They hadn't fully accepted that their parents had split, let alone the idea of someone new. Liam wanted it to seem natural, as if we were longtime acquaintances that had become great friends, who coincidentally have kids the same age. He wasn't keen on his kids knowing he was dating.

We would need to get creative.

Liam and I set about planning various "unexpected" encounters—bumping into one another at the Lego store in the mall, or magically showing up at the same pizza place on a Friday night. Our most creative—and courageous—effort was a Saturday afternoon rendezvous at the top of Rockefeller Center in New York City. It required far more time coordination than any other chance meeting. We needed to arrive in the city simultaneously, while driving up separately of course; purchase tickets; and make it to the top of the skyscraper, along with the hundreds of others in line, within fifteen or twenty minutes of one another.

Somehow it worked.

"Oh my God, I can't believe you're here—in New York City!" I said.

Liam played along. "What a coincidence!"

"Jack, look who it is. . . ."

"What are your plans for the rest of the day?" Liam asked, a bit too theatrically. "Do you want to join us for lunch?"

"What do you think, Jack? Should we?"

The boys were ecstatic, chasing each other from one side of the observation deck to another. As usual, Jack moved into warp speed, ten steps ahead of everyone.

"Can Thomas come home with us and spend the night?"

I opened my mouth, ready to object, but then paused. I glanced hopefully at Liam, knowing it was very early in this fragile process but wanting so badly to have the children connect. "Would that be okay? Could the boys have a sleepover?"

There was hesitation in Liam's eyes. Despite understanding completely, I felt a pinch of disappointment. I suddenly realized that I was far more ready for all of this than he was.

"Let me think about it on the ride home."

"Can Thomas at least come in the car with us?" Jack asked directly of Liam.

My pleading eyes were enough to convince him. "Sure," he responded.

The boys cheered and high-fived, skipping off down the street. Liam smiled in my direction, and the five of us wandered back to our two cars, agreeing to meet at Liam's house once we were home before determining if a sleepover was a good idea. The boys' new-found friendship was put on hold for the next couple of hours as both fell right to sleep in the back seat. We were halfway home when my phone rang.

"How are they?" Liam asked.

"Completely crashed. I think they were both asleep before we made it out of the parking garage."

Liam laughed. "Yeah, seems to me like they had fun. Are you sure you want to sign on for a whole night with them?"

"I'm sure," I confirmed with a huge smile that I know he could hear loud and clear.

We stopped at Liam's house to pack an overnight bag for Thomas before the three of us continued home, when suddenly I sensed it. Something had changed along the way. There had been an abduction. Alien Jack was now present in the car with us, shooting down every suggestion Thomas made for how they could have fun the rest of the night, insisting on cheeseburgers when Thomas preferred pizza, and vetoing video games in favor of watching Jack's movie of the day.

I wanted to scream, "*What . . . are . . . you . . . doing? Can't you see how great this could be?*" There was the potential here for Jack to have a built-in friend, maybe even a stepbrother someday—I hoped. Why would he ruin that?

Please, Jack, don't ruin this.

As much as Jack was programmed to push buttons, Thomas seemed programmed to concede. His easygoing nature cancelled out Jack's demanding tenacity, and the end result—thankfully—was the kind of night I had imagined we would have.

Once Liam and I crossed that all-important—rather, all-encompassing—physical divide, spending time together became a matter of necessity. Now that the kids were part of the equation, we coordinated our every-other-weekend schedules so that weekends with the kids were the same, giving us weekends without them to ourselves. All my initial uncertainty had evaporated and was being replaced by a happiness I hadn't felt in a long time. As far as Jack was concerned, Liam wasn't focused on trying to be his friend as Paul had tried. That, combined with him having a son Jack's age, meant Jack had no reason to push back on Liam's presence in our lives.

It wasn't long before Thomas was regularly spending the night at our house. If I was willing to dodge a ball and offering my world-famous vanilla milkshakes (made so by the secret addition of gobs of caramel syrup), Thomas was in. The boys' personalities were 180 degrees apart, but it was a difference that seemed to work. Jack called the shots; Thomas followed along. Jack was taxing at every turn; Thomas went with the flow. Jack exhausted and irritated me; Thomas made me smile. He was an unusually enjoyable kid whose adult-like way of interacting seemed beyond his years. I was envious of Liam and questioning my parenting. More so, I welcomed the relief. Finally, there was someone who would play with Jack, repeatedly.

Over the next several months, we settled into a rhythm that suggested the situation could potentially be permanent. Though living separately, we behaved like family. Thomas spent the night with us almost every weekend. If Liam had a golf tournament or fishing trip, I would step in to help with his kids so as not to upset the weekend-on/weekend-off schedule. If Liam took the boys to the batting cages, I would take Katie for a pedicure. Even Andrew welcomed the situation by inviting Thomas to join Jack for cookouts at his house. That felt like it was crossing some unwritten boundary, but kudos to Andrew for putting Jack first.

If Liam was bothered by Jack's behavior, he didn't let it show. He was either willing to accept it, or not wanting to say anything for fear of ruining what we were building. With two kids of his own, he seemed understanding of a child that's less than perfect. Granted, I was absorbing most of the time the two boys spent together, so his level of exposure was reduced. It was in my anxious-to-please nature to go above and beyond, and in this case, it was in my best interest to soften the blow as much as possible. With Liam only exposed to Jack every other weekend, the damage was kept to a minimum.

CHAPTER 13
Exit Stage Left

Once summer began, Liam suggested that we rent a house at the Jersey Shore for a week in August. I relished the idea of an entire week with him—and his kids. Not only had I fallen in love with Liam but with the children as well. For me, it felt as though we were already a family.

Although Jack was almost nine, he had yet to learn how to ride a bike. It wasn't for lack of trying. He was unable to coordinate the motion of pedaling and braking while maintaining balance, and time after time, the bike was wheeled back into the garage. Jack just didn't get it.

The week before our vacation, Liam insisted, "He has to learn how to ride."

"He doesn't *have* to," I countered. I was willing to sacrifice the fun of the family activity to shield Jack from failure and myself from the struggle. We had tried, he didn't get it, and maybe he would never get it.

"You can't go to the beach without being able to ride a bike," Liam went on. "It's all part of the ritual."

I didn't feel the same sense of urgency, but I valued Liam's opinion. Over the last several months, I had come to realize that he was more levelheaded than me. He seemed to have a better sense of parenting, though at the time, he may have disagreed. If he thought bike riding was a necessary, important activity for the beach, I would do my part and give Jack a crash course—literally—in the fine art of cycling. The following week I took Jack to the park every afternoon where he was able to practice on the path rather than the street, with fewer obstacles and less chance of getting hurt.

It was a muggy August evening, and we had just two days before we were to leave for the beach. We hadn't been at the park more than twenty minutes, and already I was drenched in sweat. With each encouraging push from me, Jack would pedal along briefly before starting to wobble—left, then right—and eventually end up on the ground. I slumped onto the nearest bench and wiped my forehead.

"I don't know, Jack. Maybe bike riding just isn't for you."

"No, Mom, I can do it. Can you push me just one more time?"

I looked at him skeptically. Not wanting to give up on him, I hoisted myself up, got behind him, gripped the seat firmly, and waited until he had his balance.

"Ready?"

"Ready," he assured me.

Jack started pedaling forward as I put my weight against the bike. On the word "go," I gave him one last push, and he was on his way. He pedaled away from the safety of my steady grip and just kept going. In one swift motion he was on his way along the path through the park with no support, no training wheels, and no fear. But he also had no understanding of the rules of the road or the need to give pedestrians a heads-up when headed right for them.

I saw it coming, I even tried shouting to Jack in warning, but he was already too far to hear me. His head was up. He was looking straight ahead. He had to have seen her, yet Jack just kept on his way, walloping that woman in the ass with his handlebar as he sailed right past her. He hit her so hard, with such emphasis, as if to say, "Look at me! I can ride a bike!" She was knocked off her feet. I threw a hand over my mouth to prevent a scream. Okay, so a few expletives slipped out, but I doubt anyone heard. Was I possibly far enough away to avoid claiming responsibility for this wrecking ball of a child?

No! Of course not. My Catholic guilt would never allow it. I ran over to the woman, apologizing profusely, asking if she was okay as I helped her up, before calling after Jack to make it look as though I had some semblance of control.

"It's fine. I'm fine," the woman insisted, pulling away from me to brush leaves from her legs. She wasn't happy, but she appeared willing to let it go.

"I am *so* sorry," was all I could manage—repeatedly—as I caught Jack out of the corner of my eye. He was off in the distance, cruising along with great success. *He's doing it! He's riding a bike!* Seeing that I was more focused on Jack than her potential injuries, the woman eyed me up and down disapprovingly and brought me back down to earth with a massive thud. I needed to defuse the situation immediately. Jack was rounding the corner of the path back toward us, and I would insist that he apologize the moment he stopped. But Jack didn't stop. He just cruised right past us without saying a word, without even looking in our direction.

"Jack, you get back here this instant!" I shouted. "*Jack!*"

He was easily a hundred feet beyond us before he stopped and begrudgingly looked over his shoulder. "What? What did I do?"

Oh my God, Jack. Are you serious?

How could he not know what he had done? If the woman had been willing to let this mishap slide a moment ago, she certainly wasn't now. The look of disbelief and anger in her eyes screamed exactly what I knew, and feared, she was thinking: *What kind of parent allows her kid to get away with that? What an asshole!*

Instead of celebrating Jack learning how to ride a bike, a childhood milestone, and being able to congratulate him, I needed to reprimand him.

"Jack, what were you thinking?" I asked as soon as the woman stormed away.

"She was in my way."

"You go apologize to her *immediately!*"

"Why? She was in my way." He was so matter-of-fact.

"Then you should have shouted to her and let her know you were coming up behind her—not just ride right into her and knock her to the ground. Go apologize!" I don't know why I insisted when I knew it wouldn't make any difference.

Jack reluctantly dismounted his bike. He caught up to the woman and offered her no more than a sideways glance and a barely audible "sorry." He didn't even wait for a reply before turning around and coming back to me. His half-hearted effort made no difference. If anything, it made things worse.

We rode home in silence until Jack reflexively floated, "Love you, Mom," from the back seat to the front.

DON'T do it.

I left the thought on pause.

"Love you too, bud."

Not long enough.

Why am I such a terrible mother?

I put the incident behind us. I was also very conscious of not forgetting it. I needed to get a better handle on Jack's behavior. Despite the ugly conclusion to our lessons, he was finally able to navigate successfully on two wheels, meaning we were officially ready for a week at the beach. We were going to be joined by a friend of Liam's and his three kids. Michael was going through his own divorce—a common theme among us forty-somethings, I was finding—so he welcomed the opportunity to vacation with us. While the kids spent their time in the sun and sand, the three of us could unwind and commiserate.

The week was complete mayhem.

Jack was loud and unruly from start to finish, though the week being less than picture-perfect didn't lay solely on his shoulders. Michael's five-year-old was doing her best to get herself or anyone else arrested. Trying to wrangle six kids under the age of eleven while at the beach left Liam, Michael, and me exhausted. I would say, though, that Jack was easily responsible for 76 percent of the "*Please keep it down*," 88 percent of the "*Just stop!*" and 92 percent of the "*Don't you dare*" that left our mouths.

From the start, Michael had planned on leaving midweek, and Jack and I needed to return home early for a family event. This left Liam, Katie, and Thomas with a couple of days to themselves on the back end. Liam called later in the evening the day we left, to check in and make sure we returned home safely. We reflected on the week and how it had been trying.

"After you two left, Katie said she was happy everyone was gone—and that it was just the three of us again," he said. Liam and I were aware that Jack was the main source of strain, but I hadn't realized the children picked up on it too. It was a slight punch to the gut.

Over time I would get used to it. Eventually I would learn to dodge the punches by staying out of the ring. Avoiding certain situations was easier.

In hindsight, Liam and I had been enjoying one another far too much to pay attention to the growing discord among the children. I knew it was happening, but I wrote it off as something that would eventually disappear on its own, reasoning that Liam's kids were still stung by the divorce. They hadn't gotten used to the idea of Mom and Dad no longer being together, and then Jack and I came along. They didn't like the idea of us becoming a regular part of their lives. They just weren't ready.

The real problem, though, was Jack.

His defiance and disrespect were a constant presence, testing everyone's patience. Yet I never once thought to share with Liam the shadow that was hanging over Jack. I had made a subconscious decision to forget it completely. It wasn't intentional; it just went away, and I made no effort to chase it. I was hoping that within the context of the family setting we were developing, Jack would improve. Deep down, I was afraid that if I said something was wrong with Jack, Liam would walk away. Even if I had wanted to say something, I couldn't. I had made no effort to understand or research Jack's diagnosis, let alone accept it, so how could I possibly speak intelligibly about it?

CHAPTER 14
Silver Lining

Notwithstanding my relationship with Liam, the period between Jack turning eight and twelve years old is the stretch I remember least. It was long and demanding, and I am certain that on a subconscious level, I was working overtime to block it out. At a minimum, I owe my survival of those years to the consumption of large quantities of alcohol, probably another reason my memory is clouded. Alcohol numbed me to Jack's unending challenges. It made me more willing to accept his oddities, his repetitiveness, and his demanding nature—all of which were growing in magnitude. And it enabled me to forget all the nasty looks, the embarrassment, and the fatigue. Everyone around us viewed Jack as a brat, and the fact that he was the only child of divorced parents made that easier for them to believe.

I was regretful when Andrew and I divorced, knowing that Jack would likely be an only child. I had grown up as the youngest of five and had always appreciated the richness of family. As adults, I adore my older brothers—we share the same mindset and sense of humor, and in times of need, we're unconditionally there for one another. I felt Jack deserved the same, and I wanted him to have the support of family. I didn't want him growing up, or worse—growing old—alone.

And, God forbid, what if something were to happen to both Andrew and me? Who would take care of Jack?

Yet Jack was so much to handle that not having to deal with another child at the same time was a blessing. Of course, on the flip side, not having anyone to compare him to or to help buffer his impact magnified his complexity. The only measure of comparison I had was Thomas, who was on the opposite end of the spectrum and nothing short of an angel. It made Jack seem like the child from hell.

There was one silver lining.

Baseball.

Note, if this were an audiobook, this is the moment when you would be deafened by the triumphant chorus of angels.

While soccer and basketball were still part of Jack's athletic vocabulary and would remain so for many years, both quickly took a back seat to his second attempt at baseball. Just as so many of his obsessions had started—by watching and wanting to copy what others were doing—so it was with baseball the second time around. It grabbed hold of Jack with a ferocity that seemed as though it would never let go.

Thomas was already completely immersed in the sport when Liam and I first started dating, and he was also quite good. Because we were spending so much time together, Jack and I would go to Thomas's games. The more Jack saw Thomas play, the more he wanted to play, so we revisited the idea, turning to the same organization that was already serving us well. It wasn't long before Jack was playing intramural baseball once again, but this time, he committed for far longer than just two weeks.

It was a typical intramural program—practice two afternoons

a week and a game every weekend—and Jack loved every single moment. The spring season spanned two months, and that first year it was two very chilly, rainy months. Practice and games were frequently canceled, leaving Jack disappointed and us frustrated. We had finally found an outlet for his impulsive energy and a solution to his boredom, but his access was often denied thanks to two words— "weather permitting." Luckily, the spring season soon rolled into summer, albeit more relaxed with no practices and only games, but Jack didn't seem to mind. As long as he was playing, he was happy. Finally, he had a place—*his* place. It was a place where he was welcomed, and the other kids looked on him positively. It was a place where he fit in—and where, it appeared, he excelled.

The day he was called up to play on the district team was a dream come true for him. The district teams were comprised of a select few, the fifteen best players from each age group. Jack was invited to join the 11U team, meaning all the boys were between ten and eleven years of age. Of greater significance was that the team had already been playing together for a couple of years. Jack had made enough of an impression through intramurals that the minute a spot opened because another boy had left the team, the coach asked him to join. Of most appeal to Jack was that the district team would not replace intramurals. District play was tournament play—and it would be in addition to his intramural teams. *More* baseball!

Jack was elated.

I was clearly more nervous than Jack the day of his first district game. He had been practicing with the team for a couple of weeks and seemed to be settling in, but I had this ridiculous notion in my head that the other boys were on some elite level, one that Jack hadn't quite yet reached. Of course, none of them were elite.

"Oh God, are you sure he can do this?" I asked Andrew as I

watched the coach call Jack from the bench. "Does the coach know that Jack has never pitched at this level?" Hearing myself, I quickly realized how ridiculous that question was when referencing a group of ten-year-olds.

"Relax, he'll be fine," Andrew assured me.

It was the last inning of the game, and the opposing team had a player on first—with no outs. Jack was being thrown to the wolves, in my estimation.

Please don't let them down, sweetheart.

Jack wound up and threw his first pitch. It was called a ball.

Okay, not horrible.

The batter launched Jack's second pitch into the outfield. There were now boys on first and second, and I was on the brink of heart failure.

Come on, baby, you can do this.

Jack wound up for his first pitch to the next batter, and much to everyone's dismay, it was another hit. Bases were now loaded. I wanted to escape. Jack didn't seem the least bit concerned.

Please, baby, throw a strike. Just one strike.

He wound up again, launched the ball toward home plate, and this time, the batter swung and missed.

That's the way to do it, baby! Come on, throw another!

Suddenly, Jack appeared to have some sense of control over the situation, and he was able to deliver two more strikes.

"You're out!" the umpire shouted dramatically, and Jack's team went wild.

It wasn't over yet, though. Bases were still loaded, and Jack needed two more outs. I started praying.

Please, God, just let him throw strikes.

Oddly, Jack seemed to thrive on the pressure of bases being loaded. Two more batters stepped to the plate, and both were struck out handily. If they were drafting pitchers out of the fifth grade that day, Jack would have been a first-round pick.

He was a hero after that game, proving himself to his teammates and his coaches. No longer would he be a secondary benchwarmer simply because he was the newest addition to the team. He had also proven me wrong. I had it in my mind that Jack wasn't ready or good enough to justify his spot on this team. He convinced me that he could hold his own, and it made me proud that he did it with such cool, collective calm. Baseball was a setting in which Jack seemed to fit—and we didn't want to run and hide because of his behavior.

Were it not for baseball, I'm not sure I would have been able to preserve my relationship with Liam. In it, Jack had found the perfect match for his intense self—it was the glue that held everything together. Of course, it was possible that anything could go wrong. All the good that baseball brought into our lives came with its share of bad.

What began as mere interest in the game quickly turned to full-on obsession. Jack's schedule of what felt like 558 practices and 942 games a week was soon no longer enough for him. He wanted to spend every moment of downtime swinging a bat and honing his skills in the batting cages at a nearby training facility. The cages were open for anyone to use, but they weren't free. Jack was intent on perfection, and the twenty-dollar limit that I placed on tokens for the machine quickly grew to thirty, then forty and fifty dollars. Saturday afternoons rolled into Sunday mornings—and afternoons—and Monday and Tuesday evenings. Before long, I found myself purchasing a monthly membership, and Jack made use of every penny. With every spare moment filled with practice and games, you would think that the windup of every throw, the swing of every bat, and each proper stance on the field would all be movements ingrained in Jack's brain. With so much repetition, they should come naturally.

It was a Saturday in May. The first of Jack's three district games that weekend was in its fourth inning, and it was not one of his better ones. He seemed off-kilter, but I couldn't put my finger on what was bothering him. I leaned over to Andrew, who was just a few feet from me along the third base fence. "Something's not right with him today," I said.

"Yeah, I noticed that. Is he feeling okay?"

"He was fine all morning." As we shared our unease, Jack's coach called a time-out and made his way to the mound.

"Jack, are you all right?" I heard him ask.

"No," Jack replied. "I can't pitch today."

"What do you mean?"

"I just can't pitch. I don't know. . . ." His discomfort was evident as he nervously shifted from one foot to the other and adjusted his hat several times.

"Take a deep breath," the coach instructed. "Just take your time, and you'll be fine." He gave Jack a gentle pat on the back before heading back to the dugout.

Taking his advice, Jack took a deep breath and wound up to throw his next pitch. He sent the ball toward the plate—and missed completely. To miss the plate by six feet was not like him. The coach shouted a few words of encouragement, and Jack wound up again. His second pitch hit the batter squarely, sending him to first base.

Jack was beside himself, paralyzed on the mound.

Calling time once again, Jack's coach ran onto the field, placed his arm around Jack's shoulder, and crouched to be at eye level with him. Jack immediately brought his glove to his face.

"Hey, Jack, relax," the coach said calmly. "I've watched you pitch a thousand times. You can do this. Everyone has bad days now and again." Jack fell apart. He started bawling—and walked right off the field. It broke my heart. A slight crack had just formed in his super-hero veneer.

This was more than just Jack having a bad day. Something had changed. It was as if he had developed baseball amnesia. Despite his compulsive practice habits and his obsession with being the best, his ability to throw strikes consistently in every game, and his tendency to hit at least one home run per game, there was suddenly no guar-antee of which Jack might show up to play on any given day. It might be the ten-year-old baseball god that his teammates and coaches had come to revere, or it might be the Jack that had suddenly slipped into a pattern of reversion, having no clue how to swing a bat or throw a ball. One day he could play brilliantly, the next it would be as if he had never played before.

It was all eerily reminiscent of something that had happened shortly after Jack started first grade. He had fallen from a swing on the school playground and broken his right arm. That evening, he agonized over not being able to use his right hand to practice his writing. While the other students in his class had not yet even enter-tained the idea of cursive writing, Jack was already self-taught. I had bought him a practice guide for writing that summer because he had expressed interest. Each page illustrated how to form the various letters of the alphabet in both upper and lower case, and there were plenty of blank lines for practicing. Once Jack began fashioning dif-ferent letter shapes, he became engrossed in the art of cursive writing and perfected his form. With the thought of a penmanship setback weighing heavily on his mind, he spent the entire evening teaching himself to write—and color within the lines—with his left hand. The next day he went off to school, confident that his newly trained left hand wouldn't let him down.

His fixation on perfecting his penmanship became more pronounced as that year progressed. While his classmates tossed about oversized, loosely shaped letters, Jack's handwriting grew more and more precise—and increasingly smaller. It became practically microscopic, yet it was perfect in form. He could also render every detail of every Pokémon character with exacting precision, all completely from memory.

At some point without warning, though, his flawless penmanship reverted to illegible chicken scratch, and his complex character drawings changed back to stick figures. We couldn't understand why he had been able to write and draw perfectly for months on end but then couldn't remember how to hold a pencil correctly.

It was the same now. The motion of swinging a bat had been forever imprinted on his mind we thought, but as quickly as he had trained himself to be the best, he just as quickly forgot how to do it at all. Jack looked for solutions everywhere. He spent hours watching the professionals in games and game highlights. He studied every top player and did his best to mimic them. On Saturday he was convinced that Miguel Cabrera's stance was the right one for him. Come Sunday, José Reyes was the man of the hour. He moved from one player to the next, following every movement, imitating every angle. When that didn't work, Jack convinced himself that it was his bat that was all wrong and using his teammates' bats was the key to success. As soon as he realized that barreling through every bat in the dugout wasn't the answer, he became hyperfocused on teaching himself to be a switch-hitter. He had become so unpredictable that I went from proudly wearing my "mom" jersey with our last name across the back, to questioning if I should wear it inside out. From that day forward—the day of the mysterious meltdown on the mound—nothing was the same. Still, Jack was obsessed. And he wasn't letting go.

CHAPTER 15
Fix It

As we moved toward winter, baseball season thankfully transitioned to soccer and basketball. Jack's inexplicable amnesia didn't seem to carry over to those two sports, so I put my worry aside.

Liam and I were chugging along happily, still maintaining a schedule of weekend on/weekend off with the kids. Every so often, Liam and Jack would butt heads over something obnoxious that Jack did or said. In every instance Liam was right, but he rarely complained. When he mentioned something that bothered him, his irritation was brief, and he generally let it go. He took it all in stride, it seemed.

It wasn't until the following summer that the situation came to a head.

"Are you sure you want to give this a second try?"

"I'm sure," Liam insisted.

I'll admit, I was pleasantly surprised by Liam's willingness to plan another week at the beach, given how poorly the previous year had gone. Rather than rent a house at the Jersey Shore, he proposed we rent one on the Outer Banks of North Carolina. We had never been there and had heard that it was much better than the Jersey beaches—quieter, less crowded, less of a scene.

At six-plus hours away, it was quite a drive. Although check-in wasn't until 4:00 p.m., we decided that we would leave at 6:00 a.m. It meant we would arrive early, but hopefully we would arrive ahead of every other renter, and we could fill the gap by having lunch somewhere and familiarizing ourselves with the island. At worst, we could find a spot on the beach to unwind for an hour or so.

The decision worked in our favor. Because the kids had been up since 5:00 a.m., it didn't take long once we were on the road for them to fall back to sleep, and the first three or four hours were smooth sailing. When they came around, we were already far enough south that the landscape had changed, providing enough interest to get us through the remainder of the ride without complaints. We crossed the bridge onto the barrier island with ease just after noon, and our first stop was the realtor's office to inquire about an early check-in. The house was not yet available, the realtor informed us, but they were confident that it would be clean and ready by 2:30 p.m., rather than 4:00 p.m. With keys in hand, all we needed to do was find a suitable lunch spot and wait for their call.

The island was beautiful and, as advertised, more relaxed than New Jersey. We took our time winding along the coast until we came upon a restaurant overlooking the inlet. With the sun shining brightly and a cool breeze, the back deck seemed like the perfect place to eat lunch and wait out the next couple of hours. I was sure it would set the stage for a great week, the five of us enjoying vacation together once again. This year would be different, better.

After being cooped up in a car for six-plus hours, I didn't object to Jack getting up to wander. It would allow him a little time to unwind before our food arrived. Knowing that we had just arrived in town and were all very hungry, the waitress was quick about delivering lunch. I was about to get up from my seat when Jack bounded around

the corner of the deck toward us, arms flailing, a tsunami of unintel-
ligible sounds gushing from his mouth.

The air had shifted.

No one else sensed it. They never did. No one else possessed the
same level of sensitivity I had acquired after ten years of day-to-day
exposure. I had become vigilant, constantly standing guard, await-
ing that slight shift in equilibrium that signals the appearance of an
intruder, one that isn't exactly a welcome addition.

"Jack, come sit down and eat," I calmly instructed him.

He slammed into the open seat next to me with fingers out-
stretched, directed at my face. "Is that a threat? Are you threatening
me?"

"No, Jack, I'm simply telling you what you need to do right now."

"You know what I hate?" he went on. "When people disrespect
me." I knew that the words spewing from his mouth weren't his.
Alien Jack had arrived in the Outer Banks and decided to dine with
us. Standing to smother his burger in half a bottle of ketchup and
dump a pool of it onto his plate for fries, Jack hovered over the rest of
us while we ate.

"Jack, *please!*"

"I'm tired of sitting."

"I know, but we're eating lun—" Before I could finish my sentence,
it happened.

Jack farted.

Not a subtle "Oops, sorry about that!" kind of fart. It was a shock
wave of massive proportion that made its presence known to anyone
within fifty feet of us.

What—is the appropriate response to *that*?

If Liam and his kids couldn't feel the winds of change now, they
were all out to lunch (yes, pun painfully intended). This was the exact

opposite of what I had envisioned. Both Liam and I immediately yelled at Jack, but the damage was done.

I forced him back into his seat. "Don't you dare move or say another word! Do you understand?" The blank expression on his face signaled his lack of understanding as to why I was angry, and worse, he seemed unfazed by it. This was not my child; he couldn't possibly be. I contemplated removing him from the table, but I didn't trust him to wait in the car alone, and the ramifications of him not eating would be more damaging. It was taking the easy way out, more likely irresponsible or lazy, but it was all I could manage.

"Love you, Mom."

I glared at Jack. *Don't bait me.* I didn't say another word to him for the remainder of lunch, or the next twenty-four hours. When we headed to the beach later that day, I had a football catch with Thomas. Jack asked if he could join in and I walked away. Jack asked me to ride waves with him. I ignored him. When I pulled out my camera to take photos, I didn't take any of Jack, despite his repeated requests. "Love you, Mom" was tacked on to every request and it took all my energy to let it slide off. I assumed, hoped, my strategy would have real impact and enlighten him to the seriousness of his actions.

My strategy had no impact whatsoever.

Jack had zero understanding that it was not okay to do what he had done—to let one rip in a public place while people are enjoying lunch—and I couldn't figure out why. It was always when we were in public, as if he were going out of his way to ruin everyone's day. He was completely incapable of reading the clues, the reactions of those around him telling him that he had taken something too far. Instead of a relaxing start, it was a predictably maddening prelude to another stressful week at the beach.

Trapped with Jack.

———

Shortly after returning from the Outer Banks, Liam called and asked if we could have dinner that evening. The sober manner in which he posed the request gave it away—something was wrong.

As soon as we were seated, Liam turned to me and in a very straightforward manner said, "Something needs to change. Jack's behavior is really tough to take. . . ."

My heart sank. Clearly Liam hadn't been as oblivious as I thought.

"When I took the boys over to get the fish that one day, Jack was kicking the back of my seat the whole way, and I'm sure it was intentional. I was also standing in the kitchen the other morning, and he walked right up behind me and elbowed me in the back, for no reason. . . ."

"Why didn't you tell me?" I pleaded.

"And if something doesn't change," Liam went on, ignoring my question, pausing as if to be certain of his next thought, "I'm not sure I can stick around."

No. PLEASE, NO.

I couldn't lose Liam. But I also couldn't argue. I didn't want to stick around myself. How could I expect him to tolerate Jack's behavior? There was no need for a response; my tears spoke for me.

Seeing me upset, Liam's tone softened. "Maybe you should try therapy again—or maybe consider medication." He floated the latter gently, knowing that Andrew and I were opposed and saw it as a last resort, but maybe it was our only alternative. We had no clue how to handle our son.

"We need to do something. He's unbearable." I threw the words at Andrew as if the problem of Jack was his fault. Of course, it wasn't Andrew's fault, but I wanted it to be. I was on the verge of losing Liam, and I wanted to blame Andrew. I wanted him to do the hard work of fixing Jack and to make all this tension disappear, but I regretfully knew that the responsibility rested on both our shoulders. We agreed to give therapy another chance.

As far as therapists go, anyone would be better than Lucy. Despite our lack of success with her, we reached out to the same practice of therapists and asked if they could recommend someone else.

Jack's next victim would be Charles.

"Jack can call me Mr. Sagers," Charles announced at our first appointment, directing the order at Andrew and me more so than Jack, as if to inform us that he would not tolerate any lack of parental control.

This relationship is doomed.

When it came to Jack, control was not our strong suit, and the moment you tell Jack what he can't do is the moment that he does exactly that. Much to my surprise, Jack proved me wrong and succeeded in learning to address Charles as Charles wished, but beyond that, he resisted Charles with gusto. Jack spent most appointments wandering about Charles's office, pulling books off the shelves, fiddling with the blinds, ignoring all his questions—never once looking him in the eye—and pointing out that Charles was either wearing an ugly tie or his shoes were stupid. I'll admit, I couldn't quite connect with him, either. He had an unnerving air of superiority that came off as "You're not good parents, and you're doing everything wrong." While that may very well have been true, his approach was not constructive.

After half a dozen meetings with Charles, we had exhausted the therapeutic possibilities and moved on to Rebecca, and I must give her credit—she cut right to the chase. Rebecca wasted no time in telling us that she couldn't and wouldn't help us. We were stunned. I'm not sure what Jack did in our two meetings with her—we were sitting beside him the whole time—but clearly, she was thinking on her feet and got out while the gettin' was good. A bit harsh but smart.

Following Rebecca's exit, we were assigned to Jack Lewis.

"I'm pretty sure you're going to like him, Jack—the two of you have the same name!" That was my way of telling Jack that he better be receptive to the new Jack. I wasn't sure how many options we had left. Personally, I was a fan right from the start. Jack Lewis had a relaxed demeanor, he appeared to genuinely care, and he was obviously smart—not in the "I'm not touching this one with a ten-foot pole" way that Rebecca was smart. Rather, he was smart in a clear-headed, "We're going to get to the bottom of this" manner. Jack Lewis was interested in helping us, and he truly tried. He came at Jack from every angle, trying to determine what made him tick, but he was no match for Jack's resistance. Despite every effort, he was unable to crack the code of what drove Jack's behavior and continuously came up short on ways to help him.

It wasn't surprising that therapy was a disaster. What is the key ingredient for it to be successful? The ability to share thoughts and feelings, which requires social interaction on a very personal level. Jack couldn't interact socially on any level. Ask him to share what he was thinking and feeling, and you were more likely to get an exhaustive outpouring of nonsensical babble or worse, a direct insult regarding your physical appearance or personality. We had gone into every one of these relationships armed with reports and evaluations, providing as much information about Jack's issues as possible. We had bared our souls to these people, yet none of them seemed able to break through the disabling clutter within which Jack was right at home.

Andrew and I had been resistant to the idea of medication because the last thing we wanted was for Jack to become a doped up zombie, and from a parenting standpoint, it felt like a cop-out. But with each difficult day, we moved closer to the idea. We had hit a wall in helping Jack, and maybe medication was the ladder we needed to get over the wall. But how could anyone know what to prescribe for him when they didn't understand the complex labyrinth of his mind? Despite being told that the dark figure in the driver's seat of Jack's life was Asperger syndrome, none of them seemed to understand what that meant. They had no understanding of or experience with Asperger syndrome, and I got the sense from all of them that they were simply ignoring that one crucial piece of information.

Why wouldn't they? We were.

As we stumbled our way through therapy, Jack's behavior at school settled down due in large part, I'm sure, to his IEP, which we continued to tweak with each school year. Academically he was doing well enough. He also continued in his social skills class, though beyond practicing the basics of proper manners, it wasn't helping much. Good social skills require being able to infer and read subtle cues provided by the opposing party. In Jack's world, social cues were a language of unknowns, and he could neither interpret them nor determine the appropriate response. Achieving success in social skills class would be a huge miracle. We were happy enough for smaller ones—such as Jack being able to keep himself contained for the duration of the school day.

School aside, daily life was still a struggle. Keeping himself under control from eight in the morning until three in the afternoon meant Jack let loose the moment he got home. He began bouncing off the walls the minute he entered the house.

"Bubble butt, bubble bubble bubble butt," Jack launched at me as he barreled through the door after school, heaving his backpack against the wall before tearing up the steps to his room.

"Jack, can you please stop?" I called after him. I couldn't manage *hello* anymore.

"Booty how. Booty, booty, booty, booty, booty . . . hooooooowww," echoed down from above.

"Jack, please."

"Yahtz, booty botch!"

"*Pleeease*, Jack! Just *stop!*"

"Love you, Mom."

Serenity now.

Every day was Groundhog Day, and baseball wasn't the only thing on repeat. Jack maintained a strict diet of three foods—macaroni and cheese, spaghetti and meatballs, and cheeseburgers. Lime tortilla chips were a constant snack. No other chip was acceptable, and because Jack's devotion was undying, the word "limechips" quickly became a popular choice for account passwords. Downtime was filled with one of two activities—playing catch or playing Scrabble. After dinner, the same show played night after night. I've seen close to five hundred showings of *Twister*, and I can assure you, I will not live in Kansas.

To some degree, I relied on the monotony. It enabled me to stay one step ahead of Jack and prevent upset. Introducing anything new to the routine came with risks. New could be met with hellish resistance—or it could easily become the next theme of the day for today, tomorrow, and every day thereafter until it was replaced by the next new thing. I had to tread lightly. Monotony was preferred.

Perhaps it was the sameness of every day that lulled me into a false sense of security. Small signs were popping up that I'm certain I had been missing for some time. Any one on its own didn't say much, but gather them together, read them as a whole, and they spoke volumes. Behavior that until now had been nothing more than obnoxious, disruptive, and repetitive was taking on bizarre new facets that couldn't be ignored.

Jack was undoubtedly sensitive to temperature. He had always hated the heat. In the summer months, he would completely lose it the moment we climbed into the car, unable to wait the few minutes it would take for the air-conditioning to kick in. You would think I was dangling him over a boiling cauldron. Even with winter in full swing, Jack struggled to stay cool at night. His favorite bedtime companion wasn't a well-worn stuffed animal, but an ice pack under his head. Combined with the ceiling fan on high, it was the only way he was able to sleep. So it made no sense when Jack started piling on the clothes—layers upon layers of clothes. In the midst of winter, I could relate, but as the colder days melted away into summer heat, it was a different story.

"Jack, how many pairs of underwear do you have on today?"

"Just two."

"And how many pairs of pants?"

"Um"—momentary pause so he could count—"three."

"Jack, you don't need *three* pairs of pants." I glanced at my watch. We needed to be out the door in exactly seven minutes so I could drop Jack off for the day and get back home in time for a nine o'clock conference call. I didn't have time to argue with him about the fact that he had dressed himself for summer camp using the entire contents of his closet. "You need to take off at least one pair of underwear and one pair of pants."

Given Jack's obsession with fashion when he was younger—the wristwatches, bags, plaid shirts, belts, and of course, the suit—it was no surprise that we were focused on attire once again. But this was different; this was dangerous. The day's forecast called for ninety-plus degrees, and I couldn't bear to get another call from Jack's camp counselor worried that he might suffer from heat exhaustion. He didn't seem bothered. His response was always the same: wearing multiple layers *feels good.*

The excessive layers weren't all that was worrisome. Jack had simultaneously developed a perplexing relationship with shoes. Granted, all the boys his age were fixated on the latest sneakers, so it wasn't any surprise when Jack became fixated as well. But in typical Jack fashion, he took it to another level.

He refused to let his shoes bend.

The slightest crease in his sneakers would set him sideways. A crease meant they were ruined. The only way Jack could prevent them from bending was to walk without flexing his feet. To ensure he wouldn't forget this, he went one step further and didn't bend his knees, either. His robotic motion was agonizing to watch. My son was physically paralyzed by too many layers of clothing and an irrational fear of imperfect leather. Could medication even help with these issues? I was at a loss. It was getting harder to keep pushing through our days, hoping that someday we would emerge on the other side unscathed.

CHAPTER 16
Actually, I'm Not Sure

"Can we get a dog?"

I had heard the question repeatedly.

"We are not getting a dog."

"Why not?"

"Because, Jack, dogs are a huge responsibility. If we get a dog, there won't be any more spur-of-the-moment trips to the beach. We won't be able to zip up to New York City for the day. What if we get a cat instead?"

Jack pondered this. "I really want a dog."

"No dog."

He pondered a little longer and eventually gave in. To this day, I wish he had pushed harder. Getting a cat was a mistake. Some cats have personality—this cat had zero—and it was just a matter of time before the original question resurfaced.

"Can we get a dog?"

It was Jack's eleventh birthday when I finally gave in to the pressure.

I saw the bus drive past the house, meaning Jack would be coming through the door momentarily. When I heard it close, I yelled down from my office.

"Hey, sweetie, can you come up here for a moment?"

"What's wrong?" he asked seconds later as he entered the room.

Without saying a word, I pointed to my screen. Jack's eyes grew wide.

"I want *that* dog!" he exclaimed.

I laughed. "Me too! Isn't he adorable?"

My only criterion for having a dog was that it couldn't shed. After educating myself about various breeds, we finally settled on a golden-doodle—half golden retriever, half poodle. I had researched breeders and found one with a litter that would be available toward the end of July. Jack's birthday was in August, so the timing was perfect. All the puppies were spoken for, except for one. She had sent me a photo earlier in the day, and it was love at first sight. There was no question that he would be Jack's.

"What do you want to name him?" Jack didn't have an immediate answer, and we spent the next few days tossing ideas back and forth.

"I know," he said one afternoon. "How about Mark?"

"Mark? Really, Jack? I'm not sure that's the best name for a dog. I can't see myself opening the back door and calling out, 'Here, Mark!' or 'Mark, you sit.'"

Jack laughed. "I guess you're right, but I like it."

Mark was so literal, though that was to be expected coming from Jack. This was going to be his dog, though, so I had to let go of the reins.

The following night, I was making dinner while Jack sat watching TV when he blurted out, "Mom! I've got it!" I turned to see him pointing at his basketball sitting on the floor and there it was, sprawled across the ball in big black script—Wilson. Now there was a name I could get behind, and one perfectly suited for the dog of a sports-obsessed boy.

———

We brought Wilson home on July 23, and the situation did not unfold as I expected. I had envisioned Jack being completely attached to his new best friend and immersed in his care. Beyond the car ride home, though, and our stop at Liam's house to show off his new puppy, Jack had zero interest in Wilson. Despite his insistence that he would feed, walk, and pick up after him, responsibility for the newest addition to our household fell solely in my lap. It was as if Jack had never wanted a dog at all. I was hoping all he needed was time to adjust.

It was just three weeks before we were headed to the Outer Banks for a second time. I was hoping, praying, that having Wilson with us would prevent Jack from a repeat performance of the previous year. Even though he was less than enthused about the dog, I was hopeful that boy's best friend would be enough of a distraction that Jack wouldn't do something as rude and uncalled for as farting aloud at an oceanside restaurant. (Yes, it pains me to type that for a second time.) To some degree, Wilson's presence did the trick. Jack wasn't his usual handful, at least not at first.

"Thomas, what would you like, a burger or a hot dog?" I called down to the boys as they played football in the sand below the deck.

"Burger!"

"Got it! What about you, Jack?"

"Burger. And a hot dog. No, wait, just a hot dog."

I leaned over the railing. "What's it going to be?"

"Actually, I'm not sure," he replied.

I shook my head and decided to make both, just in case. As I stood over the grill watching the burgers and hot dogs sizzle, Jack climbed the steps from below to join me on the deck.

"Do you want to take Wilson for a walk on the beach after we're done eating?" I asked him.

"Yeah, sure," he replied with what appeared to be a high degree of certainty, before adding, "Actually, I'm not sure."

I laughed at his repetitiveness. "A little unsure of yourself today, Jack?"

"No, we can go."

As the week progressed, it seemed Jack was becoming more and more unsure. He was answering almost every question with the same phrase. We found it humorous at first, posing questions in just the right way so we could hear him say it again. It wasn't until later in the week that Thomas informed us that Jack didn't seem right and his repetition of "Actually, I'm not sure" had reached an extreme level. This no longer appeared to be a joke, so I went looking for Jack and found him sitting on the porch swing, rocking back and forth, staring out at the dunes. It worried me immediately. It wasn't like him to steal off on his own. Jack always wanted to be in the middle of everything.

"Jack, are you okay?" As soon as the question left my mouth, I knew what was coming.

"Actually, I'm not sure," he replied before collapsing against me, his tears soaking my thigh.

I wrapped my arms around him tightly. "What's wrong, sweetie?"

"I'm hearing voices. They keep telling me to do bad things."

"What kind of voices?"

"I'm not sure. They say I'm a bad person."

Oh God.

I kept close watch over Jack for the remainder of our vacation, not fully understanding what was happening, but knowing that something was definitely wrong. He vacillated between incessant babble and being distant. In those distant moments, he appeared to be fighting off the voices and breaking down over the battle. The moment we were home, I called Andrew.

"He needs help," I told him, recounting the events of the week. "I hate to say this—I haven't wanted to go this route, but I think we need to try medication. He's got me scared."

"I agree," Andrew said. "I think we should see if we can get an appointment with Jack Lewis as soon as possible."

Jack hadn't been to therapy in at least six weeks. It hadn't been helping, but Jack Lewis seemed the most engaged. In our sessions, he had indicated that what Jack needed was not a psychologist, but a psychiatrist. He needed someone who had a medical degree, was familiar with different medications, understood which ones might work, and could prescribe them—if that's the route we chose to pursue. He couldn't outright say, "Your son should be on medication," but he could tell us how to go about doing it and then place the ball in our court.

I called his office and explained our urgency. Because of a cancellation, we got an appointment that afternoon. He was as understanding and helpful as possible. He could see that Jack was frightened by the voices, though he was unable to reach a solid conclusion as to what it all meant or what was causing Jack to feel the way he was feeling. Nonetheless, by the end of our session, we were all in agreement—including Jack—that medication was worth a try. We scheduled our first appointment with one of the practice psychiatrists.

Immediately, I had concerns about Dr. Sado. Jack struggled with her from the moment we set foot in her office. She was quite pleasant, not aggressive like Charles or dismissive like Rebecca, and she appeared to be as genuine, if not more so, than Jack Lewis. But she was Filipino and had a very heavy accent. The last thing we needed was another communication barrier. She had a patient demeanor, but I feared she would grow tired of us asking her to repeat herself. To Jack, her accent meant that she "talked funny," therefore she was different, and that gave him justifiable reason to throw up a roadblock. It also didn't help that, once again, we were starting from scratch. Our first few meetings consisted of nothing more than rehashing the results of every evaluation and backtracking through the tangled woods of Jack's childhood.

Because Jack's issues were a complex mix of ADHD, high anxiety, obsessive-compulsive behavior, and Asperger syndrome, there was no obvious starting point—it was a shit show that required trial and error. The only way to find the right balance of the right medications would be by process of elimination. Because it was the easiest, Dr. Sado wanted to try tackling the ADHD piece of the puzzle first. Typical treatment is with methamphetamines, which take effect immediately, so we would know right away if it was helping Jack. She wrote a prescription for an immediate-release stimulant and sent us on our way. We would need to check back with her in thirty days.

Jack lasted ten days before I found myself calling Dr. Sado to tell her that the medication was making him feel worse and he had stopped taking it. Because there are numerous options available, she prescribed another, thinking that Jack might have better success with an extended-release medication.

In the meantime, spring break was right in front of us. Wanting to expand his world, I had established a pattern of traveling regularly with Jack over spring break. Each year, we would decide together where we were headed. So far, we had driven to Boston, with stops at both the Baseball and Basketball Halls of Fame. We had made our way to San Diego and Sea World and had hit San Francisco and Chicago. Every trip was perfect. Jack was enamored by seeing new places and having incredible adventures, and together we were creating lifetime memories.

Not exactly.

In retrospect, my perception was more than a bit skewed.

Every trip was difficult in its own way, and Jack's rigidity was by no means left at home. It followed right with us. When we went to Boston, all Jack wanted was a Kevin Garnett jersey, but when we went to the Celtics game, he refused to take his coat off because he was too embarrassed—in an arena packed with Kevin Garnett fans! Our flight to San Diego was marked by uncontrollable sobbing because it was taking too long. In San Francisco, we had dinner at the same restaurant every night, because it worked the first evening and Jack was not open to experimentation. Chicago was cold and windy—making Jack wild and unwieldy. Jack may have been seeing new places, but he lacked the focus needed to appreciate them, and the number of adventures we could have was limited by his tolerance for how long any one activity might take. Still, I kept signing on for more. Some of the best, most memorable moments of my life have been on trips with Jack. I was taking him out of, and well beyond, his comfort zone, and I can't help but wonder if the very process of pushing through that discomfort is what made every detail so memorable.

Our next stop was Vancouver—where Jack was utterly uncomfortable, at best.

I'm not sure he even noticed that we had just landed in a spectacular landscape of mountains and evergreens, but that was okay; it wasn't lost on me. When we arrived, the weather was cold and damp, so we spent the first day and a half meandering through the city, weaving in and out of the shops and visiting a couple of museums. Once it improved, we rented bikes and spent more than one long afternoon circling the harbor. Not wanting to get bogged down by repetition, I made a suggestion.

"I have a great idea, Jack. You like to go snow tubing at home, right? What if we take a trip to Whistler?" I couldn't imagine a better adventure for an eleven-year-old boy than tubing down one of the grand mountains of British Columbia.

"That sounds fun—can we?"

"Of course!"

With help from the hotel concierge, I scheduled a day trip to the popular ski resort. It meant a two-hour van ride with four other people, and Jack was not at all comfortable. He spent the entire drive with his head buried in my lap, not wanting to be seen or to engage with any of these strangers. Of course, to these strangers, an eleven-year-old having his head buried in mommy's lap appeared to be anything but normal. Once we reached Whistler, Jack discovered that their facility was different and not what he was used to. There was no conveyor to carry us to the top of the mountain—we would need to walk, pulling our tubes behind us—and he refused to go. It was too far outside his comfort zone, so I spent three hours tubing solo while Jack sat in the snow at the bottom of the mountain. We then piled back in the van, where his head sank into my lap for another two-hour ride back to the city. All of that was nothing, though, compared to Jack's overwhelming anxiety around the lack of internet service in our hotel room.

"I need to do my draft." His voice cracked as he paced from one side of the room to the other, on the verge of tears.

"Your draft? What are you talking about?"

"I have a draft tonight. It needs to be done by four o'clock, and there's no service in this room. Can we go down to the lobby?"

I was clueless. I had no idea what he meant by "draft" or where this was coming from, and I certainly wasn't aware that he was committed to a four o'clock deadline for anything. But I knew enough to know that a meltdown was imminent. I escorted Jack to the lobby, where I sat him in front of an available computer—only to discover we had yet another problem. Computer use was not free.

"How much time do you need, Jack?"

"I don't know. Twenty minutes?"

I purchased thirty minutes just in case. While the urgency—or meaning—of the draft was not yet clear to me, this upheaval did explain Jack's wanting to visit the Apple store three times the day we arrived, hoping to use one of their laptops. I handed Jack the login information and waited to make sure he was able to access the internet, before I headed across the street to a coffee shop. Jack would be fine working away in the lobby for the next thirty minutes.

Wrong.

When I returned, Jack was sitting in front of a blank screen, crying.

"Sweetie, what happened?"

"My time ran out, and I just lost everything. Can I please do it again?"

While I hated to see him upset and on edge, this was getting ridiculous. Our day had been commandeered by some need of Jack's to "draft," a need about which I had zero understanding.

"Jack, can you explain this draft thing to me?"

Sure, Mom. This is just the beginning of what will become a significant obsession that will completely disrupt our lives and go on for ten, fifteen years, maybe longer. Love you, Mom.

At our next appointment with Dr. Sado, I recounted the events of our trip and voiced my growing skepticism over the efficacy of the ADHD medications—in Jack's case, at least. They did nothing more than agitate him and exacerbate his anxiety. Dr. Sado convinced us to try one last option. When that had no positive effects, either, we decided to abandon the approach for the time being. We were disappointed, but she had warned us in advance that the treatment doesn't work for all children.

Dr. Sado suggested that we try the opposite approach and treat Jack's anxiety with antidepressants, though it would take much longer to see results. None work immediately, and it can take up to six weeks before seeing benefits. In addition, each works differently, so if one is not working and you switch to another, you need a few weeks for the first medication to clear out of your system and another several weeks to ramp up on a new option. We started Jack on his first antidepressant, eager to see any sort of positive result, but it was going to require a great deal of patience, so we returned our focus to getting through each day.

That was easier said than done. It was a continuous ebb and flow. At times, the waves pulled out so far, they disappeared, but those quiet moments never lasted. The further the waves receded, the harder they would return, crashing down on us without warning.

Throughout those days, I felt as though I spent more time talking to Andrew than I did Liam. I almost always sought Liam's guidance, but I had to remember that he wasn't Jack's father—and Jack wasn't the average kid. He needed more. I didn't feel it fair to put that burden on Liam when he had two children of his own, and if Andrew and I knew next to nothing about Asperger's, Liam knew even less.

Andrew and Liam were also at opposite ends of the spectrum in terms of their parenting style. I felt stuck between the two, anxious to please them both, constantly searching for my own middle ground. Andrew coddled Jack. He didn't want him feeling any discomfort, and there was a part of me that appreciated that. I also felt the need to pacify Andrew because he was Jack's father, and I was convinced that, by virtue of that relationship, he should know best.

Liam ruled with a heavy hand. His philosophy was one of, "Buck up, life is hard, and if you don't like it, that's too bad." I wanted to give the appearance that I was a stronger, better parent than I was. As much as I appreciated Andrew's approach, I respected Liam's "tough shit" attitude. Liam got it done. I was always giving in and losing credibility.

Simply put, self-doubt was the culprit behind my being stuck. I had no confidence in my own judgment. I was forever second-guessing myself, and I lacked the muscle to disagree with either of them when I felt differently.

Late one Sunday night, my phone rang. It was Andrew.

He relayed how earlier in the day he and Jack had a family party to attend, and they ended up being late because Jack refused to leave before he had finished his fantasy draft.

"It's becoming a real problem," he complained.

"We need to set some parameters," I said.

"I was wondering, have you been giving him money to keep doing these drafts?"

"No. I gave him ten or fifteen dollars initially, but I haven't given him any since."

"Same here."

There was silence between us.

"What are you thinking?" I asked, unsure of his thoughts.

"He hasn't needed to add any money to his account because he keeps winning." When I didn't reply, Andrew continued. "Don't you see? He's able to analyze the information and put together successful teams based solely on the players' statistics. That's exactly how the Oakland A's built a winning franchise with no money."

I let Andrew's thoughts sink in.

"Do you think it's okay to let him keep doing it?" I asked. "You don't think he could develop a gambling problem, do you?" The question sounded ridiculous. Jack was eleven.

"No, I don't think so. Maybe. . . ." Andrew paused, seeming as uncertain as I was, before cementing his opinion. "No, I don't think that's the case. I don't think he's fixated on the money. He likes the challenge of getting the statistics right, and I think that's okay, especially if he's good at it. But we do need to establish some ground rules. We can't allow it to become a complete disruption to our lives."

"It feels like it already is," I said. "Every time I walk into my office to use my computer, he's sitting in front of it doing another draft, and he wants me to wait until he's done. That's just not practical when I have work to do."

Andrew and I didn't resolve our newest problem with Jack with that one conversation. We didn't even come close, and in record time, Jack's preoccupation with compiling winning sports teams ballooned into full-on addiction.

The only thing that could distract him from it was baseball.

CHAPTER 17
Pivot and Rotate

When I was young, there were two options for playing organized sports: the annual school team, which you might not make, or an intramural team typically run by organizations that had no knowledge of, or experience with, the sports they were offering. Dependent upon parent volunteers, their role was merely to provide an outlet where kids could play. It wouldn't be until Jack reached middle school that there would be a school team, but we quickly learned that intramural teams were no longer the only other option for Jack's generation. There was also the bank-account-draining, pay-to-play travel-team option. As parents of this new generation of rising sports stars, we felt an unspoken pressure to pay for our son to play, or risk having him left behind. Every other parent out there seemed ready to pay, because every other parent out there believed that their kid was the next big thing. We were not there.

Yet.

I had taken Jack to the batting cages one afternoon when I was approached by a staff member. This man standing before me was intimidating, to say the least. He was big—six foot four, easily. Of course, I knew who he was, though I had never formally met him.

I knew from talking to other parents that he had once played major league baseball, and he was now giving lessons and coaching at the facility where Jack spent every free moment.

"I want your son on my team," he said to me. No hello, no introduction, just a simple statement of intent. "Any kid with that kind of work ethic needs to be on my team," he went on. He was referencing Jack's countless hours in the cages. While Andrew and I were fully aware of the excessive amount of time Jack was devoting to improving, we didn't think that anyone else had noticed.

"Okay," I replied coolly. "I'm sure Jack would love to play for you."

Yes, of course Jack would love to play for you. Jack is obsessed. If he doesn't play for you, he'll play for someone else. But of course, Jack will want to play for you because you played in the big leagues!

Suddenly, we were "there."

Welcome to pay-to-play baseball.

"Wow, $2,200 for two months of baseball—plus the cost of travel? Some of these places are three hours away. That's extreme, don't you think?" I threw this at Andrew, thinking I was being cautious. I didn't want to jump right in without weighing the pros and cons.

"Yeah, I know, but I think we should give it a try."

Too late for caution, Andrew had been brainwashed. An ex-MLB player turned travel coach for twelve-year-olds voicing his appreciation for Jack's efforts was all it took. I could tell by the tone of his voice that he was a believer. Jack had become the next big thing in Andrew's eyes, and of course, Jack would never say no to the opportunity to play *more baseball*! I wanted to remind Andrew that those who can't do any longer, teach, but it wasn't worth the energy. I was outnumbered.

Jack's first two practices with his new team were nothing out of the ordinary, though it was obvious that Jack was no longer the standout he had always been with his intramural and district teams. He was going to need to work hard to prove himself if he wanted to win the coach's favor beyond just his work ethic. Based on the coach's style, I wasn't feeling all that confident. In no uncertain terms, the coach was a hard-ass.

Jack's third practice wasn't mandatory. Showing up was like doing the extra credit homework that no one wanted to do. There were only four kids who opted for easy points, Jack of course being one of them.

From my vantage point high above the indoor field, I knew that it wasn't going well. The coach was teaching the concept of "pivot and rotate," a physical motion that, if done properly, will put all your weight behind the ball as you swing your bat and, hopefully, translate to a home run. Jack was clumsy in his attempts, unable to coordinate the motion, and the coach went after him as if Jack was lazy or clowning around. I can assure you, when it came to baseball, Jack was neither lazy (if you'll recall, it was his work ethic that got him on the team in the first place) nor did he clown around. Jack took baseball seriously *all* the time. Even if it was just a scrimmage, he was intent on winning, and he wanted everyone else to take it as seriously.

So far, each practice had ended with the boys running laps around the field. While I waited on Jack to finish, I watched the coach climb the steps from the field, turn the corner—and head straight for me.

Uh-oh.

Once again, there was no hello, just an immediate affront of his thoughts.

"Does your son have some sort of learning disability I should know about?"

I was not expecting—and completely unprepared for—that question. Maybe this brute of a man was smarter than I thought.

I offered the only answer I could, the only answer I understood—the only one I had been willing to accept. "He has OCD. And high anxiety." I mean, duh, the kid was in the batting cages *all* the time. That's obsessive-compulsive disorder, right? And the fact that he got flustered when called out for not being able to pivot and rotate? That was because he's anxious. *Highly* anxious.

Just as there was no hello, there was no thank-you. The coach shook his head in acceptance, turned, and walked away.

Oh God, did I just wreck this for Jack?

Or did I make it better?

There was no clear answer to that question. Jack wasn't removed from the team, so I hadn't wrecked it. Nor did the coach change his approach, so I hadn't made things better, either. Jack had no understanding of the tough-guy mentality. He took every criticism and every disparaging correction personally. I wanted to believe that the coach treated Jack poorly as a means of pushing him, but all it did was cause Jack to feel badly about himself. It wasn't long before he was relegated to the bench. After leaving a game in tears for the second time, Jack asked if he had to keep playing for this man.

Hell no.

Yes, we had spent $2,200 for our son to play on this team, but I was not going to allow anyone to make him feel worthless. I had shared Jack's limitations with this man—maybe not all of them, but those that I understood—and he did nothing to change his style of communication. He did nothing more than cast Jack aside as someone too difficult to bother with. Had I shared everything, would that have made a difference? What if I had been able to say that my son has Asperger syndrome, a disability that precludes him from understanding a heavy-handed manner of instruction? And what if I was aware that this disorder had stripped him of the gross motor skills needed to coordinate the motions of pivot and rotate, no matter how hard he tries? Had I been capable of and willing to say those things, would it have made a difference? Would the coach have made any concessions or offered Jack any accommodations? Or would Jack still have become invisible to him?

Over the next few weeks, as the antidepressant took full effect, Jack's attitude seemed to improve. He was somewhat calmer, a bit more reserved than his usual explosive self, and I couldn't help but wonder if he would have fared better on the travel team had he started taking the medication sooner. What was done was done, though; there was no point in overthinking it. We were finally having some success and grateful for the peace it was bringing to our lives.

Jack had started on the lowest dosage, so the obvious next move would be to increase it to see if he would experience even more success. It meant another three or four weeks of waiting, but it was worth the wait. The increased level brought more positive results, and our fears of how medication might impact Jack were quelled. Jack's improved behavior—by no means perfect, let's not get carried away—was proof that, after fighting the idea for a long time, we had made the right decision. It was okay to have taken this route. Jack wasn't becoming a zombie; instead, he was beginning to resemble an average, bearable twelve-year-old boy.

The process had taken a lot of time, but we had made progress. Dr. Sado was no expert on Asperger syndrome, but she was the only doctor other than Dr. Casey that had any knowledge of it and put effort toward understanding its impact on Jack. She began to decipher what motivated his behavior, and she did her best to provide us with understanding. More importantly, she opened the door to our acceptance. There was no judgment passed, only patience, and within the walls of her office, we were safe.

CHAPTER 18
Turning Point

"I'm spending the week at Liam's house, so I'll only be ten minutes away, okay?" I glanced in my rearview mirror at Jack sitting in the back seat, gazing quietly out the window. "If you need me for any reason, you just call me, okay?" His lack of response told me he was nervous, unsure what to expect, maybe even wishing he hadn't decided to do this.

It was July, and Jack was twelve. Several months prior, I had received a flyer in the mail advertising a week-long basketball camp being run by the Philadelphia 76ers. Jack had become a regular at so many summer sports camps that we were on everyone's mailing list, though the camps he attended were usually day camps. This was the first time he would be away from home for any length of time. He had jumped at the idea when I suggested it—*a whole week of basketball!*—but now I could see him questioning his decision. It was only a week, but for Jack, that was an eternity.

The camp was being held at a nearby military academy, empty for summer vacation. It wasn't far from Liam's, so I had decided to stay there, knowing there was no guarantee that Jack would make it through the week—or even the first day. This was a huge step for him, being away from home for a week, sharing a room in a strange place with a total stranger, eating meals from someone else's menu in a dining hall, and I was so proud of him.

I had gotten us there early so there would be plenty of time to register, get Jack settled in his room, and help him find his way around campus. It also enabled me to gauge his comfort level. It took about three minutes for me to determine that Jack was not comfortable. It was July, eighty-five degrees, with high humidity, and Jack's room was not air-conditioned.

"How am I supposed to sleep?" he asked in a slight panic.

"You'll be fine, sweetie. It'll cool down." The look on his face told me nothing was fine. I wanted more than anything for him to be successful in this courageous venture, so I had to think quickly. When we arrived, I had seen a couple of kids in the parking lot carrying window fans. Clearly, they were camp veterans that knew from experience that the rooms were not air-conditioned.

"Tell you what," I said, "after we get you settled and you know your way around, I'll go buy a fan and bring it back. Would that work?"

Jack perked up. "Okay, thanks, Mom. This is going to be fun."

"Of course it's going to be fun," I agreed with a smile. "It's going to be a great experience for you, and I'm so proud of you for doing it." And that was that. Heat-sensitivity issues handled.

After unpacking Jack's clothes and setting up his bed, we headed over to the gym, where there was open play for all the kids. Jack was immediately overwhelmed, but with a little encouragement he was coerced into picking up a free ball and joining a nearby group of boys about his age. I assured him I would be back shortly and set off to procure a fan. When I returned thirty minutes later, I found Jack sitting on the steps leading into the gym. He looked so sad, and instantly my heart was broken.

"What's wrong, sweetie? Why aren't you inside playing?"

"There's no one to play with."

I peered inside the gym where there were easily two hundred kids, and I looked back at Jack in astonishment. "What do you mean, there's no one to play with? There's a ton of kids in there."

Jack didn't respond, and his eyes started filling with tears, which he quickly wiped away. "Can you just go, Mom?"

"But, sweetheart. . . ."

"Please, can you just go? I'll be fine."

What do I do here?

It hurt to my core to see him struggling, to know that this entire experience would be so difficult, to know that he had no clue how to jump in and approach the other kids, all of them unfamiliar to him. It appeared that many of them already knew one another. And Jack was all alone. I couldn't bear to leave him, but I had no choice. He needed to have this experience, and he was telling me that he wanted this experience. Removing him would be the worst thing I could do. It would send a message that it was okay to run away from every hurdle, and it would tell him that I have no faith in him. I couldn't possibly let him down.

"Come here and give me a hug." As I wrapped my arms around Jack, I had to fight back my own tears. "I'm only ten minutes away, okay?" I reiterated, forcing him to look at me. "If you need me, you call me, and I will be here in an instant."

"Okay," he said pulling himself away. "Love you, Mom."

"Love you too, bud," I reassured him as he wandered back into the crowded gym. I turned away and let the tears fall as I headed back to the car.

"How'd it go?" Liam asked as I flopped down on his couch and let out a heavy sigh.

"I felt so bad for him," I said, recounting the whole story of our arrival and Jack's obvious pain at being left to fend for himself.

"He'll be fine," Liam said. "It'll be a good experience for him."

I agreed, though I knew it was likely the experience would be short. I couldn't see Jack lasting through the night.

When I woke the next morning and realized that Jack hadn't called, I breathed a small sigh of relief. I set about my day, keeping my phone close, expecting a call at any minute, but it never came. As Monday turned to Tuesday with no word from Jack, I began to relax, believing that he had settled into the fun of nonstop basketball and would be okay. Wednesday's arrival, still free of that dreaded call, had me confident that Jack was going to make it through the week.

Not so fast.

It was eight o'clock Wednesday evening when my cell finally rang.

"Can you come get me?" Jack asked.

"Why don't you want to stay?"

"I just don't want to be here anymore. I feel uncomfortable."

"Aren't you having fun?"

"I'm having fun. I just want to come home. I can't stay here anymore."

I had given him my word. If he called, I would be there.

"Okay, sweetie. I'll be there shortly." I hung up the phone and turned to Liam. "I knew he wouldn't make it."

Before Liam could respond, my phone rang again. It was a number I didn't recognize. A man introduced himself as the camp director and said he thought it was a bad idea for me to come get Jack. "I've been doing this a long time, and I've seen a lot of kids that shouldn't be here. On a scale of one to ten, Jack is a two."

"You don't understand," I replied. "Jack has Asperger syndrome, and if he's feeling uncomfortable, I don't want to force him to stay."

Full stop.

Did I just willingly state that fact—out loud, with some degree of confidence—to someone other than a therapist?

The director pushed back. He was almost begging me not to bring Jack home. I quickly got the sense that he was more worried about the camp's reputation than he was about Jack. The kid who leaves early because he's feeling uncomfortable might be apt to give the camp a bad review.

"I'm not placing any blame on you," I assured him. "I just know my son, and I'm not going to force him to stay if he doesn't want to stay." Despite the director's persistence, I held my ground, hung up, and grabbed my keys. "I'll be back," I told Liam and headed out the door, feeling empowered by my unexpected admission.

When I arrived at the camp somewhere around eight thirty, I was met with mayhem. The day's scheduled activities were over, but it wasn't yet time for lights out, and kids were running everywhere. Despite the commotion, I managed to locate the dorm supervisor and introduce myself, waiting while she went to find Jack. After a few minutes, Jack appeared carrying his pillow and suitcase—followed by several kids.

"Come on, Jack, you can't leave."

"Yeah, Jack, you have to stay!" another boy said.

The entire group was coercing Jack to stay, but he seemed oblivious. He high-fived a couple of them before turning to me, saying, "Hi, Mom, are you ready to go?"

Confused, I confronted Jack as soon as we left the building.

"Sweetheart, are you sure you don't want to stay? It seems like those kids really want you to stick around. What's going on?"

"Yeah, they're my friends," he replied matter-of-factly. "We had a lot of fun."

"Then why are you leaving? Did something bad happen?"

"No, I just can't stay."

I looked at him with uncertainty.

"I did my best," he went on. "Are you mad?"

"No, sweetie, I'm not mad. I just don't understand." And I let it drop.

None of what Jack was saying made any sense, but I could see that nothing was going to convince him to stay. We started home, and over the course of the next ten to twelve minutes, I heard every last detail of Jack's three and a half days at camp. For that short time, he'd had fun. I should be happy about that, but I continued turning it over in my mind. What had gone wrong? Maybe he truly did feel uncomfortable but couldn't verbalize why. Jack was a fish out of water in almost every circumstance, demonstrating repeatedly that he has no understanding of the nuances of genuine friendship. Aside from Thomas, Jack had no true friends, and I was even skeptical of the legitimacy of that relationship. It was a relationship of convenience, given that Liam and I were always together with the kids. More so, it was one of obligation. Thomas was consistently empathetic, never wanting anyone to feel bad or left out. The only interaction Jack seemed capable of understanding was within the context of organized sports, and that was likely the reason for his few days of success.

When I woke the following morning, the events of the previous night came rushing back. I was in my own bed, rather than Liam's, and Jack was asleep in the next room, not in a dorm room at camp.

Had I made a mistake letting him come home?

If I consistently catered to his discomfort and never forced him beyond his comfort zone, he'd never grow. But maybe him making it through three and a half days truly was the best that he could do. And for the first time, I had been able to state what's true—my son has a disability. He has Asperger syndrome, and I'm not going to keep running and hiding from it. I would allow Jack—and myself—a success.

I didn't have a tremendous amount on my plate for the day. I could easily take care of what few tasks were on my list while Jack was still sleeping, and that would free me up to do something with him later. I climbed out of bed to start some coffee.

Later that day, we took Wilson for a walk down to the old paper mill. It was one of our favorite spots, with plenty of tree-covered paths and a hidden creek where we could skip rocks while Wilson went for a swim. We spent most of the walk reliving the details of Jack's few days at camp. As we wound our way lazily toward home, Jack spotted something in the dirt.

"Look, Mom," he said, pointing down at the dusty path. Brushing the dirt aside, he picked up what appeared to be an award ribbon and flipped it over. I couldn't believe my eyes. Printed in gold ink on the front side of the ribbon were the words I DID MY BEST.

Smiling at Jack, I said, "That's a message from your big sister. She's up there looking down on you and letting you know that you're on the right path." He beamed, and all my second-guessing faded away. I truly believed in the power of the universe and positivity. Even though Jack hadn't made it through the full week, he had done his best, and I had taken a major step forward right alongside him.

CHAPTER 19
The Next Chapter

Moving out of my house after ten years was bittersweet. Liam and I had just celebrated five years of being together. We agreed it was time to buy one house for the five of us. On one hand, I was embarking on a new phase, the next stage of my journey—life with Liam and the three kids, together as a family. On the other, this house that I had bought after separating from Andrew stood for so much in my life. It was a symbol of my independence, proof that I could manage on my own. It was a safe harbor for Jack's disability, the only place where his behavior was protected from scrutiny, and for my shortcomings as a mother. Hidden within its walls, I could let down my guard and not worry about the innumerable mistakes I knew I was making.

As I went room to room the evening before settlement to double-check that nothing had been left behind, tears welled up. I took in every bare wall, with patched reminders of photos that once hung but were now safely packed away and on their way to our new house. I marveled at the stark contrast between pristine patches of carpet, where furniture had once stood, and the rest of the room, discolored from the impact of ten years' worth of living. What once had held everything for me now looked so empty and would soon be filled with someone else's life. I let my mind replay countless memories—Jack growing from toddler to teenager and me picking myself up from a failed marriage. I realized that, yet again, Mom was right. Life has a way of working itself out. I set my house keys on the kitchen island, turned out the last light, and pulled the front door closed. As the realtor's lockbox clicked into place, I said goodbye to one chapter and hello to the next.

Despite my excitement, I knew there would be challenges in the months ahead. I had withdrawn Jack from middle school, uprooting him in December of his seventh-grade year at age thirteen, and dropped him into a completely foreign landscape. This could potentially be a disaster. But Jack had only developed one friendship in his old school, so there wasn't much to leave behind. And the prospect of playing for a different little league while still playing for his existing league was like winning the lottery. The amount of accessible baseball had doubled overnight.

We were also headed into the spring semester of Jack's seventh grade year, which meant that his first opportunity to play school baseball was just two months away, and he couldn't possibly be more excited. It didn't hurt, either, that it snowed continuously for the first three weeks of the spring semester and school was cancelled almost every day. Transitioning isn't hard when it means playing video games with Thomas in the basement, or better, having all day to draft players for your fantasy sports teams. I'm certain all those distractions were instrumental in smoothing the road, though nothing was ever total smooth sailing with Jack. Once the weather settled down and school resumed, the truth about how well Jack was settling in became evident.

Between no school for most of January and moving to a different school where everything was unfamiliar, Jack's grades plummeted. Wanting to stay on top of it, I called Jack's counselor and asked to meet. She assured both Andrew and me that what Jack was experiencing was perfectly normal. She had seen it countless times before with kids that transition in the middle of the school year, and with the added variable of bad weather, Jack was doing better than expected. With reassurance that the academic piece would figure itself out, I turned my attention to Jack's social life.

"Yeah, Mom, we're really close."

"Really close? Jack, you just met this kid."

Jack ignored me and headed back out into the yard where he and one of the boys from his class were tossing a football. Collin would not be the only classmate with whom Jack would become "really close." There were several of them, and with each, the relationship lasted two, maybe three weeks. Jack's perception of friendship, his idea of being really close, was anyone that would spend time with him, regardless of how long. When Collin, Patrick, and Will dropped off, Jack moved on to Danny, Alec, and T. J. It was a repeat of his elementary school years.

Jack seemed unfazed by this inability to establish lasting friendships. He still had the one friend in our old neighborhood, and in his mind that was enough. With schoolwork starting to turn around, Thomas at home to spend time with, and Nick in the old neighborhood, Jack sank into a rhythm that appeared to work. I let my concern fade, hopeful that everything would fall into place. Of course, when a call came from the school nurse one afternoon in February, that hope was dashed.

When I arrived at school, I was horrified to find that Jack's tongue was mangled and bleeding. Unable to tell me himself what had happened, the school nurse stepped in with the details. During an assembly, another student had turned around, without warning or good reason it appeared, and elbowed Jack in the mouth. This caused him to bite right through his tongue, leaving it in two pieces and in obvious need of stitches.

"Are you kidding me?" Andrew's anger rose when I told him what had happened. "Why would someone do that?"

"I don't know," I replied. "Jack insists he didn't do or say anything to make this kid angry, and Thomas backed him up on that. But you know how Jack is—his perception of circumstances isn't always accurate."

"So you don't believe him? Why would he lie? We can't let this kid get away with this! It's assault! I'm calling the principal."

Before I could voice my opinion, Andrew had hung up. This was about to be blown out of proportion, and the last thing I wanted to do was create waves for Jack, putting him in a situation at school where he was suddenly the tattletale. Teenage boys were vicious, and who knew what this kid might be capable of? But Jack was Andrew's egg—his grade school project in which the only requirement is to carry your egg everywhere for a week and not let it crack—and Andrew was determined to get an A-plus. When he called later that evening and told me what had transpired, I was in disbelief.

"You *what*?"

"I filed a police report," Andrew stated as if it was the obvious thing to do.

"You've got to be kidding me. Do you have any idea what you've just done to your son? You've just given that kid permission to beat him up!"

"No jerk of a kid is going to touch my son and get away with it!" he countered.

I hung up. It was all I could do to keep from hitting the ceiling.

While I appreciated Andrew's undying commitment to protect his son, I felt he had overstepped his bounds and likely made the situation worse. Jack's inability to communicate and understand how others communicate had become more obvious as he moved into middle school, where kids were older and social interaction was more defined. He was now at an age where bad things could happen on a much greater scale. He clearly did not understand the subtleties—or even the overt hurtful acts—of social interaction. He was doing his best to fit in, but his lack of understanding and awkward nature resulted in him being left out and, worse, bullied. I wanted to intervene and notify all kids in advance of what to expect when interacting with Jack. *Warning: He doesn't understand you and how to relate to you. He wants to control everything. He will be repetitive and annoyingly overbearing. Please don't discount him because he's different, and please don't treat him poorly, because, even if you do, he'll still think you're one of his best friends.*

But how do you do that without turning your child into an outcast? What does a conversation like that even look like, and what middle school boy is going to understand it, process it, or act on it properly? All I could do was compartmentalize the event and try my best not to worry. Baseball tryouts were a few weeks away, and I directed every ounce of positive energy toward Jack making the team. Again, he would be the newcomer, but he had proven himself once before, and I had faith he could do it again. If he made the team, hopefully he would build some meaningful friendships. Within that context, he would fit in. He would have to—because baseball was the only language Jack understood.

Jack was waiting at the front entrance of the school when I arrived, laughing with some of the other boys who had shown up for the first day of tryouts. When he saw me pull in, he gathered his gear, rushed to the car, piled it onto the back seat, and jumped in beside me. He didn't waste any time on pleasantries.

"I made the team!" he exclaimed.

"Made the team? But it's only Monday. Tryouts aren't over until Friday." I was confused. "What makes you think you made the team?"

"The coach said he's never seen anyone work as hard as I do and he wants me on the team."

Jack was beaming. Once again, his work ethic had benefitted him, and I was so proud, but I suddenly worried we might have a repeat scenario on our hands. Would the school coach be more reasonable than Jack's travel coach? That consideration led me to the uncomfortable question I wasn't ready to face—do we tell the coach that Jack has Asperger syndrome? I had found the courage to be forthcoming with the director of the basketball camp, but that was different. That situation was a one-time, short-lived event, and by the time I spoke up it was already over. When beginning a new season with a new coach, new teammates, and within the completely different context of a school team, sharing that information could be the kiss of death for Jack. But the coach should already know, right? After all, it's clearly stated in Jack's IEP.

Yes, he should know. We shouldn't need to say anything.

Jack was playing on three teams simultaneously, his talent readily apparent. As the season progressed, he appeared to get along well with his teammates during practices and games, but it always ended there. None of it was translating to friendships beyond the field the way I had envisioned. When baseball wasn't there to fill the gaps, I once again became the default playmate, ending my workdays at three o'clock with the arrival of the school bus. Jack was thirteen, yet I was out in the yard playing catch or pitching balls to him as if he were still nine years old. Despite my best efforts to keep him enter-tained, I needed to balance my time between him and my workday, and I unfairly counted on Thomas to back me up.

When we bought the house, Jack had changed schools and started from scratch with trying to make friends—obviously not his forte. Liam's kids were able to remain in their schools and maintain their established groups of friends. Naturally, Jack wanted to be included in everything Thomas was doing, and I wanted the same. But Thomas's friends didn't want Jack tagging along everywhere they went, and Thomas was tiring of the balancing act. In truth, Thomas was tiring of Jack. People need their space, and this is not something Jack understands.

I knew that blending two families wouldn't be seamless. I knew there would be hurdles along the way, but I naively assumed that even-tual success was a given. Life under one roof was becoming tough. Spending time with Liam's kids daily, I was beginning to understand how deeply Jack's behavior affected me. It killed me to watch Katie and Thomas go about their days "normally." They had friends, they were maturing, they weren't impossible. They each had their strug-gles and could be difficult, like any kid, but they both appeared to be on the right track toward becoming independent people living regular, successful lives.

Liam's kids weren't filling the house with meaningless noise.

Liam's kids weren't delaying dinner because they weren't finished assembling their fantasy teams for every game being played that night.

Liam's kids weren't monopolizing the television because they needed to watch all the day's sports highlights to ensure that the fan-tasy team they had already assembled, the same one for which dinner was delayed, was in fact a winning team.

Liam's kids weren't at all like Jack. He was a source of tension, and he wasn't exactly anyone's favorite person. I felt responsible for that tension—it was my fault for not having more control over him. I should have taught him better and worked harder to understand him. I should have better educated myself and become his primary advocate. I should have been stronger.

I could have, would have—should have.

If Angela were alive, she would be a tremendous source of tension because of her immense needs, but people wouldn't look poorly on us, as if we had failed. On the contrary, they would take pity on us and treat us kindly, because her disability would be apparent. They would see it. Jack's disability isn't so readily apparent—even to those who have been around him for years. What you see on the surface indicates that interaction with him should match up to what's generally expected, but interaction with Jack almost always guarantees friction.

Not a day went by that I didn't feel badly about myself. I would forever be apologizing and making excuses for his behavior. I would never be relieved of the responsibility of fixing the problems he caused, and I would always be asking, "What if?" What if Jack wasn't saddled with this disability? How would my life be different?

These thoughts were magnified by never having felt like a natural mother in the first place, and failing to grasp that feeling resulted in immense guilt. Why wasn't I more like my mother, or every other woman out there who steps up to the job with the grace and ease of a seasoned pro? Instead of accepting Jack's limitations and developing strategies, I was continuously trailing behind him, sweeping up his destruction and resenting every whisk of the broom. In turn, as much as I wanted to be a second mother to Liam's kids, Jack's struggles made that impossible. Watching them succeed was painful.

Selfishly, I felt a bit of satisfaction any time they stumbled—which made me feel even worse.

There was something different about Jack that I couldn't change, no matter what I did or how hard I tried. I couldn't allow it to define me, yet I couldn't escape my feelings of inadequacy as a mother—the responsible party.

Of all people, I should know how to fix him.

CHAPTER 20
Cat's Out of the Bag

"Will he still be meowing when he's thirty?"

Dr. Sado's mouth was agape while directing a blank stare at Andrew, but Jack and I fell apart laughing. It sounded so ridiculous.

"I mean, seriously," Andrew continued, adding a slight chuckle of his own, "he never stops making noise. He walks around the house meowing like a cat all day."

Looking from one to the other, searching our faces for an explanation, it was obvious that Dr. Sado had no understanding of what Andrew was saying, so I stepped in.

"Jack doesn't actually walk around *meowing*," I began with another laugh. "He babbles—constantly—and generally the babble makes no sense."

"Tell me more," Dr. Sado replied with a soft smile, as if a bit of understanding was settling in.

"I don't know. . . ." On the spot, I suddenly realized I had no idea how to define or explain Jack's "meowing." I looked at Jack for a little help, but he was useless. As far as he was concerned, his babble was a perfectly normal part of every day. As I searched for words, it suddenly hit me. "Better than telling you, I can show you," I said and pulled out my phone.

While playing catch with Jack the week before, an endless string of seemingly disconnected thoughts erupted from his mouth. It was so unusual, so comical, that, using the voice dictation feature on my phone, I had made notes of everything while we played. I quickly opened my notes app and handed the phone to Dr. Sado so she could see it in black-and-white.

"It's all 100 percent true. I didn't make up a single word of that," I said, not sure Dr. Sado was believing the authenticity of Jack's unusual soliloquy.

"I'm not sure what impresses me more, Jack's very colorful expression . . . or the fact that you were able to capture all of it," she replied, handing the phone back to me. "Based on everything you've shared with me, and certainly after reading that, it's clear to me that Jack's *meowing*, as you say, is a vocal tic."

"A vocal tic? Are you saying Jack has Tourette's?" Andrew's tone hinted at skepticism.

"Yes, that's exactly what I'm saying. It's very common in people with Asperger syndrome. So, to answer your original question, yes, Jack will likely still be meowing when he's thirty."

While that appointment had some degree of levity, none of it felt all that funny. Every time we drilled down deeper toward Jack's core, we hit another layer of complexity. I walked away wondering how much more would be heaped upon our son.

Once we were home, needing confirmation that Dr. Sado was right or maybe just wanting to feel useful, I found that book written by Tony Attwood I had once insisted I was going to read from cover to cover. I needed to dig my head out of the sand. I flipped to the index, found the words "Tourette's syndrome," and there it was on page 108: "There's increasing evidence that some people with autism and Asperger syndrome develop signs of Tourette's syndrome." The book went on to describe how vocal signs of Tourette's include "uttering uncontrollable and unpredictable sounds such as repeated throat clearing, grunting, snorting, or animal noises. . . ."

Meowing like a cat, maybe?

I read on to find that vocal manifestations also included repetition of one's own words, labeled as "palilalia," or repetition of someone else's words, "echolalia." That certainly would explain the perpetual jibber jabber. It also begged a question—was Jack's repetition of those three little words, "Love you, Mom," an example of echolalia? I can remember as a child my mother constantly showering me with "I love you," and I had undoubtedly carried on that practice with Jack, as if saying it over and over would wrap him in an impenetrable cocoon. I knew that Jack's routine use of it was habitual to some degree, but now it appeared as though no part of it was within his control. He was at the mercy of another frustrating aspect of this syndrome.

I let out a deep, exasperated breath, wondering what other valuable information this book contained, this book that I had bought years ago and ignored. I flipped the pages and stopped at a chapter referencing motor clumsiness, which revealed that some children with Asperger syndrome don't start walking until months later than most. Well, there's your explanation for why Jack didn't start crawling until he was ten and a half months old—or had trouble learning to ride a bike and coordinate so many other physical motions.

Other potential problems included "difficulty in learning to tie shoelaces and an odd gait when walking or running." No wonder Jack's arms flailed about on the basketball court and he looked like a rag doll when running bases. And tying his shoelaces? It was painful to watch the formation of first one big ear, then another, then somehow marrying the two together in the middle with a twist of the lace that barely resembled a knot but somehow managed to keep the laces in place.

I closed the book and returned it to its pile. It was better off there. If I were to hold onto it much longer, I might be inclined to burn it. Why had it taken me so long to open my mind to learning about Asperger syndrome and how it drove Jack's behavior?

After further discussion surrounding his meowing, Dr. Sado proposed that Jack try another medication in addition to his antidepressant. The drug, Guanfacine, is typically used to treat high blood pressure, but it has also been found to be effective in treating ADHD. It's unclear as to how it works in that instance, but unlike other drugs used to treat ADHD, it's not a stimulant, so Jack would tolerate it well. She was suggesting it because among its many benefits was impulse control, making it effective in people with Tourette's. We decided it was worth a shot.

CHAPTER 21
Strange New World

As a toddler, Jack had been tough. As a young boy, he had graduated to complete pain in the ass. Still, he was young enough that you could write it off as him being one of "those" kids, a lot to handle. At least through middle school, guardrails were still on the alley. With Andrew, Jack's teachers and coaches, and me, there was enough adult supervision and intervention to keep Jack on a straight path. Patiently camped out in the back of my mind was a naive notion that eventually he would grow out of this maelstrom. His strange behaviors would evaporate, and until then I would continue making excuses. I had become masterful at predicting bad situations and defusing every bomb before inevitable detonation. I would immediately remove Jack from any equation if the results weren't adding up as they should. But the older Jack got, the more firmly rooted he was in his unique grade of soil. He wasn't growing out of anything. Jack rolled right into high school with all the same patterns.

As weary as I was of explaining away his behavior, I would gladly continue doing it to avoid the alternative. Sending Jack off to high school—alone—felt like feeding him to the wolves. In high school, he would have no protection from the strange looks and annoyed reactions. No one would be there to make excuses and coerce the general population into accepting him. Jack's Asperger syndrome no longer translated to simple disruption. It now defined him in the worst possible way for this temperamental age group. When fitting in is the primary objective, being different is a death blow, and "different" was the only way to define Jack. Still, I was hopeful. A larger pool of kids would surely offer more opportunities for connection.

"My friend from school asked me if I want to hang out tonight. He invited me to go out to dinner with his family. Is that okay?" Jack said one Friday afternoon shortly after the start of his freshman year.

"Friend, what friend?" I asked, hoping my surprise wasn't evident.

"Kevin. He said it's okay with his parents."

As Jack provided more details, I quickly thought it over. I had no idea who Kevin was, but there must be something wrong with him if he wants to hang out with Jack, and if there isn't, it's just a matter of time before he changes his mind. *Oh God, do I really have that little faith in my son? What happened to my hopeful outlook?* Not wanting to squash his excitement, I gave Jack permission to go. How bad could it be?

"Where are you having dinner?" I asked.

"Sushi Ginza."

"Are you aware that Sushi Ginza is a Japanese restaurant? You can't get a burger and wings, or spaghetti and meatballs, at a Japanese restaurant."

"That's okay," Jack replied without flinching.

"What will you eat?" I grabbed my laptop, pulled up the restaurant's menu, and searched it for a suitable replacement for Jack's standard fare. "Get the chicken teriyaki," I instructed and sent him on his way.

———

Much to my delight, Jack's evening with his new friend was a success, so much so that he was invited to spend the night. Grateful though I was, I was skeptical. The only thing that had ever been of permanence in Jack's world was baseball. But when I arrived to collect him the following day, I was met with the news that Kevin had invited him to come back once Jack was done with his game that afternoon. I couldn't have been more wrong in my initial assessment of this burgeoning friendship, and I couldn't have been happier.

Had Jack actually managed to establish a real friendship, someone with whom he could develop a bond, with whom he could experience all the ins and outs, ups and downs of his high school years? Someone with whom his connection would grow so deep that their relationship would continue throughout college and for all the years to come, taking fishing trips together, being in each other's wedding parties and godfather to one another's kids? *Is this really happening?* I wondered.

Okay, I was getting carried away, but a mother can hope, can't she?

Remarkably, my hope wasn't completely misplaced. What began with one dinner out and one overnight quickly developed into a string of weekend gatherings and sleepovers. Jack was soon spending every weekend at Kevin's. I offered numerous times to reciprocate, but Kevin's house was always the center of activity. After seeing it for the first time, I could understand why. It clearly had far more to offer than our modest split-level. With more boys added to the mix, week after week, I was happy to allow Kevin's parents to manage the festivities. Kevin and Jack were soon joined by Logan and Connor, twin brothers from school; Anthony, one of Jack's intramural teammates; and eventually Thomas. I had no interest in hosting half a dozen fourteen-year-old boys, weekend after weekend—a generous gift card for Kevin's parents would express our gratitude nicely.

After several successful months, it seemed as though Jack had settled into an unexpected social groove, forming a solid pack with Kevin, Thomas, and the others. I truly couldn't believe it. I sincerely hoped it would last.

I regretfully accepted that it wouldn't.

"Where's he going?" I asked Liam one evening as Thomas strolled out the door, jacket in hand.

"Kevin's house, I think." Liam never paid much attention to the boys' whereabouts. As long as they weren't at home, he was fine with wherever they were.

"Do they need a ride? I'll give them a ride," I offered, naturally assuming that Jack was joining him.

"I think Thomas took his bike."

Hmm, that's strange.

I climbed the steps to Jack's room where I found him lying in bed, engrossed in his phone, fingers moving at warp speed.

"Hey, bud, what are you doing?" I don't know why I asked the question. I already knew the answer, and I knew that Jack would take it at face value. What I wanted to know was *why* he was doing what he was doing—and not with Thomas on his way to Kevin's house.

"Doing a draft."

When will I learn?

"Thomas went over to Kevin's house. Why didn't you go with him?"

"I don't know. I don't feel like it." Jack's tone was matter-of-fact, but it was laced with something else that I couldn't quite place. It wasn't sadness—confusion perhaps, maybe apathy.

"Since when? You've been over there practically every weekend for the last six months? Did something happen with Kevin?"

"No, I just don't want to go. Is that okay?"

"Of course it's okay." Not wanting Jack to sense my concern, I let it go and left him to the complexities of assembling his team.

While Thomas continued to spend time with the group on a regular basis, Jack receded into the shadows. Clearly something had changed, though I wasn't sure what. I envisioned the boys sitting around Kevin's basement, behaving like teenage boys, maybe sneaking beers from the refrigerator—and all the while Jack having his face buried in his phone, assembling his fantasy lineup.

If my assumption of what happened was correct, that the group had decided Jack was "weird," Jack didn't have the awareness to pick up on their change of attitude. As far as he was concerned, they were all still "good friends."

What began on a positive note, with a single invitation, trailed off and faded away to nothing. It had been months, not days or even a couple of weeks—months—that Jack had been spending time with Kevin and the others. I thought for sure that he had finally found a place for himself socially. Maybe some of his behaviors had been tempered over time, but he wasn't any better able to relate to his peers now than when he was seven.

There had to be more to it, something I was missing. Thinking back to my own high school years, I saw everyone around me as being socially awkward. I certainly felt that way myself. It's a time of great transformation, and most kids don't yet know who they are.

But they know enough to pretend.

For the average kid, high school years are all about appearances, doing whatever it takes to make it *look* as though you belong. Jack couldn't talk the talk, or walk the walk. He was incapable of pretense. He put nothing more and nothing less out there than his whole, honest, unfiltered, unapologetic self, for better or worse. Neither his decrease in social activity nor his increase in isolation seemed to bother him, though. He simply fell back on those things he knew best—baseball and fantasy drafts.

In middle school, the same boys that played together in seventh grade had naturally evolved into the eighth-grade team. High school, however, meant the merging of two middle schools, significantly upping the stakes. Making the freshman team was key if Jack expected to play on the varsity team. And with his sights set on playing in college and then, of course, the major leagues—he was the next big thing, after all—making the varsity team was a must.

"Do you think we'll be done by 3:05?"

I looked at my watch. It was 1:37 p.m., which meant we were a bit early for Jack's 2:00 p.m. appointment. His mentioning of such a precise time exposed the source of his concern.

"Yes, sweetheart. I think we'll be done by 3:05," I replied, with just enough tone to inform him he was being silly.

"I need to have my draft done by 3:05."

Of course you do.

I assured Jack it would be fine as we entered the doctor's office, signed in with the receptionist, and took a seat.

Two o'clock came and went, and by two thirty, Jack still had not been seen. He had spent the time zooming back and forth between player bios and recent game performance, assembling his team, disassembling it, reassembling it. Each flick of the screen prompted another shift in position, each shift becoming more emphatic, his discomfort obvious and growing.

"Oh my God!" he finally blurted at top volume. "What's taking so long?"

"Jack, keep your voice down. I'm sure it won't be much longer."

"I can't sit here anymore. This doctor is a moron."

All eyes in the waiting room were on us.

"Jack, sit down," I insisted, tugging at his shirt to pull him back into his seat. "If you want to play freshman ball, you need to have this physical."

"Can't we come back? I need to get my draft done."

"No, we can't come back. You have an appointment, and we're not leaving until the doctor sees you and fills out this paperwork. Why don't you just finish the draft now?"

"I can't. The internet in here sucks!"

"Let it go, then," I snapped back, furious with him for his petulant behavior.

It was 2:50 p.m. when Jack was finally called into the exam room. He had spent those remaining twenty minutes doing something on his phone, which told me there wasn't a thing wrong with the internet. With signed sports forms in hand, we finally left the doctor's office at 3:25 p.m. I said nothing to Jack as we crossed the parking lot to the car. His mood had visibly improved, and I knew that he had finished his draft. Having witnessed his behavior just moments prior, I wondered how it was that he had even made the team—this rigid brat of a person. How long would it be before they figured him out? How long would it be before he pulled a similar stunt during practice, or worse, during a game, and the coach was prompted to confront the parents? Was it possible to buy my way out of being one of said parents? I knew I was putting the cart before the horse, but I also knew Jack all too well.

Jack's need to draft fantasy sports teams had become acute. He was drafting teams at a rate of speed that even the best of obsessives couldn't match—and with a success rate high enough that the money earned could feed the obsession indefinitely. Night in and night out, with a thin thread of blue light below his bedroom door, we engaged in the same repeated exchange.

"Jack, turn your phone off. It's time for bed."

"I'm almost done. I'm just checking my lineup."

I worried about the negative effects of his obsession. The speed with which he flicked back and forth between screens must have been bad for his eyes, not to mention his attention span. Watching him for more than a few seconds was enough to make me carsick, but getting him to stop was a futile effort. I wondered if there could possibly be an upside. Seeing him move so deftly—assessing each player's statistics, calculating their cost, balancing that with the unexpected variables of injury rate and unforeseen management decisions, and instantaneously deciding which players were worth the expense and which were not—it was more than just impressive, it was mind-boggling.

But was it okay?

We had never mentioned Jack's Asperger syndrome to his middle school coaches. Now that Jack had made the high school freshman team, I was once again questioning the wisdom of that decision. My thinking was that the school knows, and the school as a whole includes the coaches; therefore, they too must know. Andrew thought that Jack was good enough that it shouldn't matter. To hell with the school and their coaches. If they can't see that our son is the next big thing, well, then. . . .

The season started off well enough, with all the boys receiving equal playing time so the coach could assess their skill levels and how they fit together as a team. Jack possessed the necessary skills, no doubt. But baseball is a team sport, and at this higher level, another aspect of the sport was coming into play and becoming equally as important.

Camaraderie.

When it came to being one of the "baseball brothers," as Jack dubbed them, he fell short. I think he had awareness that something was changing, but he didn't understand it. At the grade school level, there's little analysis of who fits and who doesn't. Common interest is enough to welcome someone into the group. Baseball was the common interest, and Jack was good at it; therefore, he was well received. It had always been his way of fitting in, and he couldn't grasp that it was changing, let alone why.

"It's all politics," Andrew insisted, as we sat watching yet another game where Jack was spending more time on the bench.

"What are you talking about?"

"Can't you see that Jack is better than all these kids?"

I had no reply, only a need to understand why Andrew thought Jack should receive some sort of preferential treatment. It was the coach's decision whether or not to play him, and maybe the coach thought differently. But Andrew insisted that Jack was being singled out because he didn't fit the mold.

Maybe Andrew was right. Maybe the coach was questioning what's wrong—or at least, not quite right—with Jack. He certainly didn't look the part of a "baseball brother." He refused to wear a belt, which meant his jersey was always hanging halfway out of his pants. He routinely wore plaid boxer shorts, which were readily visible, under his white baseball pants instead of slider shorts and a cup like everyone else. At least it wasn't two or three pairs of boxers.

Jack's baseball amnesia had also reared its ugly, uncoordinated head more than once since the start of the season. When he should have been smashing easy pitches into outer space, he was swinging and missing. He was more than capable of throwing strikes, yet he was lobbing most pitches into the dirt.

And he was completely missing the picture when it came to relating to his teammates. While jokes were flying between them in the dugout, Jack was hyperfocused on his next at bat. A "What's up?" between his teammates took the form of a hearty rolling laugh combined with a high five and a half hug. A "What's up?" from Jack was an emotionless, expressionless greeting. His interaction with most of his teammates was awkward. None went out of their way to include him, and none were exactly friends.

It seemed that there was no place for him within this developing picture of a winning team. Unable to wrap his head around the concept of camaraderie, Jack didn't understand the culture that was suddenly attached to this game and its environment, within which he had always felt at home. The meaning of team sport had changed, and while all the other kids were privy to that subtle nuance, Jack was in the dark.

Maybe we should say something to the coach.

Maybe not.

Jack was still playing on an intramural team with much less pressure to conform and no emphasis whatsoever on image, but that did little to temper my worry. The social interaction it provided was shaped by the limited extent to which Jack could communicate and connect with his teammates. Within the context of games, he managed well enough. But remove that structure, and Jack retreated inward, and his teammates lacked both the interest and energy to coax him out.

He was more removed now than ever. With his world narrowing, there was little to occupy his time, and I could no longer bear to watch the choreographed dance of his fingers through yet another fantasy draft. Flick, flick, flick of the thumb, down to the bottom, full throttle reverse and back to the top. Slide to the left, shift to the right, tap, tap, tap, tap, tap.

And . . . again.

I just couldn't stand to see him so isolated and doing nothing productive. It was time for Jack to enter the working world.

CHAPTER 22
When All Else Fails

"**D**o everything you're asked to do, and do it happily. If you're overwhelmed by all the things they're telling you, ask them to tell you again. Be confident and have faith in yourself. Don't be afraid to tell them you have Asperger syndrome."

Yeah, right. I can barely say it myself.

"Okay," Jack replied robotically. One sideways glance at him and I could see that his focus was elsewhere.

"Don't complain. Don't roll your eyes. Look for extra things to do that would be helpful. Cases of bottled beer are heavy, so be very careful lifting them. You don't want to drop one and have it smash all over the floor. Okay?"

"Okay."

"Be respectful of the customers. That means greeting them with a smile, saying please and thank you. Offer to help them take stuff to their car. The better you do the job, the sooner you'll get a raise. When in doubt, text me, or sneak into the bathroom and call me. Make sure you alert them about your baseball schedule in advance too. Okay? Got it?"

This was my advice to Jack as I drove him to his first day of work, his first real job, at the local beverage store. I knew it was too much to throw at him all at once. Jack couldn't absorb more than one or two thoughts at a time, but I couldn't help myself. I had to cover every base and cover them all more than once. I had my doubts, with good reason, that any of my advice was permeating. Nonetheless, after just a few days, his new career was taking off, with his boss singing his praises and vowing to hold onto him for a long time. He was getting big tips from customers, and he even earned himself a Christmas bonus after just two months.

I was shocked and proud.

As with everything in Jack's orbit though, the good times didn't last. He was overwhelmed and confused but never asked questions. He dropped several cases, each time letting two dozen glass bottles smash to the floor, spilling beer everywhere. Based on his own reports of how things were going, which were often exaggerated in Jack's favor, I'm certain he rolled his eyes at his boss more than once. Mention his Asperger's? Nope, not a chance.

Maybe he just got bored. Initially, the newness of the experience and the positive reinforcement he was receiving kept him interested. Once the novelty wore off and his boss began asking more of him, he lost interest, started making mistakes, and even worse, didn't care that he was making mistakes.

Although I'm sure his boss was extremely frustrated, ultimately, I believe it was "the stinky" that prompted the demise of his beverage store career. Reminiscent of his Outer Banks farting incident, Jack moved his bowels in the bathroom and didn't bother to flush the toilet. I was appalled when Jack told me, but the inappropriate nature of such a gesture was completely lost on him. As a result, his first job came to an end. By the time this unfortunate incident occurred, it had been an entire year, so it wasn't a complete failure. At least he had gotten some experience that would facilitate getting another job.

Shortly after turning the beverage world on its head, Jack took a job at the local supermarket stocking shelves, gathering carts, and performing other odd jobs. The upside was that this job was far more structured, which ideally would translate to greater experience and skills. The downside was that he would be making minimum wage—just $7.25 an hour—and had to pay taxes. Although he wasn't making more than minimum wage at the beverage store, the pay there wasn't taxed and it was supplemented by tips, which some days were considerable. Jack's only hope would be to get a raise, and the one way to do that was to become a cashier.

The process didn't seem that difficult. While simultaneously being trained to operate the cash register, Jack needed to learn the store's forty different produce items and be able to recognize at least thirty-two of them. The day of the test, I picked him up from work with high hopes.

"So how did you do?" I asked before Jack was settled in the car.

"I only got twenty-eight right. I needed to get thirty-two. I'm the only one that failed."

"Oh, sweetie, I'm sorry," I replied, feeling instant disappointment. Although he said it wasn't a big deal, I could sense that he was dejected too.

Immediately, I started placating myself with excuses—*He's not a good test taker, he never was*—only to push right back on my thoughts—*He didn't study hard enough, I'm sure of it. He needs to put forth more effort than the average person, and he's too lazy to do it.* My disappointment turned to annoyance. As I was flip-flopping between sympathy and irritation, Jack added that the people at work were being mean to him. They told him to go home after the test.

How dare they treat him poorly!

I had to stop myself. As Jack's mother and protector, it was easy to get sucked into Jack's side of every story. Were they really being mean, or is that simply how he interpreted it?

"It's just like the beverage store all over again," he acknowledged in defeat.

It was true. His previous boss often got angry because Jack couldn't remember the prices of all the different beverages they sold. I guessed that he wasn't getting mad as much as he was exasperated, and Jack doesn't have the ability to distinguish between the two. Part of me wanted to go to the manager of the store and tell him that Jack has a disability, but I talked myself down. What difference would it make? They likely wouldn't give him another opportunity to pass the test, and admitting a limitation would only discount him from other opportunities.

My mother called later that day, full of excitement. "Guess who was training at the register this morning when I went to the supermarket?" She didn't know yet that Jack hadn't passed his test to officially work the register, and I immediately felt resentment. *Didn't she get it?* Now I had to explain to her that he wouldn't be checking her out next time—that he had failed once again. This was my mother, Jack's grandmother. It's not like she doesn't know Jack. She had been deeply involved with him since day one, and I resented that despite all that time spent, she still didn't understand his limitations—this person that I had always counted on to understand everything and make everything right. I was so disappointed for Jack, and I couldn't bear to tell her this news and have her be disheartened too. He deserves to succeed, but I'm continuously wondering when he will.

Every parent has moments when their child does something that stands out. You feel a sense of pride that lures you into thinking that they've finally figured it out, they're on the right path at the start of something great, they're going to be okay! We had several of these moments with Jack. But they were always short-lived.

I urged Jack to consider volunteer work, insisting that it looks as good on a resumé as a paying job, sometimes better. If he could get involved with any organization, I would gladly pay him myself. It would be worth the expense.

"Why don't you consider working at the Y?" I suggested one afternoon when he got home from school. I had been there earlier that day and saw signs announcing their Leader in Training program, which was a prerequisite for becoming a summer camp counselor, reasoning he might be good at it given his passion for sports.

"Yeah, that might be fun. Why don't we try?"

"Not *we*, Jack. You." His inability to disconnect himself from me was concerning. He was old enough now that he should be doing these types of things, like applying for jobs, on his own, yet I couldn't help myself. If he had any chance of being accepted into the program, he was going to need all the help he could get with the application.

In theory, the ideas we assembled weren't too far off base. In reality, they were a joke. Jack could barely take care of himself, let alone watch over a group of children. He's incapable of making decisions and lacks good judgment. Nonetheless, we (I) wove a great tale:

I really like kids. I love sports, and I'm an outdoor person. Most importantly, I like to play. I attended summer camp myself for many years, and I have great memories. I think my good experiences will help me to create good experiences for other kids.

I have a lot of experience playing sports. I've been playing baseball since I was ten, I played for my high school freshman team last year, and I have played on multiple travel teams. I understand the importance of teamwork, but because baseball is also very much an individual sport, I also understand the importance of needing to be your best at all times. I play intramural basketball during the winter months, as well as in an annual summer league. I also played soccer for many years and, last year, I was a member of my high school bowling club.

I am very creative and love arts-and-crafts-type activities.

I'm eager to learn, and I think this would be the kind of experience that would teach me a lot, and I am willing to work hard.

I love animals. I help at the SPCA by organizing neighborhood collections and going to walk dogs whenever possible. I'm planning to become a formal volunteer this summer or next fall.

My goals include wanting to play baseball in college. I would like to have a sport-related job someday, and that might mean coaching. Working with kids will help me to understand what that might be like.

I also want to be more independent. Guiding and caring for kids on a daily basis will teach me a lot about how to care for myself.

The fluff seemed to fly. Jack's (and my) application was well received, and he was accepted into the training program.

However, Jack went off to the program each morning as if he was a camper, not a counselor. He came home each afternoon as if he were an eight-year-old that had just had a fun-filled day at summer camp.

"All the kids love me," Jack exclaimed. "We went on a field trip this afternoon, and they were fighting over who got to sit next to me on the bus."

"That's great, Jack! Are you enjoying it?"

"Yeah, this morning I taught them how to play knockout."

"Knockout? Isn't that a game where you try to hit one another with a ball?"

"Yeah, they loved it."

"Jack, I'm not so sure that's the best game to teach little kids. One of them might get hurt."

"They were fine. Well, except for one girl. She started crying, so we had to stop."

I was horrified. But there was more!

"I taught them how to arm fart," he proudly announced.

It was game over for being a camp counselor. On to plan B.

For several months we had been making regular visits to the SPCA to spend time with the dogs and take one or two for a walk. Each time we visited, the kennel soundtrack was the same—a chaotic, deafening symphony of barking and whining. For someone with Asperger's, this might be overwhelming and unbearable, but not for Jack. The animals brought perfect calm over him. He had also been organizing neighborhood collections of old blankets, jars of peanut butter, and other items on the approved SPCA list. I helped him make a flyer to distribute to all our neighbors. Okay, I made the flyer myself, but he did the rest. He hand-delivered them, fielded calls from neighbors wanting to donate, and went house-to-house collecting bags and boxes of goods, but he wanted to do more.

After submitting the appropriate paperwork, the facility called to schedule Jack for a training session so he could begin regular volunteer work. He would learn about the quarantine process for newly arriving dogs. Before being introduced to the other animals, all new arrivals are quarantined for two weeks to ensure they are healthy and won't cause a threat to either the other animals or staff. For this reason, the dogs can't be exposed to human germs. Jack was doing something good, and I was so proud of him.

Despite the summer heat that afternoon, I was out in the yard pulling weeds while Jack was at his training session when I heard my phone ring. I glanced at my watch, thinking it was much too early for Jack to be finished, so I ignored it. Thirty seconds later, I heard it ring again. Jack is the only one who will repeatedly stalk me by cell phone. If I don't pick up, he'll immediately dial again until I do pick up.

I shed my gardening gloves and ran into the house. "Hey, bud, is everything okay?"

"Can you come get me?"

"You're done already?" When I dropped Jack off, Mary, the director of training, had said the session would last a few hours. I glanced at my watch again. He couldn't have been there more than forty-five minutes. "Is everything okay?"

"Yeah. They told me I could go."

Everything was not okay. I had enough experience with these situations to know that Jack being told he "could go" actually meant "we don't want you here."

"What happened?" I asked as he slid into the car beside me.

"It was really hot."

"Okay, what does that mean exactly?"

"They wanted me to wear a suit, and it was too hot."

I could see Jack was reluctant to give up details and I would need to pry them out of him.

"What kind of suit, Jack?"

"I had to wear a hazmat suit and these thick gloves. I was so hot, and I was sweating so I took my gloves off."

"And?"

"They told me I couldn't take them off."

"Did you put them back on?"

"Yeah, but then I took them off again. And they yelled at me."

"Jack, there are reasons why they need you to wear that protective clothing. You need to do what they say to protect the animals."

"They told me I can't be a volunteer."

Just like that? The good that Jack had started doing was over?

"Are you sure? Maybe you should call them when we get home." I wasn't willing to let this slip away so easily. They would have to give him a second chance.

"Do I have to?" I could see that Jack was uneasy. As far as he was concerned, this whole experience was already behind him.

"You need to at least send Mary an email and apologize to her. I think you should tell her that you have Asperger's and you are incredibly sensitive to heat."

For God's sake, say anything that will appeal to this woman's sense of compassion.

The idea of sending an email versus making a phone call sat better with Jack, and he agreed. Mary was very appreciative of the email, vaguely understanding of the Asperger's piece—if Jack did, in fact, share that with her—and unyielding in her position. Rules were rules, and the procedures in place were for everyone's safety. Jack would not be volunteering at the SPCA.

He just couldn't win. Was this what he had to look forward to? Was his life destined to be a meandering, haphazard path of dots all connected by one commonality—each representing a failure of some sort? He didn't have any understanding of decorum, he was incapable of the critical thinking required to make informed decisions, and he lacked the communication skills to assemble the right pieces in the right order to be able to carry out assigned tasks without some sort of misstep. Ask questions? Never!

What if he makes a mistake that has repercussions down the line? An innocent mistake that he makes because of his disability—not because he intended to, or because he's stupid, or because he doesn't care. What if he makes a mistake that causes someone to get hurt? If he hasn't disclosed his disability, can it be held against him? His Asperger syndrome almost always gives itself away. If he were to mention it from the start though, he might not be hired in the first place.

It wasn't all Jack's doing, or lack of doing, that had him consistently stuck between a rock and a hard place. It was my own inertia and indecision about whether or not to say something, and if I did choose to say something, when to say it. I was forever trapped between embarrassing him, and failing him.

CHAPTER 23
In the Driver's Seat

Jack's freshman year undoubtedly set the stage for the remainder of high school. He never fit in, but he didn't exactly stand out, either. He flew under the radar. There were no dances or proms. That would be too awkward. There were repeated Friday and Saturday nights at home, alone, watching sports and sports highlights. There was freshman baseball but no junior varsity, and subsequently no varsity. He tried in earnest to make each team, but Andrew had been right. Jack was discounted because he didn't fit the mold. And it went without saying, there would be no attending graduation. Sitting in oppressive heat for hours, listening to speeches drone on, watching the trail of graduates, none of whom had befriended Jack? No chance.

On occasion, Jack's flight path would get picked up, and there would be some sort of midair collision. The jerk of a kid who had elbowed him in the face in middle school, splitting his tongue in half, resurfaced at the start of sophomore year, this time hurling a full bottle of water at Jack's head during lunch.

"Jack, why are you sitting with this kid? You need to stay away from him. He's not right!"

"We're actually good friends, Mom."

Uh, Jack, sweetie, a full bottle of water thrown at your head gener-ally means that someone doesn't like you.

There was the occasional email from a teacher: "I found Jack sleeping on the floor in the hall before French class. I'm afraid of what the other kids might think."

Or: "Jack farted again today during history. Could you please talk with him?"

Again, Jack? Oh, come on!

Compared to elementary and middle school, though, those moments of conflict were fewer and further between. Through it all, Jack seemed neither happy nor especially unhappy. Flying below the radar was easier than trying to figure out the complex dance required to take center stage.

I had hoped that high school would bring with it a clean slate, that Jack would somehow make new friends and find his place, but that wasn't the case. I accepted that four unremarkable years were preferred over continuous struggle and conflict.

I worried that his having no place was my fault, that moving and changing schools was the root of his social problems. All the other kids had been together since elementary school. They had formed tight bonds early on that they carried with them through middle school and into high school. Even though they had been Jack's class-mates for two years, he was still on the perimeter, an outcast. Would anything have been different if we had remained in our old neighbor-hood? Jack hadn't formed tight bonds with any of the kids he started kindergarten with, and most likely the distance between them would have been just as pronounced.

Social interaction is a give-and-take, and Jack, I finally realized, was incapable of both sides of that exchange. The world communicates not only with words, but through mannerisms and visual cues that leave thoughts and feelings unsaid and are often in fact different than what is said. Jack lacks the ability to decipher that code. He has no clue how to deliver his own thoughts or portray his moods in any other way than to hit people in the face with them. He wears all of it on the surface. There's no need to pretend he feels differently than he does. There's no need to censor the honest things he says. And there's no need to look out for anyone but himself. In his world, everything is black-and-white—there are no shades of gray. The rules of social interaction are unwritten, existing in a gray area between what's real and what's implied, and when you view the world in black-and-white, what's unwritten doesn't exist. How can it possibly be understood?

Once I was able to see our world through Jack's black-and-white lens, the distinct pieces started coming into focus—and questions started finding their answers. I was gaining some understanding of Asperger syndrome and what it meant for him, though I reluctantly accepted that it had meant something different at every stage of his life to this point, and it would mean all manner of different things with each stage moving forward. What I was understanding today would likely change tomorrow.

High school brought with it one highlight—Jack getting his driver's license.

"I'm not putting my face against that thing. It's disgusting," Jack announced at top volume in the middle of the DMV.

"Jack! Keep your voice down. You need to do this. Everyone does it."

"I'm not doing it."

The poor soul whose job it was to funnel one sixteen-year-old after another through the eye exam for their learner's permit flipped his eyes up at us, dropped his jaw, and made it clear that he wasn't inter-ested in dealing with this drama.

"I'm so sorry," I said. "Could you give us a minute?" I pulled Jack aside and told him in no uncertain terms that he was going to press his face against the machine and take the eye exam. Making it pain-fully clear that he wasn't happy, he finally agreed and successfully completed the exam.

"Okay, good. Now you just need to pass the test."

"He failed the permit test," I told Andrew later that afternoon after recounting our battle over the eye exam.

"How could he fail? He studied for it. He knows all the answers."

"He was so grossed out by the fact that other people had pressed their faces against the eye machine, I think he wanted to fail."

Andrew let out a sigh. "Okay, I'll take him again next weekend."

The following weekend, Jack surrendered to the eye exam once again, this time without a fight, and managed to pass the learner's permit test.

Worry takes on new meaning the moment parents put their chil-dren behind the wheel of a car. Can they handle the power of the car? Are they aware of everything going on around them? Will they be able to navigate a parking lot without running over someone?

The worry is all-consuming and paralyzing when that child has Asperger syndrome.

But what's the alternative? What would life look like for Jack if he's never able to drive? Relying on Uber isn't practical, neither from a time nor a cost perspective. Would he have to live in a city some-where where public transportation is readily accessible? He would hate that. I would hate that, knowing he hated it. How would he ever take a girl out on a date—pick her up on his skateboard?

Despite my fears, I took him out for his first lesson. My small hatchback was easily manageable, so I assumed he would feel comfortable. As we inched along, I peeked out the corner of my eye, knowing this person beside me was only sixteen, but expecting to see a ninety-five-year-old man. *This is good*, I thought. *He's being cautious.*

"Jack, it's okay to go a little faster." Despite my encouragement, he didn't increase his speed, and he continued to roll along as slowly as he possibly could. Eventually we reached a stop sign, at which point, Jack made a right turn—and kept turning—until we drove right up on a neighbor's lawn.

He wanted no part of driving again.

An entire year passed, and still, Jack had no interest in learning to drive. His permit expired and we renewed it, knowing that we couldn't hide from this forever. At some point he would have to try, and renewing his permit would buy him another year.

Once Jack was willing again, Andrew and I made further attempts to teach him, and we both agreed that neither of us felt safe getting into a car with Jack driving. We didn't care how much it cost, we were willing to pay someone with experience—and a second set of brakes—to do it.

Jack was enrolled in driver's ed at school and, to ensure that he was as educated as possible, with a private driving tutor as well. Because we weren't convinced that two rounds would do the trick, Jack took the defensive driving program twice more. Four rounds of driver's ed should be enough to guarantee that Jack was fully prepared to operate a motor vehicle, as well as promise the safety of every other licensed driver on the road. Come December of his senior year, a year and a half after first getting his permit, Jack was finally armed with enough driver's ed that we felt comfortable letting him take the test for his license. He passed on his first try.

He was eighteen—and it felt like we had just given a twelve-year-old permission to drive.

It scared the shit out of me.

With money that his grandmother had left him and a bit of help from Andrew, Jack bought his first car. Andrew and I went back and forth about which made more sense—buying an inexpensive used car that could take the abuse of a novice disabled driver, or buying something new with all the latest safety features. We both agreed Jack needed all the protection he could get.

It was a few days after Christmas when Andrew took Jack to the dealership to pick up the car he had chosen, and my phone rang.

Andrew was in a panic. "Are you aware that he has no idea how to pull into a parking spot?"

"What are you talking about?" Jack had successfully completed four rounds of driver's ed. How could he not know how to handle one of the most fundamental aspects of driving? More importantly, how could Andrew and I be surprised? All the education in the world is no guarantee. Jack forgot how to hold both a pencil and a baseball bat. Who's to say he wouldn't suddenly forget how to operate a car? The thought of that happening quadrupled my fear.

Jack's relationship with driving got off to a rocky start. In the first six months alone, determined to cut corners and run things over, Jack had four flat tires. They would be the first in a line of many. He was also completely naive about his role, not understanding that every now and again, he would have to give this relationship a bit of gas. It was news to him that when the gas runs out, the car stops running. Various other misunderstandings surfaced along the way. He couldn't quite grasp that if you exit the turnpike through the E-ZPass lane when you don't actually have an E-ZPass, you'll be charged the full fare. Ouch.

Then the tickets began to pile up.

For the most part, his violations were all innocuous mistakes made simply because he lacked experience. Still, moving violations are moving violations, which come with unforgiving points against your license, and I'm certain his response to every state trooper at his window was quintessential Jack.

"Oh my Gahhhhhd, are you kidding me?" would be his retort with a pound of his fist on the steering wheel and an overblown roll of the eyes. What little savings Jack had from his job at the beverage store was quickly depleted to hire a lawyer so those points could be erased and his driving privileges salvaged. Each time, the story was the same. Needing to go to court because of a traffic violation—that was his fault—was stupid. The cop was a jerk and the judge an idiot.

There were a few major mishaps too. Granted, the deer and the fire were not his fault. The laws of physics say that the accident in the school lot was not his doing either, but I still have my doubts.

Nonetheless, Jack having a driver's license opened up doors. It presented him with complete freedom for the first time in his life, and it gave Andrew and me a welcome break from being Jack's chauffeur and also his main source of entertainment.

Jack's car became his haven. It was the one and only place to which he could escape, be all alone, and be free from analysis and judgment. It was also the only place where he could have the air-conditioning on high at all times, even in the dead of winter. There might be a complete breakdown or jail time, but there would be no discomfort.

Jack's newfound freedom drove him right back to sixth grade and granted him access to something he so desperately needed—a true friend.

Jack and Nick met on a baseball field when they were twelve. From day one I couldn't help but love the kid. A bit pudgy, slightly shorter than Jack, brown-eyed and apple-cheeked, he had one of the most contagious laughs I've ever heard. He could be a hothead, but only when pushed and needing to stand up for himself. Nick didn't take crap from anyone.

Their friendship was the only one from our old neighborhood that had potential, but moving out of the area did nothing to strengthen it. Despite remaining friends, it was logistically more difficult for the two to spend time together once we moved. Eventually, Nick's visits to our house came to an end, and time spent together was limited to those weekends that Jack was at Andrew's. But their friendship remained intact, lasting through middle school and into high school. Jack now having the ability to go where he pleased, when he pleased, changed everything for the better.

In no time at all, Jack and Nick became inseparable. They arranged to get themselves on the same intramural baseball and basketball teams. They saw movies and wrote rap songs together. They went to concerts and sneaker campouts, discovered favorite places to eat, and spent evenings at the gym. Nick became Jack's purpose, eclipsing baseball and fantasy drafts. I worried that he might become Jack's sole focus, his next obsession. I wanted to believe otherwise, praying that Jack's Asperger syndrome didn't run that deep, that it didn't have such a hold on him that he was incapable of understanding the demands of true friendship or being able to fulfill that commitment.

Jack bore most of the weight of their relationship, always going to Nick, and that bothered me. I understood that Jack had his own car while Nick was forced to share one with his older siblings; still, I worried that Nick was taking advantage. Deep down I didn't trust the authenticity of their relationship. No one had ever wanted to spend time with Jack to the degree that Nick did. I wanted to believe that his desire was genuine, but I was leery.

"I'm not sure if you're aware," Andrew relayed to me one afternoon, "but Nick was diagnosed with Asperger syndrome."

"Are you serious?" I was in disbelief. "Nick doesn't have Asperger's. He doesn't behave at all like Jack. He's so outgoing. That just can't be."

"I didn't believe it at first, either, but after thinking it through, it might be true." Andrew went on to give me several examples of Nick having done or said something that sounded exactly like something Jack would say or do. He was seeing Nick more frequently now, so he would know. Still, I didn't believe it. Nick seemed so "normal," and I struggled to comprehend what made him different. Never at any point in Jack's childhood was there a kid that honestly wanted to spend time with him regularly. Thomas did it out of loyalty. Nick was doing it by choice. He understood Jack in a way that no one else ever had and didn't seem bothered by any of Jack's odd, overbearing ways. He didn't care that Jack was immature, that he rambled on endlessly about nothing, or that he was rarely flexible enough to try something new. Nick accepted Jack as is, no questions asked. In so many ways, he was the best thing that had ever happened to Jack, and to us. I said numerous prayers that their friendship would last.

CHAPTER 24
Onward and Upward

"Test-ahhhhh, Testa one, two . . . one, two. . . ."

Jack put his nonsense on pause and turned serious for a moment.

"Brandon Testa scored a sixteen hundred on his SAT," he said. "I guess he won't be needing a Test-*ahhhhhptional* school."

"Now that was funny," I said. Jack had never been able to comprehend the nuances of humor, so it strikes me hard when he says something witty. Brandon was one of his travel teammates, and he was in fact incredibly smart. It didn't surprise me that he had earned a perfect score on his SAT. Jack, however, wouldn't be so lucky. Acceptance to college, any college, was going to require significant effort. He was never a good test taker, and I didn't want him being limited solely to test-optional schools, so I decided to hire a tutor. Based on input from his school counselors, we were all in agreement that Jack should take the ACT and not the SAT. The latter required more conceptual thinking, which was not his strong suit. He had a better chance for success with a test that was literal in its presentation of questions.

After researching the numerous test-prep services in our area, I realized Jack was going to need a tutor with a greater level of skill than most, one who understood his limitations. I eventually found someone who had experience working with kids that were academically challenged.

"Wow, are you serious?" Those were the only words I could muster after learning it would be $250 per session and Jack was likely to need between eight and ten sessions. I didn't see another option and accepted the expense as part of his college tuition. If tutoring would help him on the ACT, broadening the array of schools he had to choose from, it was worth it. I agreed to the cost, and Jack was soon meeting weekly with Stephen at our local library. Each meeting was followed by an email to update me on progress:

Jack and I worked on English and math yesterday. He was a little more animated, singing while working on math problems and making hand gestures off into the distance, like a smoking gun. I am doing my best to keep him engaged and focused.

I could picture it perfectly—Jack doing strange things akin to his moves in front of the mirror in the karate studio. His behavior undoubtedly signaled his discomfort with being trapped in a library study room with a middle-aged man. I'm sure it was completely inappropriate and awkward, and Stephen was totally embarrassed, but I didn't feel terribly guilty. I was paying him a significant amount of money.

Three ACT attempts and $2,500 later, Jack finally scored high enough that some schools might accept him.

In addition to taking the entrance exam, he also needed to write an essay. If I left the writing solely to Jack, I was certain the result wouldn't exactly be college material. I could help him write it, but I worried that I wasn't capable of being impartial. I'd end up writing the whole thing myself. I had just spent $2,500 on a tutor. What difference would another $2,000 make?

Prior to Jack's first meeting with Jessica, I decided it would be best to come clean and prepare her for the daunting task at hand to maximize my investment.

"So I just want to let you know in advance . . . Jack may be a bit tough to work with. He doesn't communicate all that well. He has Asperger syndrome."

Momentary pause.

"Thank you for sharing that information. I appreciate your honesty," she said. "I'm certain I have worked with other children on the spectrum, but their parents never said a word. I wish they had. Knowing as much as I can about my students helps me to help them as best I can." She went on to say she was ready for the challenge, and her earnest reception put my mind at ease.

I promised to send her samples of Jack's writing but quickly questioned whether I had anything of value to share. Every high school essay he'd ever written had been elementary at best, but I reminded myself that it was now out there on the table—she knows that Jack has a disability and his communication skills are lacking. If his writing samples underwhelm her, she can't say she wasn't warned.

I sat down at my desk, opened the folder on my hard drive labeled JACK, and sifted through the numerous files. What I found wasn't only unexpected—it got my wheels turning. I had no idea what had been hiding in that folder. Why had I not remembered any of it?

After setting several files aside, I quickly dashed off an email to Jessica. I attached a couple of standard essays along with several poems and added a quick note stating that they were the best examples I had. I stopped myself there, wanting to hear her thoughts before sharing my own, hoping they would be the same.

A few hours later, my phone rang.

"You know, Jack's writing is actually quite good," she said, a hint of excitement leaking through the line. "These poems he wrote are very creative. I was thinking, well. . . ."

She seemed hesitant to put the idea out there.

"What do you think of this idea?" she went on. "What if Jack were to write a poem instead of a standard essay? The one that's titled 'I Am,' the one about baseball, would make a great foundation. What do think of that idea?"

What do I think? That's *exactly* what I was thinking!

"I was hoping you would say that," I replied casually but warmly, letting her know I was appreciative of her foresight, without letting on that I was thrilled.

At their initial meeting, Jessica shared with Jack her idea of using his baseball poem as a foundation for his essay. He liked that approach, so she asked him to come to their next meeting with a list of as many qualities about himself that he could think of starting with the phrase "I am."

"I just want you to know, sweetie," I informed Jack on our ride home, "I'm paying Jessica a lot of money to help you. You need to put forth as much effort as possible."

"I know. I can do this," he replied nonchalantly.

And he did. Jack walked back into Jessica's office for their second meeting, clutching two sheets of paper, each covered with every last detail about himself. It looked like nothing more than four pages of illegible chicken scratch, but it was all Jack. He was engaged in the process, and she was impressed.

Unfortunately, Jack's engagement was limited.

He had done what Jessica had asked, so as far as he was concerned, he was done with this college essay assignment. The entire poem still needed to be assembled, finessed, and edited—all implied parts of the process—but Jessica hadn't said anything to him about those steps. To Jack, they didn't exist. Jessica was left to do the heavy lifting, and I'm certain it was accompanied by numerous uncomfortable moments with Jack in her office. But again, I was paying this person a significant amount of money. It was her job to get him through this process.

Jessica did not let us down. She was masterful in guiding and managing Jack, and the result was an absolute masterpiece of self-expression. I can't say it was 100 percent accurate, but it was a work of art.

I Am

I am kind.

I like making people laugh.
I respect others and help them when they need me.
I work hard in school and at my job.
Cases of soda are heavy, but I am strong.
It is not easy for me to make conversation with customers as I haul beverages to their cars.
But I am happy that I do.
I have a lot to say, but words do not always come easily.
I am thoughtful. I am honest. I am giving.

I am Asperger's.

I put everything into what I want to accomplish.
That is how I meet my goals.

Sometimes, I pretend to be untouchable.
But disappointment tackles me when I do not succeed.
Luckily, dark clouds never put me in a bad mood.
And dogs always make me happy.
I think four dogs are better than three.

I am imaginative.

I love drawing, painting, ceramics, and photography.
Because my memory is amazing, numbers, facts, and statistics are trusted friends.
Why can't someone creative like me also be a gifted statistician?
I analyze the performances of every single athlete in almost every major sport.
With thousands of contestants in a nationwide Fantasy Sports competition, I placed first.
Chemistry is numbers, facts, and formulas.
Maybe that is why it is one of my favorite subjects.

I am a competitor.

I pick up most sports easily, except lacrosse.
I scored my one and only goal against my own team.
Baseball is my favorite sport.
I train every day because striking out is not acceptable.
When it happens, I work harder to succeed.
Having teammates that accept me, makes a good team great, regardless of the score.
I want to contribute—for myself and for them.

I am proud to have made our high school's freshman baseball team.
I did not make our baseball team sophomore or junior year,
But will try again senior year.
I do not quit, and I never give up.

I explore my options.

I play for a travel team.
It is important to keep my head in the game because I can get silly when I am bored.
On the diamond, I hear chatter from the dugout.
I smile at the noisy, clapping crowd cheering me on.
I feel like Babe Ruth at the plate and on the mound.
I touch my smooth brown baseball bat and wait.
The bat cracks, and the ball goes out of the park faster than an airplane.
I dream about making it to the major leagues.

I wonder about my future.

Will I hit a home run?
I question how I'll fit in at college.
I am not sure about a major.
I wish it was possible to major in baseball.
What will my roommate be like?
He needs to love sports and dogs.
I ask myself if I can handle living alone.
Is there a job for who I am?
Is it possible for me to grow from cheeseburgers to avocado

salads?

Doubtful.

Will I have my own dog—or four dogs, because four are better than three?

I am determined.

I want to be the best at everything, even when I struggle.
My way of staying organized might not look like yours, but it fits me perfectly.
I am never late—ever—and I am always early for baseball.
I strive to be a leader.
I am focused. I must be.
I am resilient. I must be.

Comedian and actor, Dan Akroyd
Artist, Andy Warhol
Filmmaker, Tim Burton
Author, Lewis Carroll
Animal Scientist, Dr. Temple Grandin
Baseball player and statistician, Jack Somers

We are Asperger's.

That was Jack's college essay.

When he first completed it, I shared it with everyone I knew. I wanted to share it with the world. It was a concrete piece of evidence, other than home runs and stolen bases, that painted a positive picture of who he is and spoke of his tremendous value. It was thoughtful, meaningful, and so full of self that I envisioned him getting emails and phone calls from every admissions officer that read it, to congratulate him on writing such a moving and engaging piece, and instantly offering him admission into their school.

More likely, it would be nothing more than a $2,000 exercise, receiving barely a quick glance from one or two people. I'm sure Jessica had a huge hand in crafting it, but it was done, and it was done well. It would go a long way toward compensating for his less than outstanding test scores.

Jack had two requirements as far as a college was concerned—it needed to be a small school, and it couldn't be too far from home. If those two variables could be combined with the opportunity to play baseball, it would be a done deal.

Our first college visit was to a local state university. We were less than halfway through the tour when I realized it was not the place for Jack. He would be lost at a school that size, nothing more than a number. He required guidance and an extra level of attention that didn't appear to be available in a larger setting.

We toured another school later that same day—a small private university just fifteen minutes from home. The campus was beautiful, but I worried that its small size meant it would be lacking in resources and opportunities.

"This is where I want to go to school," Jack announced as we parked the car.

"You haven't even seen the campus yet. Let's tour it first and then decide." I was a firm believer in gut reactions and following your intuition, but Jack was an expert in impulsivity, and I didn't want him making an uninformed decision.

"It just feels right to me," he insisted.

"What if you're not able to play baseball?"

He didn't respond. The likelihood of his being able to play baseball was growing slim. Despite all the prospect camps he had attended and all the games with college coaches in attendance, this school's coach included, Jack had failed to procure a spot on any team. If he wanted to play, it would mean either attending a no-name school that probably wouldn't meet his requirements of being small and close to home, or attending the school of his choice and trying out for the team, hopefully becoming a walk-on. That would be taking a big chance.

Throughout high school, Jack had been playing travel ball. It wasn't exactly the glue that held everything together—it was more like Scotch tape—but it was a much needed constant that filled the gaps and provided exposure to college scouts. Jack wasn't capable of following a straight line, though, and never developed continuity with any one group of kids. He bounced from one team to the next, playing with a team for a season, then deciding he couldn't or didn't want to play with that team again the next season. He didn't like the other kids. He wasn't getting enough playing time. The coach was a dick.

Jack, please don't say that again.

It wasn't until Jack's junior year that the right team came along.

"They want him to play on the Warrenton team," Andrew informed me regretfully.

"Warrenton—that's forty-five minutes away!"

"I know, but we're out of options. If Jack had stuck with one of the other teams he started with, we wouldn't have this problem, but now it's too late. It's either make the drive, or don't play."

After much discussion and Jack's adamance that he wanted to play, Andrew and I conceded. Game locations were the same for all teams, so where your team was based mattered only for practice. We agreed that we would share the burden of driving back and forth and find a way to muddle through for a few months.

Perhaps it was a slight bit of maturity, or maybe it was because the clock was ticking toward college, but everything started to click. Jack had finally found his comfort team, one in which all the pieces fell into place. Not only was he playing exceptionally well, but he was accepted by his teammates. There was no need to fit the mold. With the boys coming from various high schools, travel ball was more about the play rather than appearances.

Unbeknownst to Jack, his coach was friends with the head coach from a small college in Delaware. They needed a pitcher, and Jack's coach suggested that he come out to see Jack play. After watching a few games, the coach was quite impressed and offered Jack a spot as a starting pitcher at his school, which was small and private, with the type of setting in which Jack would feel comfortable and hopefully thrive. Jack's efforts had paid off. There was just one problem—the school was ninety minutes from home.

"We should at least go look at it, Jack, don't you think?"

"I guess it can't hurt," he said with a degree of disappointment.

"Who knows, you might love it." I did my best to sound encouraging, though Andrew and I were both equally as disappointed as Jack. He finally had a shot at something, but his pint-sized comfort zone would probably prevent him from taking advantage of it. It would take a mountain of convincing, and even if we were successful, how comfortable would he be with the choice? The last thing we wanted was for him to go off to a school that was an hour and a half from home and find himself uneasy and panic-stricken. Nonetheless, Jack and I scheduled a time to tour the campus and meet with the head coach.

The campus was small, as we expected, but older than I hoped.

It was a few steps shy of falling into disrepair. The campus was tree-lined and quaint, sitting in the midst of a welcoming neighborhood, but the facilities themselves felt run-down and a bit less than homey. Let's call it what it was, though—our only reason for even considering it was so Jack could play baseball.

After our guided tour led by a senior student athlete, who went above and beyond to sing the school's praises, we were taken to the admissions office for our meeting with the coach.

I didn't want to be the one doing all the talking. It was important that Jack engage with the coach, ask questions, and be in charge of this decision, so I had given him explicit instructions on our drive down as to what he should say and how he should behave. I didn't want Jack giving the coach any reason to dismiss him.

Once we had all the information, I presented the one potential hurdle.

"The one thing that might keep Jack from deciding to attend your school and play baseball for you is the distance. He doesn't want to be that far from home."

The coach chuckled slightly in disbelief. "It's only an hour and a half. It's not that far."

Not responding, I offered the coach a half smile because I already knew how this was going to go. *It might not be that far for you or me, but for Jack, that distance is likely a deal-breaker.*

"So what did you think?" I asked, stealing a quick glance at Jack as we pulled away from the admissions office.

"It was okay, I guess. What do you think I should do?" His perpetual need for direction was always so immediate.

"Well, it's not exactly where I picture you going to school, but if you can play baseball, maybe it's worth a shot. What's the worst that can happen? You go for a semester, and if you decide you hate it, you transfer to another school."

"I guess."

I could see he was struggling, and it was all because of the distance.

Jack went back and forth about the decision for months, one day excited about playing college baseball, the next day questioning if it was the right school.

"Nick says that if I go there, I'll walk away with a Macaroni and Art degree."

"That's not true, Jack. It has a good reputation," I replied with a laugh, not wanting to let on that I had concerns of my own about the quality of the education. I wanted so badly for him to have this opportunity to play baseball, to shine. At the end of the day, though, it needed to be his decision.

Jack's desire to play eventually won out, and he agreed to give it a shot. We submitted his application, wrote a deposit check, and it was decided.

But it seemed that the moment we made it official, fear took up residence in Jack's head.

"Mom, do I have to go?"

I let out a heavy sigh.

"No, sweetie, you don't have to do anything, but don't you want to play baseball?"

"Yeah, I want to play, but I don't want to be that far from home. I just don't want to go there."

"I wish you had decided that before I wrote a check," I said, raising an eyebrow at him but not feeling surprised. It wasn't a big check, and it wouldn't be the last needless expense due to Jack's inability to think things through and make decisions.

"If you are absolutely positive that you don't want to go, then you need to let the coach know, and you need to do it soon, so he has time to find someone else to fill your spot." Deadlines for application—at all schools—were upon us, meaning Jack would need to make a quick decision about where he did want to go.

"Okay, thanks, Mom . . . love you," he added. It was the period at the end of every conquered hurdle. At the end of everything. And it was as necessary as breathing in and out.

"Love you too, bud."

Though I urged him strongly to call the coach, Jack was uncomfortable, not wanting to explain himself, not wanting to hear a response that would undoubtedly be negative. Disregarding my direction, he sent an email instead, and it appeared to have been met with sincere understanding. Not wanting any of it to reflect poorly on Jack, I followed up with an email of my own, asking the coach if he had a few minutes to chat by phone. I felt it necessary to explain Jack's months of hemming and hawing, his eventual commitment, followed by his eleventh-hour retraction of that commitment, yet I had no idea how to tell this college coach about my son's disability. How would Jack ever have been able to hide it, though? He is so athletically gifted, but his limitations would eventually surface and upend everything. The idea of telling this man, out loud, that Jack has Asperger's sent me into a panic. It led me to the darkness of the basement, seeking shelter from the painful conversation about to be had, hiding from the finality of it.

"Coach, I really appreciate you taking the time to talk, and I can't apologize enough for Jack's last-minute decision not to play for you. It's just that the distance is too far for him."

"I understand. . . ."

"No, you don't understand."

I was convinced that this couldn't be that easy. I needed to get this out in the open, to take ownership for every inconvenience my son had ever caused.

"I'm not sure you realize," I went on, "but Jack has Asperger syndrome, and being ninety minutes from home, well, for him, he may as well be on the other side of the planet, and. . . ." The words, the thoughts, the years of analysis and second-guessing, the vague explanations offered to various coaches, things gone unsaid to most—it all came rolling out with the force of an unchecked locomotive on a downhill track. And it did nothing more than disappear into silence on the other end of the line. There was no anger, no protest, no assigning of blame for an inconvenience that shouldn't have happened.

"It's okay. I understand," the coach offered again. "I know Jack has Asperger's. I knew it before I went out to see him play the first time."

I stopped breathing for a moment.

We've just made a tremendous mistake.

Jack had just passed up the one and only opportunity that was likely to come his way. He had declined an offer to play baseball—*college* baseball—for someone that was not only aware of his limitations but accepting of them, someone that was viewing him as an asset, not trying to decipher him. And Jack was saying no thanks.

What have we done?

He went on to express that he was genuinely interested in having Jack on his team and should Jack change his mind at any point, the spot would be his, even if that point was a year from now. I heard his words, pretending to let them comfort me, not for him but for myself, because I knew the truth. Jack had made up his mind, and there would be no rewind.

I sat in the dark basement dumbfounded. I was relieved that this man had been so understanding, but suddenly I was faced with processing something so much bigger than this simple, matter-of-fact conversation—my grief over the loss of baseball. This entity that had been living with us for the last ten years, dictated practically all of Jack's middle and high school years, and essentially defined every aspect of Jack's personality was over. Just like that, with one decision, in a single conversation, it was over.

This sport had commandeered our lives for a decade. It was an all-consuming inconvenience at times. I should have been thrilled at the prospect of shedding it, releasing it into the past so Jack could move on to more realistic prospects. Instead, I felt immense disappointment. I wanted Jack to prove everyone wrong, specifically all those people throughout high school who thought he wasn't good enough. All those people who thought something was just a bit off. All those who decided Jack didn't fit. I wanted him to be able to say, "I am more than good enough—and better!" I wanted to be able to say, "Look at *my* kid. Look at what he's doing and all that he's accomplished." Until then, I hadn't been aware of how important Jack's playing baseball was, not only to Jack but to me. I had been clinging to it for years because it was proof to the outside world that Jack was worthy.

Despite the sense of loss and needing to accept that Jack would no longer be playing his favorite sport, I felt a huge sense of relief. His stress over this decision, and the fear of being too far from home, had been obvious for months. My heart had been aching at the thought of him being away from us, alone and unprotected. I knew the idea made him tremendously uncomfortable, and that crushed me. Choosing not to go relieved us of that weight. With only weeks to spare, we scheduled an appointment with the admissions office at the small local college he had fallen in love with at first sight. Jack submitted his application, received their acceptance letter, and we gave them a deposit.

"If you dig up a tree and plant it somewhere else, the leaves are likely to fall off. It needs to take root before it can start to grow again."

Leave it to my brother, the gardener, to come up with that analogy. He said this to me shortly before school began, knowing I was worried about how Jack would adapt to this enormous change. It was his way of gently saying that he may experience some setbacks, but ultimately, he'd be fine. I wished that I had a fraction of his confidence. Jack had slept away his last summer before school began, and I was fearful he was in defense mode, keeping his anxiety at bay by remaining in a semiconscious state.

I had spent nineteen years trying to understand Jack. Just when I thought I had him figured out, he was going off on his own, and I was worried I would lose my handle on him. I had been so attuned to his various modes and had trained myself to recognize all the signs of a bad day or triggers for a potential meltdown. Without being in step with him, the likelihood of any situation becoming a nightmare was exponentially greater.

After much back-and-forth, we decided that Jack would be better off not having a roommate. Having a safe space to which he could retreat and untangle his days in private would serve him far better than the company of a stranger that he no doubt would have difficulty relating to. After he was granted a single room, I backtracked. I became fixated on everything that could go wrong. How lonely would he be? Would being lonely translate to depression? Would he know who to go to when he's feeling down and needs someone to talk to? Would he even be willing to talk to someone? And would he know what to do if he got locked out of his room? Because we knew that would happen.

It was causing me significant anxiety, which translated to stressful interaction with him. I knew my stress would only weigh on him, but I couldn't help myself. I felt he was so unprepared despite all I had done to prepare him. I didn't want him to fail, yet I knew he needed to make mistakes and learn from them. My fear was that failure would somehow put him in harm's way.

He's only going to be fifteen minutes away.

Within days of moving in, Jack had made friends with two of the boys living on his floor. One had chosen to attend solely because he was offered a spot on the swim team. He appeared not much different than Jack's "baseball brothers" from high school—your standard jock with an image to maintain—but for the moment, he made a good partner for shooting hoops. Their friendship would be over before October.

The other boy was a science major, somewhat nerdy and a bit of a loner like Jack, and the two quickly established a mutual agreement: "We're stuck in this mess, let's weather it together." Ryan, it seemed, needed Jack as much as Jack needed him. I hoped it would last.

Despite having a companion at school, Jack still wanted to spend every weekend with Nick. It was obvious that he was dependent on Nick, though he didn't see it that way. Even if he did, he never would have acknowledged it. He wasn't capable of understanding that concept. Their friendship provided routine, and the safety and comfort he needed to keep his world stable. While I had no doubt that Nick saw Jack as his best friend, he was far more extroverted and capable of handling changes. Also living away from home, Nick had freedom to explore new experiences and meet new people. I worried that Jack would eventually be left out.

It was yet another Friday morning when Jack called, wanting to see if I could pick him up once classes were over for the day. Since school began, he had come home every weekend. Because freshmen weren't allowed cars on campus, Jack's need for his weekly Nick fix was becoming a nuisance.

After discovering that no firm plans were in place, I got the uneasy feeling that Jack was about to be blown off. No matter how many different ways I've tried explaining it, Jack doesn't understand the subtleties of friendship. He wants what he wants, and he assumes that everyone around him exists to give him what he wants. In Jack's mind, you're his best friend, therefore you should do everything together. Jack insisted that he and Nick were going to do something, so I didn't push the issue. He was getting his car from our house, going to meet Nick, and spending the weekend at Andrew's. If Nick were to bail on him, at least Andrew would be there to pick up the slack, I reasoned.

Nick bailed on him.

Jack returned home about five o'clock Sunday evening, ready for me to drive him back to school. His quick hello and sour tone told me he wasn't in the best mood.

"What's wrong, sweetie?"

"Nothing. I'm fine. Can we just go?" Anytime Jack is bothered by a situation, he immediately wants to move on. Let's not discuss it, let's not overthink it, let's just ignore it. He wasn't giving up any information about his weekend or why Nick didn't want to get together, so I talked about other things on our ride back.

Once we arrived at school, Jack texted Ryan to see if he wanted to play basketball or video games. When he didn't get an immediate response, his mood turned dark. I helped him take his clean laundry and a few other things up to his room, and before I could give him a hug goodbye, he asked me to leave. It killed me to see him feeling down, but I had to let him be.

I was on my way out of the building when Jack called me. "Love you, Mom."

"Love you too, bud. If you need anything at all, even if it's just to be on the phone with someone, please call me. Okay?"

"Okay," he said, his tone sounding a bit lighter.

"There's a big group of kids sitting in the common area watching football. Go join them. Make some new friends—so you're not revolving your life around one person. Okay?"

"Okay. Love you."

I paused. Jack's words were habitual in this moment; I could hear it. Nonetheless, I welcomed them, even if the sentiment was less than genuine. It was comforting not only for him, but for me as well. It assured me that his downcast mood had taken a turn.

"Love you too, bud."

Regardless of the situation with Nick, Jack was 100 percent committed to their friendship and continued coming home every weekend. He had placed Nick on a pedestal and was willing to go above and beyond for the sake of their relationship. Since the day he first picked up a bat, baseball had been the cure-all for Jack. "Everything will be okay once I can play baseball," he used to say. It was when Jack got his driver's license that things changed. Nick had become Jack's cure-all. I let go of my concern for the time being. During the week, Jack was hanging out with Ryan, and together they had made a few other acquaintances, so I considered his first semester at college a small social success.

Academically, it was a much different story. Throughout high school, Jack had been bringing home As and Bs with regularity. More than once, I questioned their validity. His school was historically ranked very high for the state. I sensed that they doled out good grades to everyone, whether earned or not, wanting to push the kids through so they could maintain their reputation. When I saw Jack's grades at the end of his first semester, my fears were confirmed. High school had done absolutely nothing to prepare him for college.

"Sweetheart, this is a real problem. If you don't get your grades up, you're going to lose your financial aid, and if you lose your financial aid, it's game over. I can't afford your tuition otherwise."

Jack looked at me with the same lack of concern he exhibits over every other setback.

"I will," was his uncomplicated response.

"Jack, you need to get your grades up. You just have to!" I felt the need to repeat myself, because clearly he wasn't understanding the urgency.

"I will," he repeated.

I was beside myself. How could he have gotten in such deep trouble with his grades? Wasn't anyone paying attention?

Of course not! He's in college now!

I found myself grappling with a new curse—out of sight, out of mind. With Jack away at school and out of sight, it was easy to believe that everything was fine. It was easy to forget about the challenges he faces every day. I assumed he was gaining independence and able to handle things on his own. I had started to think he was going to be okay. But then something would happen, or he'd say something to remind me that he's never going to be totally okay. There will always be some problem trailing after him like an unshakable shadow.

Asperger syndrome.

My first thought was to reach out to his guidance counselor, or better yet, the head of the Disabilities Resource Center. But I decided to have him reach out.

"They assigned me an academic coach. Her name is Amanda. I need to meet with her once a week." Jack stated this development as if he had just been handed a death sentence. I had significant doubts about his ability or his desire to pull through this dilemma, but I needed to stop chasing him to constantly clear the rubble. At some point he needed to take control.

Jack's second semester got off to a better start. He adjusted his attitude toward Amanda, and thanks to their weekly meetings, his grades crept up. I was hopeful that he was beginning to understand the importance of maintaining good grades, and more importantly, communication. I was grateful, too, that there was a third party responsible for looking over his shoulder. He may have been out of my sight and mind, but it was now her job to keep Jack on her radar.

Too bad there was an unexpected, ominous presence on the horizon, waiting to disrupt Jack's progress.

CHAPTER 25
Isolation

My cell rang, and it was Jack. *He had better not be calling to say he's not coming home for dinner.*

It was Friday, a night I didn't ordinarily cook. Jack had gone to Andrew's house to use his gym, and the only reason I was making dinner was because Jack had specifically requested that I make spaghetti and meatballs. Earlier in the day, I had sensed that he was off-kilter in some way, and if pasta could fix it, I was willing to get it done.

"Hey, what's up?" I said.

"I'm on my way home," Jack replied. "Is dinner ready?"

"Not just yet. The meatballs are still cooking."

"Okay. Do you think we'll be going back to school in the fall?"

His question smacked me in the face. It wasn't the first time he had asked it, but when we're in the middle of discussing meatballs, it felt like it had come out of left field.

"Yes, sweetie, I do." Whether or not I believed it, the only answer in that moment was yes.

"Okay. I'll be home soon."

I hung up, knowing this wasn't good.

———

It was March 2020, Jack's second semester. Campus had been closed abruptly, temporarily at first, but then for the remainder of the semester thanks to the Covid-19 pandemic. Jack's college experience, the one he had spent his high school years waiting for, the one that had started out well enough and was just beginning to feel familiar and comfortable—his fresh start—had just become a wholly virtual experience.

Jack sat down at the kitchen island and was fit to be tied. I knew that mode better than any other. He was miserable, and nothing would pacify him.

"I need to purchase a code from the school bookstore, and I have no idea how to do it," he unfolded with aggravation.

"What does that mean?" I had no idea what he was talking about, so to me that seemed like a legitimate question. To him, it was an exhausting exercise. In his mind, I should know exactly what he's talking about and how to rectify the situation. He gave me that shrug of impatience, of frustration, of "I'm about to implode."

"What exactly do you need to do?" I asked him calmly, trying to break down the problem.

"I want to major in business management, and to do that, I need to purchase a code from the bookstore, but it's not working. I can't find it. I don't even know how to get into the bookstore. I just want to get this done." Ever since he was a child, Jack had an impulsive need to handle every task immediately. If he wanted a pair of sneakers, it had to be done that day, that hour, right now. If he realized his car needed an oil change or inspection, the appointment needed to be scheduled immediately, for that afternoon. Acknowledge it, and address it. Black-and-white.

I don't know why I can't always see it, but at some point in the midst of these scenarios, it becomes crystal clear. Frustration over not being able to purchase whatever he needed to purchase from the school bookstore was just a symptom.

"Have you had anything to eat today?" I asked, already knowing the answer.

"This virus is ruining my life," Jack threw at me, as if he were the only one in the world impacted, failing to acknowledge that the immediate issue was that he was starving. The look on his face, his mood, his entire being in that moment was broken.

This freshman year of college was the first and only time in his life that he had reached any real degree of comfort. It had been so unexpected. He hadn't amassed a social circle hundreds of friends deep, not even a dozen deep, but he was finding his place. He was finding a way to fit in on his terms.

And now this. A once-in-a-lifetime pandemic. Social distancing. You would think for Jack that would be the perfect scenario: not needing to attend class or engage with his teachers face-to-face, to talk with someone who might sit down with him in the cafeteria, to socialize in any way. But it was killing him. He couldn't go anywhere or do anything to exercise his newfound independence.

He was bored.

Of all the things for Jack to experience, boredom is the kiss of death. It's one of the reasons why playing on three baseball teams at one time had always been so essential. Don't give Jack downtime. Don't give him time to think too long or too hard. Don't give him reason to behave like a complete jerk. Keep him occupied. Keep him entertained. Keep him going. At all times. It had always been an endless cycle, and the cycle was still going, even at age nineteen.

I fixed him his plate of spaghetti and slid it in front of him.

"This is ruining everyone's life," I explained. "What you are experiencing is nothing. There are people out there right now that have no idea how they're going to pay their bills this month. There are people out there who have lost family members this week who were perfectly healthy last week. Yes, this is impacting you, but it is *not* ruining your life."

It seems like we've spent Jack's entire life at the edge of a precipice. It always happens in the same way, and surprisingly I still don't see it coming. Jack has a meltdown. I talk Jack off the ledge. Jack eventually comes around. Crisis averted, right?

Wrong.

The meltdown is nothing more than the opening act—the prelude to everything in his life being wrong. It announces a string of bad moods, abrasive days, and unresolvable conflicts, and how long it will last is anyone's guess. The pandemic provided just the right blend of toxic circumstances for a breakdown. Jack was on his way to losing it.

School reopened for the fall semester, but nothing was the same. More importantly, nothing about it was the way Jack wanted it to be. Classes were in person 25 percent of the time at most, and when they were in person, class size was limited. The remainder of the time was virtual. I was paying thousands of dollars for room and board, and he could have been having the same empty experience from home.

"I don't want to go back to school for spring semester," he announced. "Not if it's going to be the same as fall. I hate it. This sucks. Covid has ruined my college experience." He was adamant about his decision, and I couldn't argue with him.

"Covid has changed your experience, yes, but it hasn't ruined it," I reiterated, trying my best to keep him grounded. "If you want to take the spring semester off, I'm behind you, but you need to do something productive with your time. You can't sleep it away."

Jack made the necessary arrangements for taking a leave of

absence and agreed to find a job. Options were not only limited, they were practically nonexistent. Delivering takeout was the only possibility. Fortunately for Jack, that idea worked. Becoming proficient in delivery apps like DoorDash and Grubhub wasn't much different than learning how to draft fantasy teams. He quickly mastered the system, figuring out where and when to go to get the best tips, and the fact that he was making good money was positive reinforcement for maintaining a dedicated schedule. Good life lessons were being learned, I decided. Jack would never be a nine-to-five, work-in-a-cubicle kind of guy. I questioned if he would ever be a report-to-someone-else kind of guy. He was better off calling his own shots.

The time away from school, though, wasn't good.

"I'm worried about him." One part of me wanted to reel the thought back in, pretend I hadn't said anything. I valued Liam's opinion, but hearing it was generally hard. I needed to lean on him, though. What was going on with Jack just didn't seem right. It didn't seem normal.

Ha. Did it ever?

I said it again, "I'm worried about him. I'm worried about Jack."

Liam stopped and looked up at me. "He's fine."

"He's not fine." I wanted to share my fears but didn't. I never wanted Liam to know the full truth. Even after twelve years together, I still worried that he viewed Jack negatively.

"Look," Liam continued, "he has a year and a half of college under his belt, and he would still be there if it wasn't for Covid. He's working. He's making money. He'll go back to school in the fall. He'll be fine." Liam paused. "What you do need to do, though, is stop allowing him to sleep until three o'clock in the afternoon."

He was right. Jack was spending far more time sleeping than anything else. It was his escape from everything that was wrong. That he was delivering food primarily at night made it okay in my mind. What worried me was that delivering food was all he had. He slept all day, got up and delivered food all evening and into the night, then came home and watched sports highlights until the early morning hours. He was completely cut off from life, except for Nick, and even that situation had become tenuous. There wasn't much they could do together, because they couldn't go anywhere. Also, Nick had found himself a girlfriend.

"She's weird," Jack complained. "You should see her Instagram posts. Every day her hair is a different color. And she hates me."

"Of course she hates you, sweetie. You pose a threat. She wants Nick all to herself." I had seen this day coming, and I had tried to prepare Jack for it. I knew it was just a matter of time before a girl would come along.

"I don't understand what he sees in her."

"He's a twenty-year-old male. Once you have a girlfriend, you'll understand." Even though I said the words, the thought of Jack having a girlfriend seemed impossible. That would require relating on a level that was completely foreign to him.

It was obvious that Jack's feelings had been piling up. How long they had gone unnoticed, and how long we had before he collapsed under their weight, I didn't know. There were still eight months between "Okay, this works," and the start of the fall semester. Would we make it? And if we did, would he be able to pick up where he left off, or would that be another impossible task, leading to more setbacks?

I didn't push back on Liam's counsel. I kept the details of my concern to myself: Jack's inability to understand that everyone was dealing with the same isolation; to have the presence of mind to do more than just sleep, deliver food, and watch sports; to have any motivation or level of consciousness whatsoever, any plans for his future. And I vowed, to myself of course, to try harder.

My concerns went far beyond the pandemic and Jack's forced downtime, though I couldn't quite pinpoint the challenges. He handles so much on his own, and yet, he can't seem to handle anything on his own. Trying to get him motivated, trying to explain to him where he's falling short, trying to help him understand that he needs to do more, it's all—*so hard*. It's constant friction, and frustration leads to letting him be. It's so much easier to give in than it is to do the incredibly tough job of parenting, which requires guidance and direction, laying down a set of laws and adhering to those laws, setting limits, and following through with consequences.

Letting him be doesn't help, but I can't ever seem to define the problem or identify his needs. If I could define it, solutions would come more easily. His Asperger syndrome is always right there on the surface, but still, it's so hard to see clearly. Outwardly, it appears that he's moving through life fairly well. In reality, he's moving along blindly. He is always going to be stuck halfway between assisted and accomplished. No one offers him the assistance he needs because no one can see that he needs it, and no one understands why he can't accomplish more because they can't see that he's trapped in place by an abstract force he can't control.

A few days later, I received a call from Andrew. "Are you at all worried about Jack?"

"Yeah," I admitted a bit too readily with a slight laugh, as if his question were a joke. "Every minute of every day. Aren't you?"

Andrew's reply was not immediate, almost as if the full gravity of Jack's situation was just now catching up with him.

What on earth had taken so long?

"Yeah, I'm really worried."

I didn't say anything, waiting for him to continue.

"He just doesn't seem to get it. I worry that delivering food is all he'll ever be capable of. I guess I understand it—he likes driving, he doesn't have a boss. But he can't make any kind of good living just delivering food."

"No, he can't," I said, giving Andrew's thoughts room to form themselves.

"With him not in school, he has no interaction with anyone. Will he ever have a girlfriend? Will he ever be able to live on his own?"

Andrew's thoughts began to spill all over the place. "He's just . . . he's. . . ."

"Oblivious," I offered.

"Yeah, he's oblivious. He has no clue what life on your own requires."

"I hear everything you're saying. Trust me, I've been agonizing over all the same thoughts myself," I said. "I don't know how to get him to understand that he needs to do more, that he needs to start preparing for life on his own."

"I don't think you can," he replied. "That's the Asperger's. It's. . . ."

"Detached. Not grounded in reality." I filled in the missing pieces. "There's a complete disconnect. He thinks that he's going to graduate and just magically get a job. Trying to get him to understand all the steps that are needed in between is impossible."

"Right. That's Asperger's. You can't put your finger on it, but every now and again, intangible things come across your plate that make you say, that's it—that is Asperger syndrome."

I floated my opinion cautiously. "You know, I'm wondering if it's partially his medication."

"What do you mean?"

"Well, is he oblivious—or is he numb?"

"I'm not following."

"Remember I told you I've been experiencing a lot of anxiety lately and I've had a few panic attacks? I've been taking antidepressants to combat that. I now know how they make you feel—how it's making Jack feel. They make you numb."

Andrew didn't respond.

"When my father died, I didn't cry. *At all*. Don't you think that's strange? My emotions were completely flatlined. That's the point of antidepressants. They numb you, so you're impervious to life's curveballs. I'm not so sure it's completely a matter of Jack being oblivious, I think he's just numb. And—"

"How much are you taking?" Andrew asked the question before I could get the words out.

"That's exactly what I was about to say. I'm taking twenty milligrams a day. Jack is taking *sixty*!"

Andrew was at a loss, and I was right there beside him. We had spent so many years avoiding medication, and those were probably the years when it would have helped Jack the most. Now, after years of him being on an unchanged regimen of drugs, we were left wondering how long he's been coasting along aimlessly. How much damage had we done by not being attentive enough, by assuming that Jack and medication were blissfully married? Would he be achieving more if he weren't still taking it? How hard would it be for him to stop? What if he stopped and we discovered he really does need it? Then what? Start over? And if we do need to start over, how much damage will be done in the interim?

Andrew and I agreed it was a change we needed to consider but wasn't something we should do during a pandemic. We would revisit the idea once life returned to normal.

CHAPTER 26
Girls, Girls, Girls

By the time school started again, Jack was ready to return. He wanted to go back, be around people, and be on campus. He was even looking forward to the mental challenge of academics. The dark clouds were clearing. The only piece that hadn't righted itself was Nick and the ever-annoying presence of the girlfriend. With Nick available only half the time, Jack decided to strike out on his own and find himself a girlfriend. He went from zero to sixty—in one afternoon. How else would a socially awkward, sexually inexperienced twenty-year-old interject himself into the dating world?

"I need your help," Jack said. "I need to wash an outfit for tonight."

An outfit? For tonight? Naturally, I assumed he had plans with Nick. But when did he start caring about how he dressed for Nick?

"You know how to do your laundry," I said. "Oh, wait, you want to wash them without wrecking them—is that what you mean?" I marveled at how I had become an expert at interpreting "Jackanese." After years of translating his obscure, inarticulate language, I could fill in the blanks anytime Jack opened his mouth. "Where are you headed?"

"I'm hanging with a girl."

"What? No, you're not." My disbelief insisted it wasn't true.

Jack informed me otherwise. "Her name is Logan."

A girl. Named Logan. More details, please.

"Where did you meet this girl?"

"On Bumble."

"A dating app?" I asked incredulously.

"Yeah. You should see how many matches I'm getting."

My mind went to sixteen different places at once. I allowed this news to seep in slowly, absorbing it with some level of practicality. If Jack was going on a date, I wanted to make sure he was prepared.

"You need to do two things," I informed him. "First, you need to take that filthy car of yours and run it through a car wash. Then, you need to get to a drugstore and buy a box of condoms."

There wasn't a second of hesitation. "Okay," he agreed.

"When you get home, I'm going to show you how to use them." *On second thought*—I flashed back to the day I tried to teach Jack how to drive—*maybe that's not a good idea.*

When I shared the news with Liam, he was stunned.

"I just want him to know what he's doing."

Liam's expression said it all. "People have been having sex for millions of years. How do you think we got here?"

I laughed. "True, but Jack is clueless about how life works. Do you really think he'll know how a girl works?"

Liam dismissed my worries with his standard response: "He'll be fine."

"So, what was she like?" I asked Jack when he returned from his date that evening.

"She was okay," he offered half-heartedly. "She wants to hang again tomorrow."

Really? Unfortunately, my optimism didn't last long. Jack's second date with Logan wasn't as successful.

"She said she's getting back together with her ex. Then she blocked me."

Feeling sudden disappointment, I paused before responding. Was that the truth? I could picture Jack sitting next to this girl with his head buried in his phone compiling a fantasy draft as she rambled on about her interests—and her deciding he was odd. I brushed it off for Jack's sake.

"Don't worry, sweetie. Someone else will come along."

Our conversation didn't skip a beat.

"I know," Jack went on. "I'm hanging with Olivia on Friday."

I stopped dead. "Who's Olivia?"

"She goes to Waldman College. She's on the basketball team."

"Now that sounds like a better match. You already have something in common." I always worried that setbacks hit Jack harder than the average person. But he had become adept at handling them. Perhaps it was due to the numbing effects of medication. In this case though, I was okay with that.

Before Jack had a chance to meet Olivia in person, Sophie entered the scene. It had only been four days since Jack needed to wash an outfit. Logan was in the rearview mirror, and Jack was looking ahead to both Olivia *and* Sophie. How was this happening?

After a quick Google search, I discovered that Bumble's platform allowed women to make the first move. How perfect for Jack. Girls were picking up slack in the one area where he was lacking, and Bumble's electronic nature suited him. He had mastered the fantasy sports draft and uncovered the secrets of food delivery. Surely, he could conquer the world of online dating. One side of me wanted to slow him down. This could get out of hand quickly. He was bound to get hurt. The other side of me wanted him to experience all parts—good and bad. How else would he ever find a relationship of substance?

The morning following Jack's date with Sophie, I heard him climbing the stairs to my office.

"Wilson is missing his undergarments," he said as he entered.

That wasn't what I expected to hear, but it was comforting to know that nothing had changed. Jack had just entered one of the most competitive stages of the race—and he was still stuck at the starting line, spewing nonsense like an eight-year-old. He volunteered his review of Sophie—two stars at best. "She was weird. I didn't really like her."

Jack moved on to Olivia, and the outcome was the same. "She was weird."

Next!

"I'm not diggin' the supermodel," Jack announced the following week.

Is my son okay? How could any hot-blooded male not dig the supermodel? Jack had showed me photos. She was stunning.

"Why not?"

"She drinks. And smokes. I'm not into that stuff."

"I'm glad you recognize that. The right girl will come along," I assured him.

"I'm taking a break for a while."

"Taking a break?" I laughed. "You just started!" What just happened here? Did the car run out of gas? Get a flat tire? Jack had gone from zero to sixty—right back to zero.

"I want to focus on school right now."

"Admirable, but I'm not buying it."

"It's just. . . ." Jack went on, trying to find the right explanation.

"I'm not very good at starting a conversation with someone I don't know. It feels weird."

"You want it to happen naturally."

"Yeah, I want to meet someone in one of my classes or something. . . ."

Now, *this* was the Jack that I knew. The Jack that was buzzing around on Bumble was the one imitating everyone else, just to fit in and keep up with Nick. The real Jack was seeing it for what it is— artificial and forced. Black-and-white. Fast forward two days though, and Jack's insistence that he was removing himself from the dating scene went right out the window. I received a text from him early that Saturday morning. I wasn't quite sure how to interpret his message.

"I went home w a 10/10 I met at the club last night. She was 23. She was from NYC, so it was only a one-time thing."

Deep breaths. Deep, *deep* breaths. I slowly typed out a simple, rational response. I can't be sure I spelled everything correctly because my hands had started to shake.

"What does that mean exactly?"

It meant what anyone with half a brain knows it meant. Jack had lost his virginity. Not waiting for a response, I dialed his number. After getting the specifics of where he had gone and who he had gone there with, I had to ask—because I couldn't help myself.

"Well, how was it?"

"I don't get what all the fuss is about."

Seriously?

"Are you sure . . . are you sure you did it right?" I asked with hesitation, not certain I should even be asking or how I would respond if the answer was no.

"Maybe not," he replied, his flat tone revealing his ignorance.

I felt instant regret for having asked. How would he know if he had done it right if he had never done it before? I wondered if the high level of antidepressants in his system had impacted his experience negatively, because that's what they do. I felt disappointment for him on a level I couldn't begin to express. I was happy that he had had his first sexual experience, the one that most boys spend years waiting for and all their energy trying to achieve. I was deeply saddened by the fact that he didn't seem to enjoy it. This should have been one of the biggest moments of his life and he was saying it wasn't all it's cracked up to be.

Even if his experience had been a success, what then?

There are few people with whom Jack can truly be himself. I worried that no girl would accept him for more than just a few days or weeks and be willing to tolerate all that comes along with his world. When a girl kisses him on the cheek, will he rub it off the same way he does with my kisses? How long would it be before she determines he's clueless and describes him to her friends as awkward and strange? How long would it be before Jack says exactly what he's thinking: that her new hairstyle looks stupid, or her dress is ugly? Will he ever be able to experience physical and emotional intimacy with a woman? Or will trying to get there be so exhausting that either he or she will give up? And if he does manage to establish a successful relationship, will he ever have children? What's the likelihood that his children will have Asperger's? If they do, will he be able to recognize it, *see* it? Will he know how to handle it?

I had to stop. I was getting twisted up in my thoughts unnecessarily. More likely, this was all for the best. Jack hadn't missed girls to this point, and he would be better off not having them as a distraction. He didn't deserve any additional critique of his ways—pressure to be someone he isn't—especially from girls. It was obvious he had gone down this path for two reasons: he was bored, and he wanted to be like Nick, just like he had wanted to emulate Thomas with base-ball. Neither was a sound reason for diving headfirst into the dating pool, and the last thing he needed was to become obsessed with girls in the same way he had gotten hooked on baseball.

Jack's sprint with the opposite sex was over. It had lasted two weeks.

I was never more relieved.

CHAPTER 27
Growing Pains

Jack's fleeting interest in females was nothing more than research to determine if they could fill the void that both Nick and school had left. He had waited eight months, impatiently, to get back to his "college experience," but now that life had mostly returned to normal, he was still unhappy. Something was missing and with each passing day Jack was growing more unsettled.

I'm not sure what prompted his change of heart about the small school that had made such a big impact on him. I'm certain all the stopping and starting hadn't been helpful, but maybe it just wasn't the right place. If there had been greater continuity, maybe his discontent would have surfaced sooner. Either way, the love affair was over.

"I hate this school," Jack confessed.

"You loved it at first. What's changed?"

"I hate the people here. They're all weirdos."

Jack's sentiment about the human race was always the same. Everyone is weird. They're all losers. With no understanding of how to relate—to anyone—it's no wonder he's consistently coming up against a wall. There's no part of life that doesn't require us to engage in relationships. Even meeting a stranger on the street means having an exchange. It requires a fundamental understanding of connection and how to behave. With no understanding of how to walk in step with others, Jack is constantly stepping around them. How can he possibly navigate a path forward if he's always taking a detour?

I might have worked harder to help Jack weather the social storm if it weren't for another issue that we couldn't ignore. He was completely uninterested in his classes. Like most kids, he hadn't known right from the start what he wanted to study. The only topic that ever interested him, the only one that ever brought him to life and had gotten more out of him than just the minimum was sports. In conversation, Jack typically offers up one-word, expressionless answers. Ask him about sports and he's a completely different person, speaking fluently and with confidence. The Jack that talks sports is animated and compelling, and if he could study it, this would undoubtedly put him on the road to success.

Sports management seemed like the logical choice. Unfortunately, it wasn't offered as a major at his current school, only as a minor, so Jack settled for that along with a major in business management. Almost none of his classes had anything to do with sports, and almost all of them were beyond his comprehension.

"My advisor suggested that I drop accounting," Jack informed me unapologetically.

"Again, Jack? This is the second time. What on earth is going on?"

I couldn't understand it. He was getting assistance from a tutor, but it clearly wasn't helping. He had emailed the professor six or seven times and gotten no response. No response, at all? I wanted to ask, do you have the right address? But of course he had the right address, so my next thought was, what the hell was wrong with this person? This young man was *trying*; wasn't that obvious? He was clearly looking to succeed, not necessarily with flying colors, but with a passing grade at least. I was paying this person's salary (a hefty one), so my son deserved one of two things—help from his educator, or a refund.

Then again, this is Jack we're talking about. I reminded myself to step back.

"Sweetheart, are you sure you didn't do anything to anger your teacher?"

"No, why would I do that?" Jack immediately became defensive, something he knows well, not being able to see that he might be wrong.

"You might not do it intentionally, but. . . ."

Before the words even came out, Jack did exactly what I was about to suggest he might have done—the very thing that might signal to his professor that this kid was lacking interest, that he's just like the rest of the kids failing her class, that he's a loser. . . .

He rolls his eyes.

Was this my fate? Was I destined to be forever stuck in that protective limbo between *My kid is not incompetent* and *Yes, I totally and completely, without any question whatsoever, understand that my kid is—unwaveringly difficult*? Uninterested. Inflexible. All those adjectives and more apply, it just depends on the day of the week, the hour of that day, and how many minutes have passed. The details weren't important. The fact remained that Jack needed to drop accounting for the second time.

"Maybe he just isn't cut out for college."

Andrew's words bore a hole through me—in that same way that every doctor's evaluation, teacher's note or email, and school report perforated my heart. I had already contemplated and anticipated this, but I wasn't willing to accept it.

Maybe he's not cut out for college. There are a million reasons why that might be true and only a handful to make me think otherwise. He doesn't have any desire. He lacks initiative. He simply doesn't want to conquer hurdles that stand in his way—he just wishes them away. They are a nonentity on his landscape. Acknowledging their presence would require thinking in dimensions beyond uncomplicated, undemanding black-and-white.

Still, I refused to give up on him. My rebuttal was simple; it was logical. "He's halfway through. The money is there. It's set aside. A degree, any degree, will only work *for* him. Not having that will be a definite strike against him right from the start. He needs every ounce of support we can give him, and if that support comes in the form of a $100,000 degree, well, then . . . that's what I'm going to give him." My urgency was surfacing. I was determined to stay afloat in this discussion, for Jack's sake.

I will *not* let him sink.

"I'm afraid of what will happen if he doesn't have that degree. I would rather take the chance, spend the money, and have him walk away with that piece of paper . . . the one that says . . . that he's capable. Because he is capable."

I wanted to believe that if he was in college and attending classes, he was worthy, deserving of something better. Having that piece of paper would make it so. Going to college says he has the ability to achieve something—anything. Not being in college signals a dead end ahead, a limited amount of road.

There was silence on the line.

Andrew knew I was right.

I knew he was right. Jack struggled in all spaces.

"I hear you," Andrew finally said, committing to weathering this never-ending storm right alongside me.

———

After much discussion and a visit to another small private school close to home, Jack decided to transfer. The new school had a great reputation for their sports management program, which was offered as a major, and its heavy emphasis on internships was a huge plus. The only way Jack was likely to get somewhere after graduation would be through an internship. Networking his way into anything was not his forte. All he needed to do was finish the semester without any more upset and focus on starting over come January.

With Jack out there behind the wheel of a car, I immediately take inventory any time my phone rings and I see that it's him. What day of the week is it? What time of day? Where should he be at this moment, and what could possibly have gone wrong? It's a way of preparing myself for the worst.

It was a few days before Christmas, late in the afternoon. Between work, the upcoming holiday, and moving Jack out of his dorm room, I was overwhelmed. My phone rang, and Jack's name appeared on the screen, and I knew. I don't know how—maybe the screen was dimmer than usual, maybe the ring was off just slightly—but my inner clairvoyant alerted me that what I was about to hear wasn't good.

As usual, he cut me off before I could say hello. "Hey, uh, I just had an accident."

I knew it. I could tell by his tone that it was bad.

"Is everyone okay?"

"Yeah."

"Where are you? How bad is it?"

"Pretty bad." Never ask Jack two questions at one time. He'll only answer the last one you asked.

"Where are you?"

"I'm at school."

More details, please! "At school where? What do you mean? Tell me what happened."

"This girl was pulled over in the parking lot, and I tried to go around her—and then, I don't know what happened. She went to turn into a parking space, and I hit her."

My mind went in twelve different directions at once. If this happened in a parking lot, how bad could it be? More importantly, if this girl was pulling into a parking space, how could Jack possibly have hit her? The only answer was that Jack was doing what he does best—being impatient and acting impulsively. I said I was on my way and hung up. Anger began a slow boil inside of me.

When I arrived at school, the police were already there. Jack was correct—it was bad. How could he have done so much damage to her front end in a parking lot? I did my best to remain calm as I examined the damage to both cars and said nothing.

After the officer walked them through the exchanging of numbers and insurance information, he gave them each a reference number for the accident report and was on his way—and we were left to deal with the aftermath. Jack's tire was punctured, which meant the car couldn't be driven. I called Andrew who, in turn, called his go-to shop for car repairs. Trust me when I say, they were all too familiar with Jack's car. The shop was closed for the day, and their tow truck wouldn't be able to get out until the morning. We would need to leave it in the school lot overnight with a promise from campus safety that they would keep an eye on it. Before emptying the car of any valuables, I took what pictures I could in the fading light.

It wasn't until Jack and I were in my car that I unloaded on him.

"Are you *out of your mind* trying to pass someone in a parking lot like that? You could have killed someone!" Every possible scenario ran through my mind. The more I contemplated what Jack had done, the angrier I became and the more petrified I grew about what this meant for him, and us.

Jack should not be operating a motor vehicle.

He doesn't make good decisions. He's impatient. He's impulsive. All of that adds up to disaster. I know I should have stopped, but I couldn't help myself. "Do you want to spend your life behind bars because you're in too much of a hurry and end up killing someone?"

Jack smashed his fist on the dashboard, screaming, "Why does this keep happening to me?"

"Because you don't think!"

I pulled into the driveway and before I stopped, Jack got out, slamming the door behind him. He went straight to his room, and I went straight to the phone. It took Andrew just two rings to answer, but I was already in tears.

"What are we going to do?" I cried. "We can't let him keep driving. He could kill someone, and then what? And if he can't drive, what does life look like for him?"

I was getting ahead of myself, yes. But as I recounted the details of what Jack had told me as well as the damage to both cars, Andrew was growing as upset and concerned as I was. He didn't want to jump to any conclusions, though.

"Listen," he said calmly, "just back off a little bit, and let me talk to him. I want to get his side of the story before we go overboard. I don't want to punish him if it wasn't his fault."

"I don't know how it couldn't be his fault," I protested, agreeing nonetheless to scale it back.

"Also, can you send me any pictures that you took?"

I forwarded the few photos that I had taken, and Andrew called me back almost immediately.

"This isn't his fault," he stated triumphantly.

"What do you mean?"

"There's not a single scratch on his front end. All the damage to his car is along the passenger side, and her front end is completely destroyed. It's simple physics. If there's no damage to his front end and hers is destroyed, then she hit him."

"But . . . how. . . ." As I processed what he was telling me, a wave of nausea overwhelmed me.

How could I be so stupid?

I knocked on Jack's door before turning the knob, and as I entered his room, he rolled over on his bed away from me, wiping tears from his eyes.

"Jack, can you tell me exactly what happened? I think . . . maybe . . . I think I may have been wrong. Please tell me exactly what happened, so I can be clear."

"This girl was pulled over in the lot, and people do that all the time at school. I thought she was waiting to pick up someone. She didn't have any turn signals on, she was just stopped, so I went around her and when I did, she tried to turn into a parking space. That's when I hit her."

"Oh, Jack, I am *so* sorry. I was completely wrong." I showed him the pictures, pointing to the evidence. "You couldn't have hit her. There's no damage to the front end of your car. *She hit you.*"

I felt sick, dizzy with shame. How could I possibly have betrayed him like that? I'm his mother. I should be the first one to have his back, take his side, defend him to the death. Instead, I made an immediate assumption that he was at fault. Hadn't I learned anything over the years, watching teachers and coaches automatically assume that Jack wasn't capable, that each failure must be his fault? Why don't I ask more questions before jumping to conclusions? Why don't I have more faith in him? He is capable—of so much—and I continuously fail to give him the credit he deserves.

When we returned to school the following morning to meet the tow truck, I took as many photos of Jack's car as possible. I wanted to be certain the insurance company could see that my son was not at fault. I also needed the proof for myself, a visual to refer to the next time I felt faith in my son slipping. This had been a major wake-up call for Jack and for me as well. I handled the situation horribly, and I needed to reverse my lack of trust.

Once Jack's car was on its way to the repair shop, we packed up his belongings, returned his room key, and bid farewell to the first half of his college experience. It hadn't gone as planned, but nothing ever did with Jack.

Wanting him to get acclimated at the new school quickly, we urged Jack to live on campus, at least for his first semester. It would enable him to get familiar with his surroundings, meet new people, and hopefully make a few friends. Figuring he could handle the transition, I took my hands off the wheel.

"How's school going, sweetie? How are your grades?"

"Good."

"Are you sure?"

"Yeah, everything's fine."

Of course it is. Out of sight, out of mind!

"What about friends? Have you made any new friends?"

"Not really. Everyone here is kind of weird. I've been going to the gym, though."

"To work out? Are you thinking about getting back into baseball?"

"No." A second of silence passed. "Maybe."

"Why don't you look into club baseball?"

"Maybe."

I was trying hard not to push, reminding myself daily, *He is capable, and I am going to have faith.* But he seemed down, and I was growing concerned that transferring hadn't been the best idea. He was struggling just as much socially in this new space, and I wasn't convinced that he felt any greater interest in his classes. I feared his grades weren't exactly "good" as he said they were. Even though Jack rarely spoke with expression, I always knew when he needed someone to throw him a line. If he could just get involved with an activity, especially one he loved, he would meet kids with a common interest, and the interaction would distract him from all the difficulty he was facing. Jack feeds off the positive, but he needed to find it first in order to feast.

Have faith.

CHAPTER 28
For Appearances' Sake

Some people need love; others need adventure. Jack needs an obsession. It's a core component of his being. For most of his life, that obsession was baseball, a solution with which we were perfectly happy. It kept him outside and active, it taught him the meaning of teamwork and the importance of perseverance, and it gave him an opportunity to shine. It appeared as a perfectly healthy facet of growing up. But baseball was no longer a part of his days.

Thankfully, Jack's friendship with Nick filled much of the gap. I decided it was best not to overthink it and to just be grateful. Making friends had never come easily for Jack. Hell, it had never come at all—except for Nick. They were like-minded people, standing on common ground and sharing the same interests. Nick was a willing recipient of Jack's attention, and that suited Jack just fine. It wasn't until Nick's girlfriend came along that Jack started looking for his next big thing, a new activity to hook onto and conquer.

"Remember that model I dated?" Jack asked one afternoon. "She makes tons of money. She said she has close to $60,000 in the bank. Sometimes she makes three or four grand just for one shoot."

"Wow, that's a lot," I said. "Maybe you should try modeling."

As soon as the words left my mouth, I knew we had just entered a new phase. Jack didn't know it yet, but I did. This time the air hadn't shifted on its own. This time, I was the one responsible for generating the force that was about to barrel through and disrupt life. And it was too late to reel it back in.

"Yeah, maybe. Do you think you could take some photos of me?"

"Of course. I would love to." And that was the truth, even though I was fully aware I had just created a monster.

That Jack would even contemplate modeling came as a surprise. Somewhere around the age of seven, his smile broke, and he decided that cameras were not his friend. I had taken thousands of photos of him as a baby and a toddler, but as he grew older, capturing any sort of normal expression was impossible. Smiling for the camera appeared almost painful. He lacked the ability to do it naturally, clenching his teeth every time, and he often adopted weird poses. Maybe it would be different now that he was older.

I did a bit of research, visiting the websites of various modeling agencies and educating myself about current styles. Urban chic appeared to be the popular look—think serious, almost cocky expressions in grungy, ripped clothing, while leaning effortlessly against a fire escape. After studying numerous examples, I decided I was ready to give it a shot, so I took Jack to a nearby train station. It was Sunday, so only a few trains were running, and they were mostly morning and evening. We would have a window of time midafternoon when the platform would be empty.

Jack completely surprised me. As a model, he was unbelievable. He was patient and accommodating, and he seemed to know exactly how to move so the camera caught his best angles. It was a hot, humid afternoon, and not once did he complain about the heat. He had managed to put his intolerance aside, and within a couple of hours, I was confident we had captured "that look." Armed with a small portfolio of amateur (albeit sensational) photos, Jack began making submissions to various agencies.

"I got a response from Impressions. They're in New York City. They want me to come in for an interview," he announced one evening.

Of course they're interested in you, baby; you're an absolute stud!

I was thrilled for Jack, but Impressions was just one of thousands of agencies, and I had no idea if they were legitimate. I wanted to keep his expectations in check without raining on his parade. He was genuinely excited about modeling, and with Nick distracted by his girlfriend, it was important for him to try new things. He needed another outlet, an interest he could throw his heart and soul into, and if he could make a buck or two in the process, all the better.

Jack booked an appointment, and I agreed to take him.

It was a long Friday afternoon and evening. It took us almost three hours to get into the city. Jack's appointment lasted all of thirty minutes and our Italian dinner on Restaurant Row not that much longer, and then it was a two-and-a-half-hour ride back home. I knew that would be the case. Heading into Manhattan on any Friday afternoon is an exercise in extreme patience.

It had been a great ride up, though. Jack was at his absolute best. He was excited about the opportunity ahead of him, and he was talkative in that mature, concise manner he so infrequently exhibits. The conversation was fun, it was meaningful, and it actually made sense. I said a little prayer to myself that his demeanor would hold through his interview.

The agency's "corporate office" was nothing more than a closet on the twelfth floor of a rundown building with dim lighting buzzing overhead, torn leather furniture longing for an occupant, and a doorman who was nowhere to be found. I immediately doubted the legitimacy of Impressions Modeling & Talent Studio; nonetheless, we were there, and we were, surprisingly, on time.

Jack pushed on the hollow wood door marked 1205, and we entered a tiny but bright corner office that was divided into three even tinier spaces—the waiting area, an office, and a photo studio I could easily have mistaken for a phone booth except that it had a couple of professional lights and no phone. Dance music was pounding through tiny speakers hung high in each of the four corners, enough to encourage me to remain positive.

A waifish young man with not a hair out of place, brilliant teeth, and a carefully orchestrated combination of garments, peered out of the office to let us know he would be with us in a minute. Jack and I sat on a lime-green loveseat that was almost too predictable for the setting. We had barely gotten comfortable when Aaron stepped out again and invited us into his office.

Aaron didn't waste any time; he was all business. He asked Jack all the obvious questions—weight, height, did he play any sports (did Jack ever not play any sports?), experience with modeling (uh, none), why he was interested in pursuing it (okay, I will admit, Jack surprised me with this one). Jack very articulately told this curious young man that he wanted to try something new (fair enough)—and that he was interested in traveling.

I stole a quick look at my son.

I always had the highest of hopes for Jack, wanting to believe anything was possible. But I always questioned, what does *that*—the highest of hopes—look like? The thought of Jack traveling, even just wanting to travel, thrilled me. But on his own? Was he capable? Or was Jack really saying that I would like to travel, provided my mother accompanies me? I suppose in this particular moment I was getting ahead of myself, but getting ahead—or more importantly, staying ahead—was a skill I had been fine-tuning for the last twelve or thirteen years.

Aaron took it all in, nodding his head, making notes, agreeing with every bit of information.

Sizing up his next sucker.

Once he was finished cross-examining Jack, he went on to explain the company business model, the nuts and bolts, the "This will only cost you X amount, and look at all that you get" fine print.

"It's simple—" Aaron stated matter-of-factly.

"You get out of it what you put in," Jack offered, cutting him off.

Wait a minute—let's back this thing up. Is this young man sitting next to me my young man?

I was so impressed with my son in those few moments—the one who so seldomly makes eye contact with strangers and has zero understanding of the nuances of banter. Rather than shutting down, Jack went with it and danced circles around Aaron.

WOW. This is a first.

As we listened to Aaron's sales pitch—an initial investment of $500, which included a "professional" photo shoot (right here in the corporate studio!), and a $40 monthly subscription fee that would provide access through their portal to thousands of modeling jobs—I could tell Jack and I were clearly hearing two different versions.

Jack instantly jumped at the opportunity. "I want to do this."

"Jack, let's think about this for a minute." While he saw it as an opportunity, I saw it for what it likely was, a scam—a business scheme designed solely to make money rather than build modeling careers.

"I want to do this. I'll pay for it."

The last thing I wanted Jack to do was throw away his hard-earned money. The savings he had built up over the last several months were quickly dwindling, thanks to his car troubles. As he persisted, my thoughts kicked into overdrive—how many tens of thousands of dollars did we throw at baseball? Was that wasted money? Of course not. He loved every minute of it. If he were to get just one or two modeling jobs, he would earn his investment back, and without question, the experience would be invaluable, especially for Jack. Casting calls would give him experience with the interview process. And if he did land a job, needing to pose or act out a role would require him to step out of his comfort zone, which was even more valuable. Maybe it would end up going nowhere, but we would never know without trying. Or maybe, like baseball, this would become his raison d'etre.

"Tell you what, we'll split it."

Jack beamed. "Okay, cool. Thanks, Mom."

After signing on the dotted line and a swipe of my credit card, we stepped back out into the afternoon bustle that signaled the arrival of another weekend in New York City, with Jack carrying his welcome packet from the agency tightly under his arm. My fish out of water was their newest potential talent.

"Well, are you excited?" I asked, barely able to contain myself.

"Yeah, it'll be cool."

I stopped in my tracks. What was suddenly cool was not this new-found opportunity—but Jack's tone. The enthusiasm he had been showering on Aaron moments ago had, without warning, vaporized into thin air. He was dropping from his high like a rock.

"Are you hungry?"

"Yeah, I'm starving."

He was spent; I knew it. The only thing that could salvage the remainder of our day was food. At twenty years old, his needs were still so much like those of a toddler—basic—with complete intolerance for discomfort. Wet diaper? Instant tears. Lack of sleep? Bouncing off walls. Empty stomach? Extreme irritability bordering on complete and utter breakdown.

I tried quickly to get my bearings. I was unfamiliar with this part of the city and wasn't sure in which direction to head. Walking aimlessly could easily be the kiss of death. I suddenly remembered that Restaurant Row ran between Eighth and Ninth Avenue. We were just a block away, and surely we would find a place where Jack could get a burger and wings.

"I think I might want spaghetti and meatballs," Jack said, softening a bit as he realized that food was within reach.

Oh, for God's sake.

"I'm sure we can find an Italian restaurant somewhere," I told him, containing my frustration while asking myself, why, of all nights, did he suddenly have to deviate from his standard menu of a cheeseburger, no lettuce, tomato, or onion and DEFINITELY NO PICKLE and wings, buffalo sauce on the side—and want Italian???

As we turned the corner, the first restaurant in sight was—God, thank you for hearing me—Italian. Not exactly a restaurant, it was more of an old rowhouse turned eating establishment. We walked up the two or three steps into a narrow, dark space. Not a soul was there—not even staff. The only sign of life was the voice of Frank Sinatra floating toward us.

"Hello?" I called out.

No response. Jack and I looked at one another, shrugged our shoulders, and quietly escaped before being found out, laughing as we stumbled back into the fading light of early evening. At least his mood hadn't soured totally.

Continuing up the block, we passed a high-dollar steakhouse, a

Mexican cantina, both Chinese and Japanese restaurants, and easily three or four burger joints.

"General Tso's?" I suggested.

"No, let's just keep going."

It was another block and a half before we found a second Italian restaurant. We scanned the menu posted at the door, noting the spaghetti and meatball option. Both patrons and staff were alive and well inside, so we agreed this was our best option. Jack was on the brink, and I didn't want him going over.

"I think I'm going to have a burger instead," Jack announced as soon as we were seated.

Are you fucking kidding me?

Okay, excuse my French. But Jack has no filters, why should I? Despite the long drive home ahead of us, I intended to order a drink promptly.

To speed up the process, I decided to keep things simple and have a burger as well. The house burger, with its caramelized onions, roasted tomatoes, and pesto sounded enticing, and it would enable us to order quickly.

I don't say this frequently, but I think Jack was clear in his request. He wanted a plain cheeseburger, not the house burger, and he didn't want lettuce, tomato, onion, or a pickle. Granted, he had to make a concession on the cheese—you're not going to get American when you're in an Italian restaurant—so there was some back-and-forth before he agreed to provolone, but he was clear in his description of what he wanted.

I knew as soon as the waiter set our plates down that something had been lost in translation. I watched painfully as Jack dissected the soggy mound in front of him. First, there was the cautious lift of the bun, followed promptly by the emphatic flick of the caramelized onions that he discovered hiding below it, which were *not* supposed to be there.

"This is disgusting. Why would they do this? Who puts onions on a burger?"

I knew at that moment that I had lost my hold completely.

The other Jack, the one that had sat next to me in the car for two and a half hours earlier in the day, the Jack that had been so engaging, the Jack that I have always wanted Jack to be—mature, aware, accommodating—that Jack had slipped from my grasp. Every now and again, *that* Jack, the one that I know is in there somewhere, rises to the surface and floats along steadily for a short while. Eventually, inevitably, he sinks back into his abyss.

"Sweetheart, just eat it. It's not going to kill you." I reached across the table to try and rid his burger of the perceived poison, but that only angered him more.

"I'm not eating this. Can I order something else?"

"No, Jack, just eat it." He was being unreasonable. I refused to give in.

"I'm not eating it. The waiter's an idiot."

Then go dissect the waiter.

Jack continued his assault on the tainted meat, eyeing each piece of onion suspiciously before shoving it to the edge of his plate. Realizing his fork was now tainted, he picked up the bare patty with his fingers and reluctantly took a bite. I glared at him, grabbed my own fork, and threw it across the table at him.

"Seriously, Jack, grow up and use a fucking fork," I hissed.

A sharp look from the gentleman at the table next to us indicated his disapproval just as the fork fell into Jack's lap. Jack burst out laughing.

I was mortified.

Yet. . . .

There was something about the purity of Jack's reaction, the absolute honesty of it—the obvious-to-him-only humor of having a fork thrown at him, the "I'm pissed that my very clearly ordered *plain* cheeseburger arrived with all this shit on it, and why doesn't anyone else see how ridiculous that is?" attitude that managed to cast a crack in the hard shell that had formed over me in the last half hour.

A slight smile slipped across my face without permission.

Jack caught it, making it too late to reel it in.

I caved and burst out laughing too.

My Jack from earlier in the day never resurfaced. He was irretrievably lost, but it wasn't the first time. I've grown accustomed to the disappointment I feel every time he slides away, but I've also come to accept that *that* Jack will never be a constant. The ride home was not as brutal as dinner, but it was tiring in ways that only Jack could make it. There was no more meaningful conversation, only senseless babble. No more thoughtful moments, only deflection.

When we finally reached home, I was happy to hear Jack say that he was going to Nick's. I didn't care what they would be doing; I didn't care what time he would be home. I was exhausted and I wanted to decompress. Hearing music from the patio, I knew where to find Liam. I grabbed a beer and headed out to join him.

"Hey, how was your day?" he asked.

Suddenly realizing just how worn I was, I collapsed in the chair beside him, grateful for a warm evening, the lively music, and promise of easy conversation.

"It was good," I replied, pausing before offering more. I gave Liam a complete recount of Jack's interview and the decision to give it a chance. He agreed that it was worth a shot, and if nothing else, it offered the potential for some great experience.

As the beer found its way into my bloodstream, I began to soften.

"I just don't get it. I don't understand him." I paused, then added, "I feel like I am forever saying that. Will I ever understand him?"

"What do you mean exactly?"

"He was great on the way up. He was excited, he was talking like a normal twenty-year-old kid, and he was downright impressive in our meeting. But then something happened. A switch flipped. He reverted to his usual rigid self, with total disregard for decorum, and then he began asking questions about Thomas, as if he was determined to find a weak spot. It made no sense whatsoever."

"Maybe it was just anxiety catching up with him. The thought of modeling might be intimidating to him, and by pointing out someone else's weaknesses, he's taking attention away from the possibility that he might fail."

That was a heavy thought, one that I needed time to process. It made sense, but I just couldn't imagine Jack being that calculating. And if he was worried about failing, why even try? The idea had been his from the start. Why go through the aggravation and the cost? If Jack were to get into modeling full-time, nothing about it would be easy or cheap. It would require a huge investment to see any kind of return. I had no answers in that moment, or even in the weeks that followed, but I wasn't going to deny Jack this opportunity. It hadn't been a perfect start with baseball, either.

It didn't take long to figure out that Impressions was a bust. Of course they had responded to Jack's photo submission. That was their business model—take anyone and everyone. It was a win-win situation for them. After the initial deposit, and every month after that, they got paid, while their so-called talent got nothing. At least, Jack got nothing. None of the job opportunities were actual jobs. It boiled down to being a social media platform where wannabe photographers could exchange time with wannabe models. There were no credible paying jobs of any substance, nothing upon which an up-and-coming model could build a portfolio or use as a springboard to start a career.

I suggested to Jack that he research all the modeling agencies in the Pennsylvania, New Jersey, and New York area. "See if any feel like a good fit, and submit your photos. What do you have to lose?"

He agreed and set to work. A few days later, Jack received a response from an agency that sounded promising.

"They want to know if I have any personality shots. What does that mean?"

"They want photos that show emotion and expression—different reactions."

Jack gave me that blank stare, the one that says, "I don't get it."

I further explained to him that it's about acting, pretending you're in a certain situation and reacting. Maybe you laugh; maybe you look amazed or thoughtful. I promised that come the weekend, I would take some personality shots of him so he could understand it better and get some practice.

The entire exercise was a debacle.

"Hold it to your ear," I instructed, handing him his cell phone, "and laugh as if someone just told you something funny. You know, pretend something is funny."

"I don't get it," he stated unapologetically.

"Pretend you're talking to Nick, and he just said something funny."

Jack held the phone to his ear, appearing utterly confused. He wasn't quite sure what expression he should make, and he didn't comprehend the need for acting. The idea that he was supposed to laugh when there wasn't anyone on the other end of the line baffled the hell out of him.

"How do you not get this?" I screamed.

"It's just not funny."

"*Pretend* it's funny!"

"I don't get what's funny about that."

After an hour of pulling my hair out, I gave up. Jack just wasn't getting it. Acting involves role-playing, much like social interaction, and it's anything but literal. It involves make-believe, and Jack's black-and-white world had always been at odds with such behavior. We managed to capture a few poses, but the process was so painful, I wasn't at all confident that Jack could pull it off at a bona fide photo shoot.

Jack wasn't about to give up, though. Despite our less than successful attempt at establishing personality, he threw himself into his new career. He discovered models on social media that he wanted to emulate and followed them. He regularly practiced various poses in the mirror and wanted to get in front of my camera whenever I had the time. He also spent a fair amount of time contacting agencies.

Eventually, Jack was invited to join the talent pool at another agency with a solid reputation and of much higher caliber than Impressions. However, they required that he schedule a professional shoot with one of their contracted photographers to get the standard shots for his portfolio. It pained me deeply, but I agreed to spend the $1,900, reasoning that it would give him a good understanding of the realities of being on a live set. We had spent a small fortune on baseball over the years; this was no different. Jack was engaged and excited about the opportunity—and for the moment, he was happy. That was worth any amount of money.

We headed up to the city for a second time, and once again, Jack was on fire. He had adopted a mature attitude, and his performance was every bit professional. As I watched him twist and turn under the lights and engage in articulate conversation with the photographer, the irony of it was not lost on me. In front of the camera, he appeared grown-up, together, no longer an awkward young man incapable of social interaction. *He's a really good-looking kid*, I thought. Based on appearance, he's a ten. See a picture of him and you would say, "Wow, he's the image of success!" He's hot, handsome, stunning. But he's also Jack. And Jack is a multidimensional, complicated creature that's rarely as pleasing as he appears.

How long would this last? How long would it be before Jack's dimensions rose to the surface, before the photo studio was too hot or too cold, before lunch was brought in and there wasn't a single thing that Jack would eat, before he couldn't understand what was being asked of him on set? If he were successful, maybe he would be able to pull it off, like he had always done with baseball. With the beginnings of a professional portfolio and representation by a legitimate agency, all Jack needed was one job so he could start to build upon that foundation. Just one opportunity to taste success and give him a goal to chase. Just one chance to do what he had always done on the field—crush it. But modeling was not about to provide Jack with instant gratification in the same way baseball had, and it was just a matter of time before he reverted to what he has always obsessed over most.

CHAPTER 29
Rude Awakening

"I'm on the club team." I could hear that buzz in Jack's voice. The one that says, "I was made for this, and I can't wait to get moving again."

"Really, just like that?"

"Yeah, they don't have enough people, so there aren't any tryouts. Practice starts next week."

"That's great, sweetie. I'm so happy for you!" I hung up the phone feeling relief. The change of schools hadn't gone as smoothly as I had hoped, and with Jack's "modeling career" not gaining any traction, I worried that he was lost at sea. Baseball was the one and only thing that could save him from drowning.

It was Tuesday of the following week when my phone rang sometime just before three o'clock. It was Jack, and I immediately ran down my mental checklist. It was his first day of practice, so I assumed he was at school and this call would be benign.

"Hel—" I started to say.

"Hey, my car is smoking."

"What do you mean, your car is smoking? Where are you?"

"I'm right around the corner. My brakes stopped working, and now I'm on the shoulder. The car is smoking."

Being forced to process this information instantly, in real time, threw my heart onto a racetrack. What could be wrong with his car? And what is he doing out this way, near home, and not at school? There was no time to consider the answers.

"Get out of the car. Immediately. I'm on my way."

I grabbed my keys and tried my best to stay calm. Knowing Jack, he could say the car is smoking, and it could be overheating. Jack could also say the car is smoking and it might be fully engulfed in flames. Before I even reached the intersection, I could see the smoke. Thick, black smoke.

His car was not overheating.

The moment I saw Jack's car on fire, a million thoughts raced through my head. First, that car is toast. Second, everything in it is toast. Oh God, that brand new laptop, the one I haven't finished paying for yet—*toast*! And the biggest one—my baby had been in that car—that's now on fire!

Jack ran over to meet me. I told him to call 911.

"I already did," he reported calmly.

"Really? Okay, good." I was shocked that Jack had had the presence of mind to place such a call. More so, I admired how he was maintaining his composure, unlike me.

Both the police and fire department arrived on the scene within minutes, and in no time, the fire was under control. Jack's car had been reduced to its shell, and there was nothing more we could do other than gather those personal items the firemen were able to retrieve and leave it behind for the tow truck.

I called Andrew as I was taking Jack back to school, to his first practice, for which he was now going to be late. "I have some bad news. You might want to sit down for this."

"What's the matter? Is everything okay?"

"Jack's car is totaled. It caught on fire."

"What happened? Is he okay?"

Andrew's need to know and understand was urgent and desperate, and it was completely my fault. I had set him up. What I should have said, with a note of levity, was, "You're not going to believe this," because the truth was, it was downright comical. Jack's car seemed to have been cursed from the start.

I should have been laughing, but that feeling of always being one step away from calamity with Jack looms over me. Clearly, I hadn't learned anything from his accident or grown at all as a parent, because I failed to see that this horrifying scene—his car engulfed in flames—was a freak event and not his doing. It had just come out of the shop after his accident, and it's possible it hadn't been repaired properly, right?

No, I was certain it had to have been some shortcoming in Jack's driving skills, or his lack of awareness regarding the condition of his car. Jack must have done something stupid that caused this horrible outcome. I was convinced of it. Even though Andrew insisted that there was no way he could have caused this, I still had significant doubt.

It was *not. . . his. . . doing.*

Jack called me later in the day, after practice, to talk about everything. Our conversation took on a life of its own, turning in as many directions as he has over the years.

"I just wasn't expecting this," he said with a hint of bewilderment. I heard his words differently, though. What I heard was his most recent mantra: "Why does this keep happening to me?"

"Sweetie, this is life. Things happen unexpectedly every day." He didn't respond immediately, so I knew I had his attention. "All you can do is try your best to be prepared. Stay ahead of all the bad things that can happen."

"What do you mean by that?"

"Think about every choice you make, before you make it. Think about what might go wrong if you don't make good choices. Plan ahead. Remember what I told you? If you fail to plan, you plan to fail." I knew he was listening and could feel my concern, even though the direct moment of fear—that moment when you see your son's car in flames—had passed.

Jack then offered an unexpected thought. "What you said about Uncle Joe the other day, and him dying unexpectedly, that stuck with me, how one day we're here and the next day we're a pile of ashes."

I paused. Lucid Jack had floated to the surface, and a familiar sentiment settled over me—I wanted to hold him there as long as possible.

"It's true. At any moment, something could happen to either one of us. Something unexpected, just like today. It's all part of life. The more you experience days like today, the better prepared you'll be for the next time that something unexpected happens." I paused for a moment before adding, "Seeing your car in flames today scared the shit out of me."

"I'm going to live a long, healthy life, Mom." He was so matter-of-fact in his response, and his assuredness caught me off guard. Jack is never sure about anything.

"Good. You put your mind on that. If you put your mind on it, then it will happen." His adamance comforted me. He believes it to be true. I should believe it too.

"Love you," he said, this time with sincerity, not out of habit.

"Love you too, bud."

I hung up feeling relieved. This event had scared him, even if it wasn't as visible on the surface as my own fear. I knew it impacted him, and while the impact was uncomfortable, it was a positive.

He had learned something. Life is full of the unexpected. Nothing is guaranteed to last. Just when everything seems okay, expect it to change.

As much as I wanted to move on, I couldn't ignore that I had made the same mistake again. I couldn't understand why it's so hard for me to have faith in Jack. Why do I always think things are somehow his fault?

You're not right; therefore, what went wrong must be your fault.

Was I blaming him for having Asperger syndrome? Or was I looking to be relieved of the responsibility of being his mother? If it's his fault, it's not mine.

Those thoughts—that I was faulting him for being who he is, and that I didn't want to be associated with all his destruction—frightened me more than seeing his car in flames. Again, I was betraying him, and I felt an inexplicable self-loathing, a deep-seated melancholy at the thought of deserting him. There will be things in life that are his fault, but having Asperger syndrome is not one of them. And he is my son, my baby. If Jack was left to fend for himself through life, he would not survive—and *that* would be my fault.

I told myself that the complete opposite was true. Something being his fault is proof that he needs and deserves accommodation. If something is his fault, then I can hold onto him for just a bit longer and justify every bit of indulgence and all my years of coddling. Something being his fault preserved my rights as his mother to go above and beyond to protect him, love him, and give him the extra that he needs. At all times.

But why did it have to be anyone's fault?

Because it went so much deeper than this one event. I hadn't realized it until that moment, or maybe I had but lacked the courage to acknowledge it. Despite having made a conscious decision to end my marriage, I was still so weak. I had wrongly surrendered myself and all my beliefs and mistakenly accepted that Andrew was right all those years ago. I had spent almost twenty years living under the weight of my own guilt for having left him and destroying our family, for upsetting Jack's world, filling it with inconsistency and instability. I had allowed myself to believe that *everything* was my fault.

Seeing his car in flames that afternoon left a heavy mark, and I couldn't rid myself of it, any more than Jack can rid himself of his disability. It was going to take a tremendous amount of effort, but I knew it was time to burn one thought into my consciousness—I am not a terrible mother.

CHAPTER 30
Reset

"How dare you do that without consulting me first! You have no right to throw my money away like that!" I was so angry with Jack I couldn't bear to look at him, but I forced myself to stare him down. I wanted to see him squirm. *This* is why I don't have faith in him. *This* had not been some uncontrollable misfortune that landed in his lap. *This* was his fault and no one else's.

His expression, remorseful and downtrodden, said it all. The leaves had once again fallen off the tree.

I had been asking Jack repeatedly how his classes were going, and each time his response was the same, that they were going well. I didn't want to hover, because he had already been through the major transition of going from high school to college. This should not have been as tough. The two colleges were so similar. He should have known what to expect and what was expected of him. I assumed he wouldn't make the same mistakes twice.

I had taken my hands off the wheel because I felt I owed it to him. I was giving him room to be an adult, to take responsibility. I had allowed him the freedom to throw his energy into modeling and when that didn't work, toward getting back into baseball. What I should have been doing the whole time was the one thing I said I wasn't going to do—stand over him with a watchful eye to ensure it didn't all fall apart. That's what he needed, and I failed to provide it because I wanted to believe in him.

It wasn't until it was over that I discovered his first semester after transferring was an outright catastrophe. He failed two of his five classes and withdrew from another, without saying a word. I flew off the handle. It amounted to nothing more than wasted time and money, and suddenly I was questioning if I had enough to see him through to graduation. I couldn't understand why he had lied about his grades. It wasn't like him.

His only success the entire semester had been on the baseball field where, naturally, he was a standout—not that I was exactly happy about it. He had completely disregarded his responsibilities so he could throw himself back into baseball.

Because sports schedules still weren't back to normal following the pandemic, Jack's club team had just one game the entire semester. When you only have one opportunity in a season to make an impression on the coaching staff, you'd better make it a good one, and of course Jack wasn't about to let anyone down. During that one game, he successfully pitched five out of seven innings, and with four at bats, he hit a double, a single, an in-the-park home run, *and* a triple. If that's not enough to catch the attention of the school's head coach, I don't know what is—but all that effort was wasted.

"Don't you get it, Jack? You had a shot at making the school team come fall, a chance to play *college* baseball. But now you can't because your grades are so low!"

"I'll get them up. I promise."

He sounded convinced, but his words didn't reassure me. I needed to step back, get ahold of my anger, and think through where Jack had been—and where he was headed. I couldn't afford to have him hopscotching all over with his college education. It was like every other phase of his life. The patterns were the same.

I realize now that at thirteen, he hadn't been resistant to move out of our old neighborhood, because he had never developed a solid circle of friends. Moving to a new home in a different town would be a fresh start.

Transitioning from middle school, where he never settled into anything other than baseball, to high school, meant more people and new opportunities to make friends. It would be a fresh start.

High school required that Jack squeeze a square peg into the baseball brothers' round hole, and when it didn't fit, he began looking ahead to college. It would be a fresh start.

Once college started, it was stop and start all over the place.

I could no longer recall where Jack had been for any given fall or spring. It started out in the typical manner, then stopped with the arrival of the pandemic, transformed into some sort of half-assed hybrid assembly, only to come to a complete halt again for eight months. And then once there was a return to some semblance of normalcy, Jack decided he needed to transfer to a new school. It was exactly as it had always been with baseball—moving from one team to the next, no continuity, always searching for an ever-elusive comfort zone. A fresh start.

Life needed a reset.

"I just don't know how to define it," I said to friends at dinner one evening.

"But he's high functioning."

"Yes, he is high functioning. And that's the problem," I added quickly.

I had heard the same response from them so many times, I had lost count. My appreciation for their positive viewpoint was tainted by my resentment over their lack of understanding. They don't get it. They can't get it. In order to get Jack and understand how, and to what level he functions, they would need to spend their days with him. Every day. For twenty years. And even then, they might not get it. Perception and reality rarely align when we're talking about Jack.

He's attending class and doing his work. He must be a good student.

He has almost one hundred thousand miles on his car. He must be a good driver.

He's interacting with kids from school. He must be adjusting to college life and finding his way socially.

He's high functioning.

He must be normal!

Normal.

I can't tell you how much I've grown to hate that word. "Conforming to a standard; usual, typical, or expected." I've been trapped in a never-ending search for the expected, some sort of standard that just doesn't exist with Jack. He's always one layer away, aloof or detached in some fashion—a master of the unexpected.

"It's got to be the medication," I said to Andrew. "I think we should try weaning him off it. If not now, when? How much worse can things get?"

"I agree. God only knows what being on medication for this long has done to him."

"I don't even want to think about that," I said.

Jack had been taking three different medications steadily for eleven years. There was no knowing whether it was still helping him or if it was now harming him. It was summer, so we were in agreement that it was the best time for Jack to eliminate the antidepressants.

They were the one medication that we hoped he needed least. Of the other two drugs, one was prescribed to manage attention and impulsivity, the other to minimize irritability. God knows Jack is oblivious and the king of impulsive behavior, and his irritability gauge has two measurements: high and extreme. To keep taking both of those for the time being was advisable. We were about to enter uncharted territory; I knew that. But over the last twenty-plus years, we had traveled through more unknown lands than most, and we were still standing. We would find our way through whatever upset was to come.

As angry as I was with Jack for his dismal performance in school, and more importantly, his not being straight with me, I didn't want to beat him over the head about it. Jack has never responded well to negative feedback. Positive reinforcement has always gone much further toward eliciting favorable results than yelling or punishment. Rather than lament the lost time and expense, I suggested to Jack that he take accounting at the community college over the summer. It would be cheaper, and without needing to focus on other classes at the same time, it would likely be easier. He could worry about righting the rest of the ship once school started again in the fall.

"My professor thinks I should withdraw," Jack informed me regretfully.

"*Again?* Are you serious? This has become the $10,000 course!"

"Sorry, Mom. I just don't understand accounting. I don't think I ever will."

"I know it's hard, sweetie, but it's a requirement for your major. At some point you need to pass it."

"I'm not even sure if I'm in the right major."

The ground dropped out from under me. Jack had transferred schools—he had upset the apple cart and lost both credits and time in the process—specifically so he could major in sports management. And now he wasn't sure it was the right move? I have always been more concerned about him learning life lessons than I ever was about his failures, and I've always believed that if he needs to change course sixteen times before he finds the right path, then he should change course. But that sounds much better in theory than it works in practice. The prospect of running out of tuition money was now reality.

"What makes you think sports management isn't the right major?" I asked once I had calmed down. Unless we took the time to get this right, Jack would continue to fail, and best to do it sooner rather than later.

"If I can't pass accounting after three tries, I'm never going to pass. And sports management isn't really about sports. It's all about networking and sales. I'm not good at that stuff."

It was true. Jack can barely interact with people. Forget about making connections and convincing them to spend their money. I don't know why we thought it would be a good idea. Throw the word "sports" out there and Jack sees stars, so of course it felt like the right choice. I sat down with him, and together we disassembled the problem, eliminating the pieces that weren't of interest to him so we could rebuild his approach with pieces that fit.

"Don't think about an actual major. Just tell me—in plain words— what it is you want to do. What gets you excited about life?"

Jack didn't hesitate. "I love watching sports highlights. I like thinking through the player's statistics while a game is going on, and how that will affect the outcome." He rattled off his response as if it was all perfectly natural and understood. "I just want to talk about baseball."

Of course. Jack was never interested in the *business* of baseball. His interest had always been in the game itself. The individual players and their backgrounds. The rise and fall of the numbers that illustrate their success, or lack thereof. The analysis of every variable that makes baseball the complex sport that it is. As a player, he has always put forth 110 percent, and he is equally as devoted as a spectator—immersed, attentive, and knowledgeable. Baseball is at the heart of every conversation with Jack that has ever been worth having.

After an emergency meeting with his advisor and with just five weeks to go before the start of the fall semester, Jack made the switch. He would now be a communications major. It might seem a strange choice, given that Jack is inarticulate most of the time and unable to clearly convey any of his thoughts. But he has a better chance at being successful if he's discussing sports than if he's trying to network and sell his way through life. Fingers were crossed that it would get him on track toward his goals. It also enabled him to squeeze in a second summer class, one that was a requirement for his major, in hopes that it would be a jump start on getting his grades up. It helped, but not enough.

"I talked with the coach today."

Jack's tone was flat. The news wasn't good.

"And?"

"He said he's excited to have me start training with the team, but because of NCAA rules, I can't until I get my grades up. He told me to reach out to him in December, and we'll revisit the situation then."

Jack's disappointment was evident. I could feel its weight, but he was the one who had gotten himself into this mess. If he had been communicating with me through the course of the spring semester, I may have been able to help him straighten things out before it was too late. Lessons learned are typically accompanied by pain, and unfortunately, Jack needed to bear every uncomfortable aspect.

"It's okay," he said. "Everything happens for a reason."

There he goes again, shrugging off the latest setback. I couldn't see that reason, but I admired Jack's resilience and wanted to believe it myself. Emerging from under the weight of antidepressants, he appeared liberated, committed, and better connected. He threw himself into his schoolwork. I put both hands back on the wheel, making sure to check in with him almost daily, asking for a full rundown of every assignment, when it was due, and what he was doing to get a good grade.

When December arrived and Jack received his final grades, I was beyond pleased. I was ecstatic. He had emerged at the end of the fall semester with a 3.5 average—his highest GPA ever. Proud of his efforts, he scheduled a meeting with the coach. Practice was scheduled to begin the second week of January, and he was cleared to start training.

That first Monday, Jack was chomping at the bit. He couldn't wait for his first real season of college baseball to get underway.

Tuesday brought with it excitement for classes to end and schoolwork to be finished so he could focus on practice.

On Wednesday he was starting to settle in.

By Thursday he felt comfortable with his new routine.

Once Friday arrived, the newness was wearing off and he was feeling a bit tired.

Saturday found him exhausted—and questioning what he had done.

By the time Monday rolled around, Jack was ready to give the whole thing up.

Let's take five.

"It's too much, Mom," he admitted.

"But it's only been one week, Jack. Give it a chance. You worked so hard for this," I reminded him. Jack was an expert at making impulsive decisions, and this was a big one. There would be no turning back if he were to quit, and I didn't want him living with that regret. Not after all these years. Baseball was in his blood.

"I know, but I don't think I can do it. I'll fail out of school, and that's more important."

I think another five is needed here.

I couldn't believe what I was hearing. The team's training schedule was aggressive, I had to agree, with practice Monday through Friday from 8:00 p.m. to 11:00 p.m., and then again for three hours on Saturday afternoons. That left little time for schoolwork—and no time for anything else. It was more than he had bargained for, and he knew it. The way Jack saw it was, "I've done this, I've made a decision, why invest any more time than one week's worth?" Black-and-white.

While I hated the thought of Jack having worked so hard to achieve this goal only to give it up, I couldn't argue with him. My urging him to stick it out a bit longer was for me, not him, yet I couldn't be prouder of him for having made school his priority.

"You could play club baseball again, if you wanted to."

"Yeah, maybe."

It wasn't tough to read between the lines of Jack's "yeah, maybe." His perspective had changed, but I didn't know why. Baseball had always come first, and now it was as if he could take it or leave it.

I, however, still wanted to cling to it.

The likelihood of losing it had Jack's baseball life flashing before my eyes. Every home run he had ever hit. Every game with *two* home runs hit. Every time he loaded up the bases while pitching and was cool as a cucumber. Every batter he ever struck out and base he's ever stolen. Every Golden Glove or Silver Slugger Award he won at summer camp because he was clearly the best in his age group. Every school game after class that provided a legitimate excuse to cut my workday short. Every 5:30 a.m. start on a Saturday to drive two and a half hours to get to a tournament and spend the entire weekend in a folding chair next to a dugout, until it's 7:00 p.m. on Sunday and it's time to make the two-and-a-half-hour drive back home. Every hot, twenty-ounce cup of mini-mart coffee, because those early starts were typically chilly, and oh, it tasted so good. Every spin of the washer and dryer cleaning uniforms late at night because bases had been stolen that day and left their dirty mark, and we had another early start in the morning. Every new friendship made with another parent because we were in it together. Every character-building ounce of disappointment because a hard-fought game became a lost battle. Every ear-to-ear smile because the opponent was dealt a crushing defeat. Every compliment ever received because *your* kid was the reason the team won the game. Every bruised shin. Every drop of sweat. Every single penny spent on lessons and travel teams. And every last "Love you, Mom" because you were right there alongside him, enjoying the hell out of it just as much as he was.

That immense pride erased every thought that Jack is not capable. Unloading the tedium would clear the way toward new horizons, for sure. Baseball may have been Jack's everything, but that didn't mean there weren't other paths out there for him. I was just fearful that those moments wouldn't ever come so easily for him again and I wanted to hold onto them indefinitely. I had been certain that this second opportunity to play college baseball would be Jack's epic comeback, but that wasn't the case. He was firm in his decision to move on from baseball once and for all. There was no long goodbye, no regret—and no turning back this time around.

It was over for good.

CHAPTER 31
Bubble Wrap

Jack was obviously experiencing greater mental clarity since abandoning his antidepressants. His significantly improved grades and his recognition of their importance toward his future were proof. I felt a tremendous sense of guilt, worried that he had been short-changed, that he might have done better if he hadn't been taking so much medication. Perhaps he would have let go of baseball sooner and opened his mind to other possibilities.

I have always felt that, at some point, it will be his time. He will have outgrown the weight of Asperger's. He will have matured enough that he'll understand his disability, accept it, and manage it. Everything I've ever tried to teach him will shine through. He'll be able to be his honest, unfiltered self—and do it with confidence.

Maybe now would be that time.

It was the summer of Jack's twenty-third birthday. We were set to take our first vacation alone together in four years. We hadn't missed a single trip in eleven years until the pandemic disrupted our pattern, and we were both more than ready. Though never perfect and always tough for the obvious reasons, our trips together are the hallmark of our relationship, providing countless memories that we reference time and time again. Every detail, good and bad, is ingrained in my memory, because hypervigilance was a prerequisite for taking every trip. In addition to Boston, Chicago, California, and the rest, we had added visits to Utah, Belize, Niagara Falls, Toronto, Vancouver, and Aruba to our list. We also had a very unfortunate stop in Miami. Jack was nineteen, and that destination was his choice. Why I thought it was a good one, I will never know. He hates the heat, and he slept away much of the week in our hotel room because it was too hot to go anywhere.

This year's trip was going to make up for that mistake. It was going to be our best adventure ever, and everything about it was going to be perfect. It was *our* time—I was never more positive. The lonely and awkward challenges of high school were behind us. We had weathered flat tires, speeding tickets, and a car fire. We had moved from baseball to modeling and back to baseball, then left it all behind permanently. Girls, we acknowledged, would find their place. Jack was off antidepressants completely and had just had a second successful semester at school, walking away with a 3.0 average. He was getting closer to that college degree, and following the pandemic and lack of available jobs, he had finally landed a summer job that would help him reach his goal of working in the sports industry.

And above all else, he has a friend who would undoubtedly go to the ends of the earth for him. There isn't a day that goes by that I don't thank the universe for Nick. I continuously underestimate the value of his presence in Jack's life, and I often wonder what Jack's quality of life would be if he didn't have that much-needed companionship.

At this age and with more life experience, Jack would certainly be more flexible, more adaptable, more enthused. He was older, more mature, and he had been looking forward to this trip for six months.

Jack and I were headed to Seattle for Major League Baseball's All-Star Week. With the weather at seventy-five degrees during the day and mid-fifties at night, it would be perfect for Jack. We were both looking forward to leaving the heat and humidity of the East Coast in mid-July behind. I envisioned the week flowing seamlessly—sharing plenty of laughter, having quality conversation, and coming away from it feeling closer than ever.

We got off to a rough start.

We boarded our flight in Philadelphia at eight o'clock Sunday morning, as scheduled. We had aisle seats opposite one another, which meant Jack would have to sit next to a stranger. I knew the minute I saw her coming down the aisle that she was headed for our row and inevitably would be assigned to Jack's side. She was very large and this was met with an under-the-breath "oh my God" and the standard eye roll.

When it was announced that the ground crew was having trouble pulling the Jetway back from the plane, I got a bad feeling. Eventually, we taxied to the runway.

And there we sat.

We crept along, then sat some more.

Finally, the captain announced that air traffic control was rerouting us because of storms in the area. We would be returning to the gate for more fuel. While waiting for the fuel truck, a good number of passengers got up to use the bathroom, which depleted our water supply, so we then needed to wait on the water truck. A full two hours had passed before we were on our way again, and no sooner had we reached the runway when we stopped to sit again. We sat so long that we were told we needed to return to the gate because the crew had exceeded their time limit.

After five hours of sitting and going nowhere, we had to deplane. Surprisingly, Jack held up well. He wasn't happy, but he wasn't complaining. I think he was just grateful that he no longer had to sit next to that woman—who he said smelled, by the way.

Thanks for letting me know, Jack.

We were directed to a different gate and told that our flight would depart at 2:00 p.m. By this time, I had accepted that our first day in Seattle had been lost. All I wanted was to get there before Monday afternoon. To miss the Home Run Derby would devastate Jack and completely ruin our trip.

Within minutes of arriving at our new gate, we were informed that our flight was canceled.

The storms that day had wreaked havoc. I called Liam to see if he could help. Moments later, he sent me a text message saying he had called the airline, was unsuccessful in reaching anyone, and all he could do was leave my cell number for an automatic call back. I could expect a call in four hours. Our only hope was the customer service desk at the airport. The line was easily hundreds of travelers deep, but we had no other choice.

Three and a half hours later we finally reached the desk. The woman behind it looked at me unapologetically and shook her head. There was no way she could get us to Seattle before Monday evening.

This can't be happening. How do you reconcile having spent six months and thousands of dollars planning a trip to have it all fall apart within hours?

I wasn't giving up that easily and pushed her to come up with something, anything. She reluctantly started tapping away at her keyboard only to shake her head, wanting us to go away, I'm sure, as she assessed the depth of desperate travelers standing in line. I kept pushing. She tried a few other options. I begged and pleaded and made suggestions. At some point I guess she felt sorry for us. She informed me that she could put us on the standby list for Monday morning's direct flight, insisting that we had a good chance of getting on.

Are you fucking with me on purpose? I wanted to scream at her. *Why didn't you say that in the first place?*

I didn't know what to think or do. I was skeptical that she knew what she was talking about, but she assured me it was a viable option. It would mean coming back to the airport at seven o'clock the next morning, and if we didn't get on, we would need to sit and wait until 1:45 p.m. for a mess of a flight on which we had automatically been rebooked, that would take us from Philadelphia to Cleveland, and then to Charlotte, and not deliver us to Seattle until nine o'clock Monday night.

What choice did we have?

Looking me straight in the eye, she said, "Just trust me."

I stared her down momentarily, finally agreed, reluctantly thanked her, and walked away. Exhausted and starving, we arranged for an Uber driver to take us home so we could do it all over again the next day.

"So we're on this flight?" Jack asked casually as we sat waiting at the gate the following morning, me praying silently, fast, and hard.

"No, Jack, we're on standby."

Why didn't he get it? He seemed to think that because we had showed up, we would automatically have a seat on the plane. That he didn't get it exacerbated my frustration and anxiety. Unintentionally, I took it out on him.

"We need to wait until everyone boards and then see if they call our name. There's no guarantee that we are going to get there today."

I wanted to prepare him—and myself—for disappointment.

Jack grabbed the two passes the gate agent had handed me and looked at them.

"Then why do we have assigned seats?" he asked.

I quickly snatched them back and studied them.

You observant little shit.

Sure enough, they were official boarding passes—with numbered seat assignments—and no longer temporary tickets marked "standby." I was so stressed that I hadn't realized that what the gate agent had handed back to me was not what the service agent had given me the night before. I was instantly ashamed for having reacted so harshly.

I squeezed his hand and smiled. "Thank you for grounding me."

We would make it to Seattle by noon, with hours to spare before the Home Run Derby.

"Are fish and chips good for you?" Jack asked.

We had already checked into our apartment and changed our clothes, wasting no time with unpacking before setting off toward the waterfront, where we found a quaint little take-out fish stand.

"It depends, I mean . . . yeah, they're better than eating a burger, I guess," I replied, not understanding where he was headed.

"I don't want to eat burgers anymore. I'm not putting that crap in my body."

Okaaaaay. . . . Well, you can't get a burger at this fish stand anyway.

Jack ordered the fish and chips, and a good mood settled over him. He started talking about the upcoming derby, running down statistics for the various players competing, which one he thought would win and why. He had turned into my personal sports analyst, and I was grateful for it. Good Jack, the one who's clearheaded, talkative, and fun to be with, had arrived.

The afternoon and evening were everything we knew they would be. There was all manner of baseball-related activities, and the derby was nothing short of pure excitement. The entire ballpark was electric, thanks to the participation of one of the Seattle Mariners. Each time Julio Rodríguez stepped to the plate, every soul in the place was on their feet, chanting, "*Whoo-lee-oh! Whoo-lee-oh!*" Goose bumps were guaranteed.

Once the derby was over, Jack wanted Italian. We found a nearby restaurant that was expensive but looked promising. I saw that they had at least one option that would meet with Jack's approval—rigatoni and meat sauce.

"It has veal in it. Do I like veal?"

Do you really need to ask that question?

"I'm sure you've had it before. Italian meat sauce often has veal in it. You'll like it."

"Which do you think is better, the spaghetti or the rigatoni?"

"The rigatoni comes with meat sauce, and the spaghetti is just spaghetti, no meatballs. But you could order a side of meatballs, I suppose."

"Which do you think is healthier?"

I lifted my eyes from the menu, wanting to confirm that it was Jack sitting across the table, sensing that there was a new obsession in the making, and it was about to cast a pervasive shadow over our week.

The following day, Jack got a bit of sunburn on the back of his neck. Not wanting it to get worse, he didn't want to sit in the sun, nor did he want to sit in the shade because it was freezing, or so he said. Throughout lunch, he held a glass of ice water to his face to avoid overheating and consulted me every fifteen minutes about what he should wear for kayaking.

"What do you think I should do? Wear shorts or pants?"

No matter how I answered, he wasn't convinced.

"Do you think I should go with the pants? I'm going with pants."

The afternoon turned overcast, so of course Jack was "freezing" out on the lake despite having worn the pants. The sweatshirt went on, followed by the jacket. The hood went up, and he spent the next two hours tugging it tightly over his ears. The minute we were on dry land, his thoughts reverted to food.

"What do you think is better, shrimp, or fish and chips? Is shrimp good for you?"

I was afraid to provide any answer.

When not surrounded by the usual favorites of home, finding the right place to eat with Jack is especially difficult. No matter where we went that evening, every dish on every menu had at least one ingredient that was not part of Jack's dietary vocabulary. Once we ran out of options and Jack didn't want to walk anymore—because the sun was now out again and blazing—he suggested we try a nearby brewery because all breweries have "amazing food."

"They probably have the best burgers and wings."

Wait—I thought you were off burgers?

"Love you, Mom."

Our week was a maddening flip-flop from start to finish. What I had mistakenly envisioned as being a life-changing turning point was simply more of the same. It was a painful recap of every difficult moment of every trip we had ever taken. It summarized our entire journey from birth to age twenty-three—a frenzied pinball bouncing from one bumper to the next. All week it was the same questions regarding food, the ever-present difficulty with temperature, and an inability to appreciate anything because he was so damn uncomfortable.

At the foot of Mount Rainier, he'd responded with, "Yeah, it's cool" without even a sideways glance at the most spectacular, snow-covered active volcano, wanting to know how soon we could go because he was "*so* hot."

The air in our rental car went from the lowest temp at full force, to fan off, heat on. There was no middle ground. There was no finding a comfortable level and just leaving it.

We got in a taxi, and it was too hot. He lowered the window, raised it again, then put it back down with an aggravated sigh.

"Why is it so hot in here?" he yelled.

The cabbie was stunned, almost frightened. "Uh, sorry, do you need more air?"

"Yeah," Jack said angrily. "It's a hundred degrees in here!"

And if he wanted a breakfast sandwich, he wasn't having anything else. He would rather eat a shitty microwaved breakfast sandwich than a decent burger because he had some ridiculous notion that burgers were no longer acceptable.

"I'm not putting that crap in my body," he said again.

Since when? You've been filling your body with burgers and wings since you were ten!

There was no explanation for why he was suddenly so fixated on the quality of the food he ate, other than this marking the beginning of an eating disorder.

Of course! That's it! Why not add another challenge to Jack's leaden pile?

"If you really want to eat well, Jack, you need to start eating fruits and vegetables," I informed him flatly. I knew that would shut him up. There's no way in hell Jack would ever let a fruit or a vegetable pass his lips. Never in a million years would he put *that* kind of crap in his body!

"I don't want to travel with you anymore. It's just too hard!" I hurled at him as we raced our way through the airport to find a breakfast sandwich before our flight home.

I no longer like him and can't wait for this trip to be over, I thought—only to once again question what kind of rotten mother I was, feeling that way.

None of this is his fault.

Day after day, I'm convinced that Jack could behave differently if he wanted to, if he just tried, but I know that he can't. *When* will I accept that? I try to stay ten steps ahead, but it's exhausting. He's not going to change. The older he gets, the worse it seems. Not because his behaviors are worse, but because he's no longer a child, and I expect him to be better equipped to handle himself. It's striking how difficult it is for him to feel comfortable, to go with the flow, and make adjustments, so that every slight twist, turn, up, down, forward and back isn't a matter of complete disruption to his equilibrium. It's my fault for assuming the black-and-white will ever soften into some acceptable shade of gray. And I hate myself for being so hard on him.

I had hoped that this trip would be different. I had hoped that all those ways in which Jack's Asperger syndrome comes through would magically be gone. I had hoped that he could engage with people in a polite fashion without looking utterly disinterested or rolling his eyes. I had hoped that he could be in a good mood. I wanted my son to be like everyone else's son for just six days. Is that too much to ask?

Our flight home was delayed by several hours, and it was almost comical. The whole trip had been a struggle—why would the end be any different? Even though I could sense Jack's stress as we began our descent, I thought he had it under control. He had been sitting quietly, fidgeting only now and again. It wasn't until the air in the cabin turned decidedly warm that I saw the pressure building. The descent was turbulent, so he had no choice but to stay put, and I just assumed he would make it through.

"I've gotta get up," he said.

"Jack, you can't. You need to stay in your seat. Take a deep breath," I said, as I tried tugging him back.

"I can't."

"You have to. We're getting ready to land. The seat belt sign is on."

"I don't care. I can't do this," he cried as he jumped into the aisle and flew toward the back of the plane. I was stunned, as was everyone else, but I let him go—and I couldn't believe I did. I couldn't bear to see him breaking down, but what more could I do? Run after him to rub his back? Hold his hand?

At some point, I need to let him go.

It was an instantaneous realization in a moment of panic.

I can't be the Bubble Wrap anymore.

I can't wrap Jack in a cocoon and prevent him from experiencing life's curveballs. I can't continue to shield everyone else from his impact. He needs to find his own way. If it all falls to pieces, I'll help him glue those pieces back together, but I can't prevent the breakdowns anymore.

The woman sitting beside me gasped. I turned and said what I should have been saying all along.

"My son is autistic."

Go ahead—say it again, sister. Let's practice this while we can.

"I don't know what to do," I added. "My son is autistic. He's having a meltdown, and we're getting ready to land."

"Let him go," she said, not having any idea just how big those three little words were. They were exactly what I needed. A verbal crutch to lean against, if only for a few moments.

It was no longer unclear to me which side of the fence Jack falls on. He falls on the disabled side. He's not a twenty-three-year-old young man with a sensible head on his shoulders. He is autistic. Yes, technically he has Asperger syndrome, a form of autism, but the exact label doesn't matter. What matters is that Jack has a disability that constricts his movement through each and every day. It's beyond his control, and there's no advance warning. No one can see Jack's unique form of autism until it's too late, until after he has done or said something that has them scratching their heads, until after he has knocked them off their feet with a rude response or reaction. It catches them off guard because they never see it coming. Jack looked perfectly normal sitting in his seat. He wasn't saying a word or acting strange in any way. When he boiled over, it was a shock to everyone around him.

Jack's disability, his issues, limitations, oddities, challenges—whatever you want to call them—can all be felt. It's the tension at a restaurant table when his food is not what he expected, envisioned, or ordered, and he refuses to eat it. It's the irritability when the car is too hot or the sun too strong. It's the embarrassment when he comes off as being rude or disruptive.

It can be heard in all the endless strings of babble that pour from his mouth, or the complete lack of expression in every awkward thank-you, because it's the only social rule that ever stuck.

But rarely can it be seen. Jack looks normal. He's an attractive, well-proportioned young man. He's six foot two with blue eyes, straight teeth, and a heart-melting stray dimple on his left cheek. He dresses like other kids, drives a car, has a job, and plays sports. At first glance, you can't see anything out of the ordinary.

In any given moment, I find it hard to pinpoint what makes Jack different. I find it hard to make sense of what's truly happening in any situation gone wrong. I find it hard to believe that he's not like everyone else, because he appears so normal. Yet he always falls short of what everyone considers normal. I'm not seeing the whole person, because the whole person makes me uncomfortable. I see only the parts I want to see.

I would give anything to change life for Jack and for me. I want him to be like every other young man that's growing, advancing, and exploring the world around him. I want him to have the same opportunities, but he won't, because he will always be trapped within his limitations. I'm trapped there too, right alongside him, and there is unquestionably a part of me that's angry about that. There are days when I pray for something to happen to him so I can save him from this struggle of living life with a disability that no one can see, and selfishly, to save myself from the pain of watching him endure it all.

I need to accept that Jack's way of being is not a reflection on me. I need to let go of my need, my desire, to have my child be a perfect reflection. To get right down to it, he is a perfect reflection—of all my faults. I've never been a social creature, always preferring to have just a few close friends. I have a constant need for perfection, and I can't bear to be late. My anxiety level is generally as high as Jack's. I act impulsively, I get bored easily—and I hate the heat. Expecting Jack's behavior to cast a positive, glowing light on me is downright ridiculous, not to mention selfish.

I think that I'm doing what's best for him by pushing him beyond his comfort zone. But when I see how difficult that is, how uncomfortable he becomes, I think otherwise—that Jack is best off remaining where he's most comfortable. What he truly needs, though, is a balance between the two. Every time I see that balance in play, it provides me with positive affirmation that all the upset I created in our three lives in order to be the best role model I could be for my son was worth it. Jack's sweet spot of comfort will always be a very narrow space, but I will continue searching for it. I'll continue searching for my own space as well, that place where I can push him beyond his comfort zone without ignoring that his needs and tolerances are very different.

Liam often tells me that my anxiety seems unchecked. I spend too much time worrying about things I can't control.

My natural reaction is to snap back, "I'm not like you. I wish I was easygoing like you, but I'm just not. Can't you see that I need your help, not a lecture?"

I now recognize that Jack is saying the very same thing, day after day.

"I'm not like you. I am different, and I can't change that. What I need is your help, not your voiced irritation and reprimands."

I have not failed. This isn't a parenting job gone wrong. I have done the best that I can do within the circumstances. Yes, I could have better educated myself about Asperger syndrome. I could have sought out more resources. I could have been a better disciplinarian. But I didn't and wasn't—because I have my own limitations. The reality of life, with all its setbacks, was swirling around me. Raising Jack was not the only task on my plate. I was finding my way through divorce. I needed to find myself. I was making mistakes. I was being human. And I was doing my best.

I wish I had possessed the mental and emotional strength to tell people that Jack has Asperger syndrome from the very beginning. It would have made life far better, easier, more honest. Trying to hide it helps no one. I never wanted Jack to be labeled, and in turn, discounted from sports or ostracized by kids at school, yet all those things happened anyway. I have an obligation to the world and to Jack to clue everyone in so they can manage their expectations, be more understanding of his behavior, and be more receptive to learning what drives him. Jack's way of being should never be hidden from anyone. It should never be explained away.

He deserves to be seen—in his entirety.

That is the comfortable plateau I have reached after twenty-three years of struggling uphill, the space that feels right to me. It took entirely too long to get to this place, but better late than never. Not only am I wanting to share Jack's disability, but I find myself proud of it. Because "it" is Jack. He is who he is, and I love him for who he is.

Getting him to that same place is the next challenge. If I had taken ownership of Jack's disability right from the start, he likely would have grown up accepting it too, and it would be as natural to him as the fact that he loves baseball. He would have had the freedom to be himself without needing to hide behind explanations or apologies. Getting him to accept that he has a disability—this disability—and more importantly, share it with the world, is a monumental task and a catch-22 of major proportions. He needs to speak up, get engaged, ask questions, tell people what he wants and needs. But he can't ever do those things and advocate for himself because . . . he . . . has . . . *Asperger syndrome!*

Being as high functioning as he is has worked against him from day one, and it always will. He wants everyone to look at him as if he's just like the next guy—and they do—until he falls short of expectations. By not advocating for himself, he's not getting the fair chance he deserves, and he's dictating his own failure. It will likely take a lifetime, but I'm up for the challenge, and I will be by his side for as long as it takes.

The evening we arrived home from our trip, I found Liam and a close friend sitting on our back patio. I sat down with them to recount the details of our week but mostly to unwind. I had been wound tighter than an eight-day clock, all week. A few minutes later, Jack appeared at the back door and came out to say hello, with a warm smile, a firm handshake, and an all-around positive vibe. It was 180 degrees from how he had behaved all week.

I had begun my parenting journey wanting to teach Jack so much, to be the perfect role model, and I continuously feel like he hasn't learned anything. But that's not true. In the same way that Jack appears normal on the surface but isn't, he looks as though he hasn't changed or grown at all, but he has.

Our trip had gotten off to a rotten start, but he had handled the upheaval well, never complaining about our flight being canceled or having to go home and start again the next day. He was physically uncomfortable all week, but rather than hide himself away like he did in Miami, he stuck it out. At no point during the week did he say he wanted to go home, when that's most likely what he wanted. Maybe his fixation on food choices was a way of channeling his stress. Rather than unravel completely, he gave his anxiety an out, recognizing that it was my vacation too and that I deserved to enjoy it. I left Seattle resigned to the fact that I can't take Jack out of his element and have him handle it with ease. Now that we were finally home, I was able to step back and see that he had handled it all far better than he ever would have in the past.

And suddenly, I was full of regret.

If only I could turn back time and reset my expectations. Instead of assuming this would be our best trip ever because Jack had somehow escaped the grip of Asperger syndrome, I would have willingly invited his disability to travel with us and been better prepared to go with Jack's flow. I realize now that all those moments when Jack is enjoyable arise out of patience, accommodation, acceptance, and flexibility on my part.

I also understand now that it's okay to be afraid.

But it's never okay to be silent.

EPILOGUE
No Turning Back

Hindsight is twenty-twenty.

No truer words have ever been spoken. At least not when it comes to our experience with Asperger syndrome. If only I had known then a fraction of what I know now.

Then.

It doesn't matter how you define it. Even if "then" didn't extend any further back than last week, I would still be ahead of the game. If only I knew last week what I know today, yesterday's misery might have been preventable. And if only I knew twenty-three years ago what I know today. . . .

Trust me, I've thought it through countless times. If only I knew what I know now, I would have done almost everything differently. There still would have been meltdowns and train wrecks, but maybe I could have reduced the frequency of total derailments. I would have been better able to teach Jack, and I would have been better able to educate those around him. I could have promoted understanding— and prevented judgment and discrimination.

In many respects, life with Jack has been incredibly chaotic, yet his Asperger syndrome has also made it quite predictable. When Jack was young, I couldn't figure him out. Just when I would get a handle on his behavior, it would change. It's only now that he's gotten older that I feel as though I truly know him. And yet, every time he takes one step forward and I assume a second will follow, I'm surprised when he takes five steps back. He has moments of brilliance, both mentally and emotionally, yet he can't seem to string them all together. He is a fish out of water, never following conventional methods, doing everything his way.

If only I knew then.

I often wonder why I was given two children with a disorder. I truly believe that Angela was a mistake, and we needed to give her back because we were meant to have Jack instead. This is my journey. I wouldn't change it for the world. Angela came to us completely unequipped because Jack was meant to be the path we followed. If I had not experienced the brief joy of carrying Angela for seven months, followed by the extreme grief in losing her, maybe I wouldn't be as tolerant of Jack. I feel as though that loss made me so much more appreciative of him, despite his disability. The horror we experienced in terminating that pregnancy gave me the strength to love Jack more—because Jack just needs more.

Yes, he is different, but that doesn't mean he's flawed. We all have weaknesses. Very few of us are self-aware enough to recognize that, let alone have the strength to change it. Why then are Jack's weaknesses looked at with such disapproval? I wrote this book in hopes of helping people understand the cruelty of it all. Asperger syndrome often hits you in the face. It's often unbearably obnoxious. Most of the time, it's simply misunderstood. I consistently feel the need to explain it all away. I carry Jack's disability around with me like some excuse all disclaimer, a label hanging from my back pocket that serves as a constant reminder.

He's twenty-three. It's hard to believe.

WARNING: Persons in mirror are mentally much younger than they appear.

He's a good kid. He doesn't drink, smoke, or do drugs.

DISCLAIMER: Subject's choice to live a clean lifestyle has absolutely no connection to his overall behavior. A microscopic comfort zone does not allow for experimentation of any sort.

We're very close. There's never any shortage of "Love you, Mom" in our house.

CAUTION: Sudden, repetitive sounds and/or phrases uttered unintentionally or out of habit are considered a vocal tic.

The world we live in is horrifying. The word "disorderly" doesn't even begin to cover it. Dysfunctional. Disastrous. Deadly. Those are all better descriptions. Stacked up against the rest of the world, Jack's downsides are nothing. Yes, he can be annoying, and yes, he's exhausting, but when I let Jack be Jack and embrace everything that he is, I find myself enjoying the hell out of him. He makes me laugh with his silliness and babbling. He opens my eyes to so much about life and relationships. His literal perspective is often worthy of admiration.

It's moments like those that have me thinking to myself, maybe there is no such thing as "disorder." No one knows how far back in the family we would have to go to find out where and when Jack's strange combination of cells originated. The mixing of genes from one generation to the next can get sloppy, and there's always a possibility that the recipe could be a flop. When things don't go as planned, isn't it just *disorder*ly evolution?

Mention Down syndrome or autism, and everyone immediately knows what you're talking about. But when you say Asperger syndrome, there is a vague understanding, a response of "Yeah, I've heard of it, but I'm not sure what it is." Most people are unable to spot a child with Asperger's. On the surface, it's barely visible.

When I was pregnant with Angela and undergoing test after test, there was so much emphasis on appearance. Your baby is going to be made up of a hundred billion defective 9p chromosomes, but at least she will *look* normal. If that's the rule of law we follow, then Jack must be normal, right? No one *sees* that Jack is different.

Trust me, I am as guilty as everyone else of discriminating against him. He appears so capable, and countless times I have wanted to shake him, scream at him—tell him to snap out of it. *There's a normal Jack in there somewhere—I know it. I've seen him.* I have seen him respond appropriately so many times, and I assume that if he can do it some of the time, he should be able to do it all the time. But he can't. He's simply not programmed the same way as most people. That "some of the time" has come partially from repetition, but mostly I think it comes from sheer dumb luck. Those times when Jack appears to be normal are more a matter of the stars aligning than a conscious decision to behave a certain way.

He is programmed to fly off the handle if the car is too hot.

He will inevitably blow a gasket if I spend one minute too long talking with a neighbor while he's waiting to go.

If someone were to walk up behind Jack after he had just hit a walk-off home run and dump a bucket of icy water over his head, he would be more inclined to punch the guy than laugh and throw his arms up in celebration.

That is how he is programmed. He simply doesn't have the software to be anyone other than who he is. And that someone is a toddler, child, adolescent—young man—with Asperger syndrome.

It's been twenty-three years since Jack left the starting gate—with a constant companion that consistently feeds him false details about the world. It's a heavy cloak, confining him to single spaces at a time, imposing its stubborn weight on every move he makes and preventing any opportunity to break free and explore life. We have yet to determine a path through its dense fog. Setting up roadblocks are essential to its existence, making it impossible for us to find a way around it. And forget trying to outrun it—it's smarter, faster, and more conniving than all of us. Instead, Jack coasts along willingly. Perhaps that's the only way to make peace with such an obstinate, tenacious companion. Rather than wrestle free, just let its tentacles carry you along.

While writing this book, *Roe v. Wade* was overturned.

That is huge.

Without the right to choose, you wouldn't be reading these pages. Jack never would have been. Some might argue that we got what we deserve. In exchange for selfishly ending Angela's life, we were given Jack, a child whose way of being is unwieldy at its best—exasperating, maddening, and wholly overwhelming at its worst.

Without the right to choose, everyone's life would have taken a different path. Andrew and I may have stayed together. We may have divorced sooner. More than likely, I never would have met Liam. I think most about Jack, though. It wasn't his choice to be saddled with this disability, and he is the one absorbing its impact to the greatest degree. If we had known in advance, would we have chosen differently? We exercised our right to choose with Angela because her situation was so extreme, her disability unthinkable. Jack's is barely visible—and it's that lack of visibility that makes Asperger syndrome so difficult. If the decision were Jack's, would he choose to be here? So far, he hasn't chosen not to be here, so maybe that answers the question. He doesn't seem to be as bothered by his disability as I am. He's comfortable with who he is, because he's never been anyone else. He has no idea what life is like in the other camp—the so-called normal camp.

Angela is never far from my thoughts. I will forever be asking *why*. Why did we need to go through that? Why did we have to endure her tragedy to end up trudging through Jack's mud? What makes us candidates for that challenge? I will never know that answer, so the only thing to do is stop asking. Why is not what matters. How I choose to respond to what's been put in front of me is the only thing of importance. Life is nothing more than an endless string of ups and downs, and mistakes made so that lessons can be learned. I'm convinced that those moments are barely visible, so we take the time to dig in and fully experience the discomfort in order to learn and grow. I have emerged on the other side as a better person, because I was forced to dig in and deal with all that discomfort. In the process of doing so, I've learned more lessons than I can count.

The idea of writing this book about my only child and our discovery of his disability was daunting. I remember thinking that I was writing aimlessly with no forward path. I felt as though I was unrealistic and impractical in thinking that I could turn Jack's story—our story—into a book. But every time I reflected on all that he's experienced, all that we've been through as a family, and the uniquely incredible person that he has become, I realized that telling our story is not something I needed to do for myself. It's for all those other families dealing with similar circumstances who don't know what to expect or how to handle it.

My hope is that writing this book will help parents of children with Asperger syndrome to understand their child but also their own feelings—and maintain their sanity. I'm hoping I can save them from making the mistake of staying silent, and empower them to explain their child's behavior to others. I want to encourage them to swallow the embarrassment and stop apologizing. And help them to love their own child and anyone else that doesn't fit the accepted mold.

This book was not written in a linear fashion. Nothing about Jack's story has ever been linear. Just when I'm able to connect all the dots and finally make sense of a given moment in time, he does something to remind me that there are still loose ends and unresolved issues from some earlier chapter. I had made countless strings of notes along the way, a piece here, a thought there. Each note I made seemed to make perfect sense at the time, but when I would return to them later, they all appeared as senseless as Jack's behavior. Needing to organize them in some logical fashion forced me to articulate Jack in his entirety. Telling this story has forced me to chew, swallow, and digest all of life with Jack. At several points, I wanted to throw up, so if any of it gives the impression it's been regurgitated, I apologize.

I have spent years working on this book, not continuously, but if I wasn't writing, it was still top of mind. That means I've spent years living in the past, trying to conjure up memories, and I question if that's been harmful. By living in the past, has my perspective on Jack as a young adult been skewed? Have I put too much emphasis on "what was" when "what is" is now different? Yes, his disability remains, but the way in which he handles things has changed. Or has that past perspective been helpful? Delving deeply into Jack's childhood, dissecting all his responses, and questioning why he behaved the ways he did may have enabled me to see the adult Jack more clearly and better guide him.

While our journey has not led us to a definitive destination, it is a road map highlighting the twists and turns, underscoring every opportunity to make a choice, illustrating the need to backtrack at times and push forward at others. We were completely blind throughout our journey from Angela to Jack. I would like to think we haven't been completely blind, just visually impaired, in our journey since. Allowing people to step inside our world, follow our map for a while, and get to know the routes we chose may help them better understand their own situations and determine which paths work best for them. Hopefully they will arrive at their own destination without veering off course or breaking down completely.

Yes, this book details Jack's disability and its impact, his strange behaviors, and the hurdles he has faced. But it also illustrates the great impact it has had on me and my life, and how I view my child: my dreams for him; my need to keep expectations in check; my many times wishing that my son was just like everyone else's son; all the gratitude in my heart that my son *isn't* like everyone else's. His failures hit me hard, but his victories, however small, are that much greater. That sounds cliché, but learning to accept and appreciate what I do have versus what I don't has been key to success for us.

Jack is not going to change. Asperger syndrome has made an indelible impression on him, and he is going to need assistance for his entire life. But his path is unique. As my mother has always insisted, life has a way of working itself out. It may not look the way we anticipated or want, but it will be Jack's way.

Jack was six or seven when he announced that he has had ninety-nine previous lives. At the time, I remember thinking how creative that was for such a young person. Maybe he knew something that the rest of us didn't. He wasn't able to expand upon that, and he never mentioned it again, but I have no doubt he is an old soul. He has taught me how to appreciate everything, from those moments when formality is forgotten and silliness is the rule, to the absurdity of his vocal tic. He has taught me that a bad day will always dissolve away, and he is a constant reminder that positive thinking can propel you across the finish line—even if you have a flat tire. He is my heartbeat. Sometimes he skips a beat, sometimes he murmurs, but he's always there, keeping me going.

Jack is convinced that anything and everything can be fixed with, "Love you, Mom."

That isn't always true. But, boy, does it go a long way.

Love you too, bud.

About the Author

Kathleen Somers, a first-time author, holds a Bachelor of Fine Arts from Temple University's Tyler School of Art. She is a freelance graphic designer and copywriter, as well as an avid cyclist. She lives with her family in the suburbs of Philadelphia.

www.kathleensomers.com

Looking for your next great read?

We can help!

Visit www.shewritespress.com/next-read
or scan the QR code below for a list
of our recommended titles.

She Writes Press is an award-winning
independent publishing company founded to
serve women writers everywhere.